Praise for *Maggie's Breakfast* by
Gabriel Walsh

'It's a magical, true story of the friendship between an impoverished young boy and a famous opera star in 1950s Dublin'
— IRISH INDEPENDENT

'Maggie's Breakfast is an honest tale of optimism and humour, and one that remains with you for a long time. Highly recommended'
— WOMAN'S WAY

'An astonishing memoir of redemption' – IRISH EXAMINER

'A heart-warming story of an extraordinary life' – EVENING ECHO

'The story of friendship and opportunity could only come from a movie script' – THE SUNDAY WORLD

'*Maggie's Breakfast* is an entertaining, witty and often surprising account of a poor Dublin childhood' – BORD GÁIS ENERGY BOOK CLUB

'A fascinating story of the old times in Dublin' – GAY BYRNE, LYRIC FM

'Reads like the plot of a rags-to-riches movie' – IRISH DAILY MAIL

'A remarkable story' – TV3'S IRELAND AM

GABRIEL WALSH

I Dream Alone

A Memoir

POOLBEG

Published 2013
by Poolbeg Press Ltd
123 Grange Hill, Baldoyle
Dublin 13, Ireland
E-mail: poolbeg@poolbeg.com
www.poolbeg.com

© Gabriel Walsh 2013

Copyright for typesetting, layout, design, ebook
© Poolbeg Press Ltd

The moral right of the author has been asserted.

1

A catalogue record for this book is available from the British Library.

ISBN 978-1-84223-539-3

Typeset by Patricia Hope in Sabon 11.5/16.5

Printed and bound by CPI Group (UK) Ltd, Croydon, CR0 4YY

www.poolbeg.com

About the author

Gabriel Walsh was born in Dublin. He later went on to study in America. Gabriel has lectured at colleges in Los Angeles and Cork and was a staff writer for Universal Pictures in Hollywood. He has worked with actors such as Jack Nicholson, Gene Wilder and Robert Redford. He wrote the original screenplay *Quackser Fortune Has a Cousin in the Bronx* which received a Writers Guild of America nomination. He also wrote the film *Night Flowers* which received an ecumenical award at the Montréal World Film Festival. In 2012 Poolbeg published *Maggie's Breakfast*, a memoir of his early years in Dublin.

Acknowledgements

To the countless men, women and children who sailed from
Ireland before and after me, and to the passengers on the ship
I sailed on from Cobh in County Cork to New York in the
mid-nineteen-fifties: I yell from the silence of my soul the
sorrow and sadness of being detached from country and
from family. The dream of forging a new life out of tattered
memories and compromised realities has for a seemingly
limitless period of time been a constant companion to both
the willing and reluctant exiles, to keep the promise of hope
and self-discovery alive. Sailing away from one's past can be
like tears unwilling to abandon the eye. Nevertheless without
a dream for a compass one can easily sink the arrival of the
future.

Gabriel Walsh

We are such stuff as dreams are made on . . .

SHAKESPEARE

New York

The castle in Tarrytown, New York, was something like I had seen in films when I frequented the cinema in Dublin. In many ways it reminded me of places where Dracula, Frankenstein and the Wolf Man lived.

As I digested my whereabouts a woman wearing white shoes and a white apron approached me.

"Poor boy! You must be very tired," she said. She seemed happy to see me and obviously had been aware of my imminent arrival.

I didn't know whether to answer her or not, so I just nodded my head affirmatively.

"I'd say he's more bewildered than tired," Mrs. Axe volunteered as she shed her fur coat.

"Say hello to Pat – Pat is the housekeeper," Maggie interjected with a sense of instruction in her voice while looking very directly at me.

She had left Ireland a few weeks before and was settled in

at the castle, but had come to New York City to escort me to the place she had only mentioned to me a few times in Dublin.

I had so many thoughts buzzing about in my head that I couldn't settle on what to say. Hello, thanks, help me, where am I? Who is everybody? Is my father out of bed yet? Is my mother still praying in the church and is my sister still crying for me? But Maggie's presence in the vast foyer of the mansion I was standing in brought a calm and reassuring feeling to me. I looked at her and I wanted to talk, laugh and even cry. I resisted the impulse to cry because I knew it would be the last impression she'd want me to put on display at this particular moment.

As I stood trying to make sense of my situation I noticed a portrait of Maggie on the wall above a door that led to another part of the mansion. The painting depicted Maggie as a much younger woman with a broad smile on her face and it exuded a glow of contentment. Somewhat mesmerised by the portrait, I turned to face her as she stood between me and my old suitcase. With a palpable desire to express myself I wanted to say something about the portrait, but was unsure, confused and even afraid to make a comment. I didn't think Maggie would approve of me saying anything just then. As I looked directly at her I knew I was seeing Maggie in an older and sadder period of her life – I had no idea of her age and only in later years realised that she was in her late sixties at that point. For a moment or two I tried to ask myself why I was now standing in a majestic hallway in a massive castle in upstate New York with her looking at me from the wall and from right next to me with a glare in her eyes that I interpreted as an admonition for me to be on my best behaviour. The tiredness and sleepiness that was consuming me kept me from making any kind of gesture that might have embarrassed Maggie.

The lady with the white shoes and the white apron took a step towards me and, because I was having trouble standing and staying awake, I wanted to fall into her arms and fall into a deep sleep and forget where I was and who I was with. Had it not been for her radiant blue eyes and an unrestricted smile, she might in my tired mind easily have been a snowstorm approaching me.

"I'm sure you're very tired," she said.

Her words helped alert me to my whereabouts. As I attempted to act as if I was wide awake, I heard Maggie's voice bellow out: "You can see he's falling down from exhaustion!"

Having learned not to question anything Maggie said and given the degree of fatigue I was feeling, I said with as much reverence as I could muster: "Hello."

The woman in white answered me with another "Hello."

Mr. Axe, seemingly wanting to express his involvement and perhaps aware that I was about to fall down on the floor, then spoke up: "All the way from Dublin!" He then stepped away, allowing Pat to move closer to me.

"A long trip I'm sure," she said, looking kindly at me.

By now I noticed that her hair, tied in a bun, was as white as the apron she had tied around her waist and in my fatigued state she looked more like a nurse than a housekeeper.

"Eight days," Mrs. Axe joined in on the sounds and voices that were swirling around. "Stormy seas and the rest of it. Lucky to be alive." She hung her coat on a nearby coat stand. "Well, you're here. You made it, Gabriel." She wagged her head in a left and right direction like a puppy dog that had happily emerged from a cold pond. When she stopped shaking her head she smiled with a sigh of relief. The smile on her face was almost identical to the expression I'd witnessed in Dublin when I first met her. I took it upon myself to believe that she was happy that I had arrived in one piece.

Pat the housekeeper then took hold of my old suitcase and appeared to be surprised as to how light it was. For a moment or two I feared she might ask me what was in it. Had I thought about it before I left Dublin I could easily have put the contents of the suitcase into my jacket and trouser pockets.

"Goodnight, Gabriel, and welcome. We'll see you in the morning," Mrs. Axe said and walked into a room adjacent to the foyer. She was immediately followed by Mr. Axe who bid me goodnight also.

Margaret Sheridan hesitated for a moment and then reached out to me. I felt she wanted to embrace me but she didn't. Instead she laid her hand on my head momentarily. Had she embraced me I might have physically evaporated there and then. By the look on Maggie's face I wondered if she was having second thoughts about me standing there in front of her, thousands of miles away from where we met.

"Get a good night's sleep," Maggie said. She hesitated as she was about to step away from me and said, "We'll see you in the morning, Gabriel. Show him where to go, Pat." She then followed Mr. and Mrs. Axe into what appeared to be the living room and vanished from my sight.

At that moment I felt like a bird that had lost its ability to fly.

For a second or two I came out of my reverie and noticed Pat was standing patiently in front of me as if waiting for an instruction or an order. I didn't know what to say and I didn't know where to go – mainly because I didn't know where I was. I looked at Pat again, hoping she would tell me to fall asleep on the floor and end the numbness that was consuming my mind. With little ability to open my eyes and my mouth, I wondered and waited for Pat to say something to me.

Finally she broke into the abyss of my silence. "All the way from Ireland you've come."

Was she telling me or asking me? I wasn't sure. I knew I had to stay awake and, no matter the difficulty, be polite. "Yes, Dublin," I answered.

"My husband is part Irish," she said with a laugh that was welcoming and reassuring.

As I tried to think of something important to say to her, she beckoned for me to follow her and I did. In seconds I was walking up a huge marble staircase which was situated towards the back of the castle – there was a wooden staircase to the front – behind her while she talked and talked. She told me half of the mansion had been converted to office space and a large staff worked there every day of the week. Most employees were experts and advisers in the world of finance. With a movement of her hands she drew a map that told me where Mr. and Mrs. Axe's quarters were. Although they lived on the same corridor they didn't share the same suite, she explained.

"What did you bring with you from Dublin?" she inquired of me as we climbed to a higher floor.

I was afraid to tell her but I knew I couldn't escape her questions. "I didn't bring much: two shirts, a jacket, my overcoat."

"Mrs. Axe will make sure you get proper clothing," she responded and continued to walk ahead of me. She glanced back. "D'you feel okay?"

My mind was still in a fog and I couldn't yet make out where I was or where I was going. With Pat talking about her life and the world of the castle and asking me questions at the same time, I wasn't sure what to say about how I felt because I simply didn't know. I was just glad to be off the boat and not seasick.

* * *

When Pat and I reached the third floor she opened a big door that led into what was to be my living quarters. It was a long narrow room with wood-panelled walls and a rounded section that offered a view to the outside. All in all the place looked very isolated and I wasn't sure what to make of it. I had never slept in a room on my own. It was only recently that I began to sleep in a bed of my own, and that bed was a small narrow cot. Earlier in my life I slept at the foot of my parents' bed. When I got a bit older I moved to another bed and slept with two of my brothers.

The first thing I did was to walk to the window and look out at the sight below me. The grounds were covered with trees and I could see the long winding driveway that led down to the main gate. In the distance I could see the Hudson River and a cluster of what appeared to be several separated small villages.

"This is it, Gabriel. You've a nice view of the grounds," Pat said then pointed to the adjoining bathroom.

I moved away from the window and walked into the bathroom and was happy to see a bathtub that was bigger than any I had seen before, even in the Shelbourne Hotel in Dublin where I had worked. We didn't have one in Dublin and I looked forward to getting into the tub and stretching out in it.

While I contemplated the pleasures of the bathtub, I heard Pat's voice again.

"Jim's my husband. He helps maintain the grounds. In fact he helps maintain everything around here."

I didn't quite know how to respond so I just said, "Thanks, ma'am."

Pat walked back towards the door. As she pulled it shut she mumbled back to me, "I set out enough clean towels to last you a week, Gabriel."

I indicated my thanks by bowing my head.

"Get some rest. I'll see you in the kitchen for breakfast in the morning. I'll show you where Miss Sheridan stays."

Pat closed the door and I walked back into the bedroom. The absolute silence of the place frightened me and for a moment or two I wondered what was happening to me and if I knew what I was doing with my life. I shook my head and thought I might have made a mistake in coming to America. I stood next to my suitcase in the middle of the room for several minutes before I could get my body to move or turn. After contemplating whether I should even keep the leathery old thing or not, I picked the suitcase up and slid it under the bed. I was as close to being numb as I had ever been and I soon fell asleep, still wearing the clothes I had on me when I left Dublin.

* * *

The next morning I was awakened by a knocking on the door. I jumped out of bed still fully dressed and for a second or two I didn't know where I was. A few more knocks on the door and I was no longer wondering where I was.

I looked out the window and saw several cars going up and down the long driveway.

The knocking on the door continued. I went and opened it. A man dressed in overalls with a colourful kerchief around his neck was standing outside.

"Good morning! Are you ready to come downstairs?" he asked. "I'm Pat's husband, Jim McCluskey."

"I'm Gabriel. Will you give me a minute to –"

Jim interrupted me. "There's no hurry," he said.

"Can I take a bath?" I asked.

"I'll come back in twenty minutes." The man turned and made his way towards the big staircase.

I closed the door, went into the bathroom and turned on the hot water. The water burst out of the tap with such impatience I thought it might well have been waiting a hundred years for me to come and release it. I took off the shirt I'd been wearing for a week, quickly washed it and hung it outside the window. To keep it from flying into the Hudson River in the distance, I kept it in place by pulling the window down on it. In seconds the wind caught it and it flapped about like a flag in a storm.

After that I put my nakedness into the big tub and instantly felt like a new person. For as long as I could I stretched out and let the hot water dissolve away as many memories of my past as was possible at that moment.

* * *

When I entered the kitchen about thirty minutes later, Pat was sitting next to a window that gave a view of a large part of the estate. An aroma of coffee filled the air as if to underline the fact that I was now in America. A lifetime of having a cup of tea every morning had been sent into exile with one whiff of the air. I relished the aroma of freshly brewed coffee.

After Pat bid me good morning I sat down opposite her. Before I could say a word she got up and placed a plateful of bacon and eggs in front of me. She then poured me a cup of coffee. My first impulse was to show her how I could use a knife and fork and I unhesitatingly began to display the table manners I had acquired at the Shelbourne Hotel.

As I was about to swallow another cup of coffee a small bell attached to the kitchen wall began to ring.

8

Pat immediately jumped to her feet. "Mr. Axe is up!" she yelled while she pulled at a cord hanging from the bell to stop it from ringing.

She then began to prepare breakfast for Mr. Axe: a pot of coffee, toast and a bowl of cereal as well as a glass of fresh orange juice. Everything was placed on a silver tray. Pat picked the tray up and hurried out of the kitchen.

I remained at the table and as I pondered my whereabouts Pat came rushing back into the kitchen.

"He wants grapefruit juice instead!" she gasped and then hurried to the refrigerator and took out two grapefruits. She then cut each in half and squeezed them, using a glass juicer. As she poured the juice into a glass she called to me, "Why don't you go outside and look around, Gabriel, and see the garden? Come back in fifteen minutes or so and we'll get Miss Sheridan's breakfast ready together."

When Pat rushed back into the dining room I walked out of the kitchen, crossed a hallway, opened a big wooden door and stepped out into the garden. The garden was more like a forest. The grass was covered with a light coat of snow and the many trees were practically bare. The driveway that led down to the main gate looked steeper than I'd imagined when I arrived the night before. I walked about for a few minutes and wondered why I was standing in front of this huge castle in Tarrytown, New York. I strolled around to the other side of the castle and looked up to see if I could spot where my room was. I saw my shirt hanging out the window. A floor or two higher and the shirt would have been flapping in the clouds.

* * *

A voice, very familiar to me, called out, "Come in, please!"

Pat opened the door and we both entered Maggie's quarters. The place was twice as big as her suite in the Shelbourne and, like in her space there, her clothes and travel trunks were spread all about the room. She even had a record player on a small table not too far from her bed.

As I had seen so many times, Maggie Sheridan was sitting up in bed with two supportive pillows behind her: one at her back and the other behind her neck. I could feel her eyes observing me as I placed the breakfast tray in front of her yet again. This morning, however, was the first time in America. After putting the tray down I knew enough not to move, so I just stood still like a soldier at attention.

"Well, well, well!" Maggie commented on my presence. She seemed happily surprised. "I wasn't expecting you so soon. Are you sure you're not still seasick?"

I moved back from her bedside a bit and almost bumped into Pat.

"He wanted to help me, and he was wide awake," Pat volunteered.

As Maggie began to spread a chunk of marmalade across a slice of toast, she called to Pat. "Make sure he knows where he is, Pat! He's a long way from home." She looked at me and, as often in the past in Dublin, I felt she was about to lecture me. "Sit, Gabriel."

I obediently followed her instruction and went over to a chair halfway between her bed and the big window that faced out onto the estate.

"Make sure he knows his way up and down, Pat," Maggie commanded.

"Will do!" Pat responded.

By the time I'd settled in the chair Pat had left the room without saying goodbye to me.

"Well, did you sleep okay?" Maggie asked me with upturned eyes as if she was unsure of what my answer would be.

"I did. I fell asleep in my clothes."

Almost without hesitation she raised her voice and asked, "Did you take a bath? I hope you did. Did you?"

"Yes."

If she noticed how clean I looked she didn't say so. "You'll need a new suit and, looking at you now, I can say you'll need a new just-about-everything."

In a partly lost state of mind I sat awkwardly in front of Maggie as she continued to eat her breakfast. She appeared to be less frustrated and impatient than she had frequently been at the hotel in Dublin. Maybe it was because she had no one to yell at nor anything to complain about.

Maggie's bedroom had a very large window that faced out in a different direction to the room I was in. To show her that I was feeling relaxed, I stood up and walked towards the window.

"Have you been outside this morning?" she queried me as if to break what seemed to me to be a prolonged and awkward silence.

"I went out front earlier. The biggest place I've ever been in," I said with a flush of enthusiasm, more to reassure her than myself.

At that point I heard a tap on the door and Mrs. Axe, wearing a silky oriental type of bathrobe, entered the room and looked to be in a jovial mood. "How are you, Gabriel? Rested, I hope?" She seemed happy to see me and I felt a bit more at ease.

Before I could answer Maggie called out loud, "Gabriel hasn't worn anything new since the invention of wool!"

At that point I turned to leave the room and was just about out the door when Mrs. Axe called to me, "Wait, Gabriel!"

I stopped in my tracks. She moved a few steps closer to me. "We'll see you downstairs in about an hour. Dress for the weather – wear a warm coat. We'll be driving to White Plains."

* * *

The walk back to the kitchen allowed me to see parts of the mansion I hadn't noticed earlier. Down the big staircase I went, walked across the huge foyer, passed through a waiting room with sofas, armchairs and antique furniture. Seconds later I was pushing the revolving door that led to the kitchen.

As I entered the kitchen Pat and Jim were sitting at the table drinking coffee.

"Damn snow expected this weekend and Arthur's got the flu," Jim grumbled as he placed dishes in the sink. "Arthur's been workin' here for fifteen years and he always gets the flu whenever a holiday comes up."

"Plough truck ready?" Pat asked.

"Yep, it is," Jim answered in a kind of cowboy accent.

I sat down at the kitchen table but still didn't know what to do with myself. Feeling at odds as to how the rest of the day would unfold, I sat in silence while Jim continued to complain about his workmate Arthur.

With an obvious sign of impatience, Pat got up from the table and began to do routine chores about the kitchen. She talked as she put the pots, pans, glasses and plates away.

I followed her every move. I imagined it would be only a day or two until I would be on my own with regard to getting Maggie's breakfast tray ready.

As Pat rambled on she told me just about everything she thought I needed to know about the castle and the Axes, as far as she was concerned. She repeatedly related to me that Mr. and Mrs. Axe rarely dined together mainly because of Mrs. Axe's temperament and schedule. According to Pat, Ruth Houghton Axe moved about like a bumblebee and was forever on the phone talking business. If she wasn't involved with that, she was supervising her husband Emerson's schedule, particularly his cultural activities. Ruth Axe booked tickets to the opera and on rare occasions to Broadway shows. Weekdays Mrs. Axe was at the office in Manhattan and, every third week or so, she travelled about the country on company business. Mr. Axe rarely went with her. Infrequently, on weekends when they had visitors, they shared the dining-room table. Most of the visitors to the castle were individuals who were connected in some way to the business of finance and "mutual funds". The exception to the dining schedule, which included breakfast and lunch, was when Maggie decided to come down from her quarters. If she was in the mood to eat lunch or dinner she'd appear in the dining room. More often than not Mrs. Axe knew in advance if Maggie was going to be eating in the dining room and so she'd show up to eat with her and Mr. Axe. Mrs. Axe occupied one section of the castle that had a view of the town in the distance. Mr. Axe's suite overlooked the vista of the Hudson River. During the work week he would supervise the accountants, financial experts and others who worked daily close to him in the castle. Miss Barnes, an elderly spinster type of woman, who had been with the Axes since the forming of the company, was his secretary and she attended to every need he had. After overseeing the domestic operation of the castle, such as cooks, cleaners, painters and the groundsmen who kept the lawns neat and trim, Mrs. Axe made her way into the Manhattan office every morning slightly before noon. She would not return again until way past dinner time and would then spend an hour or two with Mr. Axe going over the day's business.

As I listened to Pat I guessed that the Axes didn't know they had not only hired a housekeeper but a personal historian as well.

Pat walked to the window and pointed out towards the main entrance. "That's the car Mrs. Axe uses, Gabriel," she said to me.

I leaned on the windowsill and saw a big yellow car parked under the covered archway. "I just washed and polished the damn thing," Jim grumbled further as he joined us at the window. "That's usually Arthur's job and not mine. I like being out on the grounds."

* * *

After a drive of about thirty minutes Mrs. Axe pulled her car up outside a big shop in the nearby town of White Plains and told me to get out. I stepped out of the car and followed her into the shop. Maggie remained behind in the car.

When I entered the shop it was like a warehouse. Mrs. Axe and I were greeted by a sales clerk but before he could say a word Mrs. Axe told him what she wanted. She pointed to me and gave the salesman instructions as if she had been his boss for years. The man then led me away towards a long rack of clothes. Mrs. Axe followed and began to pick out different kinds of jackets and suits as if she was going to wear them herself. She didn't ask me what I liked or what I was interested in. Mrs. Axe liked what she liked even when it came to what clothing I should wear. She had purchased a suit for me on Grafton Street and it had worked out well. She now ordered several white shirts and two black trousers. Also shoes as well as two tweed suits, a few sweaters, socks and underwear.

* * *

Two hours or so later that afternoon Mrs. Axe slowly brought the car to a halt outside the castle. I had seen almost every building and street in Tarrytown and had also learned a lot about its history and the historical characters that helped make up its overall profile. After that afternoon I knew more about Tarrytown and Westchester County than I did about almost any other part of the world, and that included Ireland.

Sitting behind Maggie and Mrs. Axe as we drove from place to place was like travelling through a time zone where every moment felt as if I was attached to a cloud of non-reality. What I slowly but surely began to embrace was that I was comfortable in that region of being away from my past and drifting in a direction where there were no signs of a final destination.

As I'd sat in the back seat of the car, Maggie had engaged in a conversation with Mrs. Axe about how I needed to be dealt with, with regard to adjusting to living in America. She outlined what she thought was the right programme for a person my age. When the time came, after I had gotten used to my new environment and life change, I was to think about attending school. Maggie was very much committed to the promise that she had given to my mother in Dublin. As she talked about work, education and even keeping clean, she also periodically would turn her head and look back and remind me that I was still a Catholic and that I was never to forget that fact. She made sure that Mrs. Axe drove by the local Catholic church so that I would know where to go when it came to attending it on Sundays and other holy days. She didn't mention the fact that the Axes were not churchgoers and wouldn't be inclined to remind me of my religious obligations. That responsibility, for the duration of her time in New York, rested solely with Maggie.

By the time I got out of the car I had been prepped on my schedule and daily routine for my life at the castle. One fact was firm, knowable and stationary in my mind: it was that every morning for as long as Maggie was residing in the castle I would serve her breakfast just as I had done back in the hotel in Dublin.

I soon learned that Maggie would regularly complain about the New York weather and just about everything else. If she wasn't going back to Dublin in three days it was three weeks. If it wasn't three weeks she would be returning in three months. One of those time periods, according to her, would be an opportune time for me to resume, or more accurately begin, my education.

My education in Dublin hardly qualified me to carry a breakfast tray. School back there was more like a prison that I was consistently and fervently attempting to escape from. I couldn't remember one day of enjoyment or pleasure or inspiration inside the walls of the Christian Brothers School, or for that matter the less draconian semi-secular school I attended before I reached the age of fourteen years, old enough to leave and join the workforce. I had barely scratched the fundamental basics of reading, writing and elementary arithmetic in Dublin. My working-class upbringing neither envisioned nor prepared me to think or imagine a world that didn't include the sight of smoke chimneys and the cacophony of hammers. The exception to answering the call of the factory horn came to me from Sister Charlotte, a nun at Goldenbridge Convent. It was she who saw to it that I had a suit for my First Communion. She, in a lesson without words, perhaps inadvertently bequeathed to me the element of hope.

As I was taking the bags and packages of clothing out of

the car trunk after our jaunt, Mrs. Axe asked me to come back down to the dining room when I had deposited them in my room.

When the three of us approached the main door it was opened by Pat. She took some of the clothing packages from me and walked alongside me as I proceeded across the foyer and headed towards my quarters at the top of the marble staircase.

Maggie called after me as she and Mrs. Axe retreated to the dining room. "Come back in fifteen minutes or so! Freshen up and come down!"

"Okay, ma'am," I responded.

Walking up the long twisting marble staircase with bags and packages was a bit of a task.

"Where were you all today?" Pat asked me as I proceeded ahead of her.

I really didn't know where I had been. I told her we drove all over the place and I also told her about the shopping spree in White Plains. As I mumbled about the day's events I fumbled with the large bags and packages I was carrying. A pair of shoes fell out of one box and landed a few steps below me. I retreated and picked them up but in my semi-blurred state of mind I dropped a few more clothing items. Pat came to my assistance and helped me pick them up.

"You're coming down in a few minutes, I understand?" Pat asked me when we reached my room.

"I'm to be down for a cup of tea or something," I answered, not really wanting another cup of tea. I was feeling tired and wished just to flop on the bed and fall asleep.

* * *

After unpacking most of my new clothes I fell down on my

bed. I was tired, confused and had no idea what to do with myself. I wanted to close my eyes but I knew I had to be down in the dining room shortly. As I lay on the bed, making every effort to keep my eyes open, I could hear my shirt still flapping outside the window. It was getting darker and windier outside. The noise of the shirt flapping in the wind made sure I couldn't fall asleep. I got off the bed, opened the window and retrieved my shirt, which was almost frozen stiff. I walked to the bathroom and threw the shirt into the tub. I then turned on the hot water and the shirt almost melted.

* * *

When I got back downstairs Mrs. Axe and Maggie were sitting at the dining-room table. A classical music piece was playing on a record player, which was situated near an enormous window that gave a view of the Hudson River valley. Mr. Axe was standing over the record that was presently playing. Several shelves laden with records were visible. A massive dining table lay in front of a stone fireplace.

"There you are!" Maggie called.

When Mr. Axe saw me enter the room he lowered the volume on the record player. "Hello, hello," he said, then cleared his throat and joined his wife and Maggie at the table. Mr. Axe had a habit of clearing his throat after he spoke. "I hear you got new clothing today, Gabriel."

Before I could answer him the swinging door to the dining room opened and Pat entered, carrying a tray with the tea things on it.

"Thank you, Pat," Mrs. Axe said with a smile of satisfaction.

Maggie repeated the same sentiment. Both women were apparently in the mood for a cup of tea.

"A few biscuits too, Pat," Mrs. Axe added.

Pat retreated to the kitchen and returned almost immediately with a plateful of colourful biscuits. Then she smiled obsequiously and withdrew again from the room.

I wasn't sure if I should reach for the teapot and pour the tea. I felt caught between serving and being served. I decided just to wait until somebody else did it. Eventually Mrs. Axe took hold of the teapot and poured tea into all four cups. She passed one to me and I felt a bit awkward. I got worried as to how to say thanks. My voice seemed to be stuck somewhere deep down inside of my stomach. I wondered if I was expected to be more open and talkative. I was happy that Maggie was in the same room and I knew she'd come to my rescue if I behaved or said anything embarrassing.

In a few seconds Mrs. Axe's voice broke into my thoughts and it was a welcome relief.

"So, Gabriel," said Mrs. Axe, "if you need anything let me or Margaret know."

Maggie then took over. "But don't get in Mr. Axe's way – he likes everything his way. He has it all pre-arranged. Don't touch anything that belongs to him."

I wasn't really sure what she was referring to.

"Miss Sheridan is referring to my chess set, Gabriel. I have it set every night and –"

"And he likes it that way!" Mrs. Axe said with a laugh.

"Yes, I like it that way," Mr. Axe added.

"Maybe you can teach him to play chess, Emerson," Maggie said.

Mr. Axe cleared his throat again. "I'd be happy to. Of course! I'd be happy to."

When the teapot was emptied and the biscuits on the plate consumed, Mr. Axe turned up the volume on the recording that was playing and all four of us sat for a few minutes listening. Mr. Axe seemed to be in another world with his music. He listened as if he was being caressed by the sound.

"Would you be familiar with this music, Gabriel?" he suddenly asked.

At that Maggie jumped in. "For God's sake, Emerson! The poor boy just got off the boat!"

Mrs. Axe laughed and took the tray with the cups and saucers off the table. She walked back towards the kitchen and Maggie followed her.

I then got up from my chair and followed Maggie.

* * *

My alarm clock rang and awakened me at seven. A quick wash and a jump into the attire Mrs. Axe had bought me: black trousers, white shirts, then down to the kitchen where Pat was in the early stages of preparing Mr. Axe's breakfast. Mrs. Axe got her own breakfast every morning way before Pat or I arrived in the kitchen. She would be up with the birds and would take her breakfast back to her bedroom where she could be on the phone doing business and eating at the same time.

When I entered the kitchen Pat was in her usual talkative mood. Mrs. Axe, according to Pat, was "the live wire" of the couple. Mrs. Axe managed everything domestically as well as holding the position of being vice president of the company. She hired and fired financial executives and the domestic staff. When she was satisfied that everything was in order in the castle every morning, she'd get into her car and drive to New York City where she presided over several executives who worked in the Fifth Avenue Office of EW Axe and Company. Apart from having different personalities and

20

interests in many diverse subjects, Mr. and Mrs. Axe shared a love for opera and almost all things "cultural".

Every time Pat lifted a spoon or a cup or a pot she made comments about everything and everybody.

Pat had placed a cup of coffee on the table for me. I drank it slowly as I watched an egg boil on the gas range. I waited for Pat to take the egg out of the boiling water and place it on the tray. She then took two slices of whole-wheat bread from the toaster. I picked up the teapot and poured boiling water into it to take away any chill that was in the pot. Maggie would know if I hadn't heated the pot before pouring the boiling water over the tea leaves. She wanted her tea piping hot and it wouldn't be if the water was poured into a cold pot. For a minute or two I might easily have been in the kitchen in the Shelbourne Hotel in Dublin. The panic and the fuss were identical.

Within fifteen minutes of my inauguration in the kitchen I was out the door and walking towards Maggie's suite with her breakfast, Pat trailing behind me. Unlike in Dublin the tray didn't have fried kippers on it: since she'd arrived in New York, according to Pat, Maggie had not expressed an interest in having fish for breakfast.

The kitchen had several exits. This time we took the door out of the kitchen that led through the main dining room and on through another room before we emerged into the hall. As we passed through the second room Pat pointed out Mr. Axe's chess area. She told me he often played chess with himself and that the chessboard was to be considered an altar that I shouldn't go near. She also mentioned that Mr. Axe was a serious wine collector. He kept a special cellar in the basement filled with wines of different vintages and seasons and was adamant that only he was to retrieve wines from the place. Before ascending the huge wooden staircase Pat pointed to a room that was Mr. Axe's personal library. Mr. Axe, a Harvard man, appeared to have an insatiable appetite for everything that was published in the arts, commerce, history and just about everything cultural.

* * *

Every meeting I had with Maggie was pretty much the same. She always wanted to know what I had done with myself since she'd seen me last.

My daily routine changed very little as the days and then weeks went by. I'd be out in the garden with Arthur and listening to his complaints about Jim. I'd go to town with Jim and Pat, following them around while they did their shopping. I'd spend time in the office mail room. I'd greet Mrs. Axe when she returned from the city every night and after that I'd either be in my room or watching television in Jim and Pat's quarters over the kitchen. The television of the fifties was awash with old black-and-white movies and Roy Rogers, Gene Autry and Hopalong Cassidy came galloping back into my life. Most of them I had already seen when I lived in Dublin. If Pat and Jim were out for the night I'd get into my car and meet up with Frank Dillon, a man I knew from a bar I had been introduced to by an employee of the Axes.

For weeks on end I had no contact with anyone who didn't live or work at the castle.

Every week Maggie played some of her old recordings in her room and had me listen to them. When she asked for my opinion I was reluctant to give one. A part of me didn't want to admit that I actually liked and enjoyed the music. It was as though the serpent of inferiority that I grew up with back in Dublin was still able to consume a large part of my existence. When it came to sharing or even admitting anything about culture or the arts in general, to Maggie or even to Mrs. Axe, I felt that if I put my social evolution on display both of them might retreat from me. On the other hand, the echoes and reverberations of the opera arias I heard in Maggie's room and downstairs in the Axes' living room stayed with me and I always looked forward to the experience.

Two Sundays in a row Maggie and I drove, with Mrs. Axe at the wheel, to a convent in Long Island where Maggie knew several nuns – an area where the Axes had a beach house they rarely visited. Although not overtly religious, Mrs. Axe seemed to display affection for religion when it came to accommodating Maggie's wishes. She even sent one of her drivers to New Jersey to bring Father Leo Clifford, a priest from the order of the Dominicans, to the castle when Maggie requested it. Twice in the last month Father Clifford, who had known Maggie in Dublin and who was now stationed in New Jersey, came to visit her and bestowed his blessing on her – presumably after she confessed her sins to him. Father Clifford had been a friend of Maggie's for years and was also her confessor. The priest was a charming, handsome man who was well aware of my relationship with Maggie and my personal and domestic situation with the Axes. When I met Father Leo on his visits to the castle he never failed to inquire about my religious practice. I always told him I never missed Mass. I even told him I went to Confession and Communion every week. Lately Maggie had exhibited a greater interest in religion than I had previously witnessed in Dublin and I think because of that she never failed to ask me if I had gone to Mass on Sunday and if I was keeping track of the church holidays. I assured her I went to Mass every Sunday with Pat and Jim (or with one or the other of them if they went separately). That was the kind of reassurance she seemed most content with when it came to asking me about my time in the castle.

* * *

An hour or two after retrieving Maggie's breakfast tray I'd frequently bump into Mr. Axe who seemed during the course of the day to be unapproachable but on occasion would stop to chat and ask me if I had heard of the author of a book he'd have in his hands or if I knew the composer of the music that was playing on his audio system. Sometimes when I'd stop to listen to him or the music he had playing I'd actually think he was teasing me. He knew I had no knowledge of classical music and I had definitely not heard of the author or the book he had in his hands. Mr. Axe seemed to derive a little pleasure from asking me questions he knew I couldn't answer. On the other hand he enjoyed answering his own questions for me and explaining the music that he was so enthralled with. Also, throughout the first month of my time in his house, I came to realise that he fancied himself as a bit of an actor and didn't hesitate not only to quote Shakespeare but to act out the lines of the play he was quoting. He spoke about Hamlet, Macbeth and King Lear as if he had been roommates with them at Harvard.

Unhesitatingly and uninvited he'd offer his opinion on characters and events in world history. His fascination with the history of World War I was palpable. He was particularly interested when I told him my father was in it. My father Paddy Walsh rarely spoke of his time in the trenches during the Great War, but whatever bits and pieces of information I had gleaned from him over the years I related to Mr. Axe.

Any bit of information unleashed a torrent of statistics on just about everything related to the war. Mr. Axe almost on a daily basis informed me of the details of the war, from its outbreak to its conclusion which ended with the Treaty of Versailles. Mr. Axe had an obsession with politicians and world leaders both past and present, Winston Churchill being his favourite target. According to Mr. Axe, when Churchill was Lord of the Admiralty he single-handedly was responsible for the greatest military blunder in World War I. This was the Dardanelles which, according to Mr. Axe, was comparable to the fiasco at Dunkirk in World War II with the exception that more soldiers and sailors from the Commonwealth perished on Churchill's orders to invade the Turkish coast. In Mr. Axe's mind, Churchill was the architect of many a bad structure.

I was perhaps for him a silent sounding board. I didn't talk back or voice my opinion on whatever he was espousing and advocating at the time. It was similar to my habit of almost non-response to Maggie when she had me listen to opera and chatted with me afterwards about the human voice and the opera composer. Dropping much of his Harvard idea of education was obviously a pleasing experience for Mr. Axe. He almost never asked if I understood anything he imparted to me. Whether the priority was him talking or me listening I wasn't always sure. One thing I was sure of and that was I didn't care if he was talking or if I was listening. Either way suited me fine.

I was convinced, after living under his roof for the best part of three months, that he was as confused about my presence in his world as I was of him in mine.

* * *

I got used to just floating about after Maggie was served breakfast and usually didn't know what to do with myself for the rest of the day. My time was essentially my own. Sometimes Mrs. Axe would call upon Jim and Arthur and ask them to take me around the estate to help them with collecting fallen branches and mowing the lawn. And often I gave Pat a hand in the kitchen just to fill in time.

Occasionally I'd meet with Maggie when she decided she wanted to eat sometime around midday. Many times we both ate in the kitchen. It was the same with Mrs. Axe. She'd come rushing into the kitchen and find Maggie and me sitting at the kitchen table and would immediately help herself to a sandwich and coffee and sit at the table also. Mr. Axe on the other hand would never be caught eating in the kitchen. He had to sit at the head of the large wooden table in the dining room and be served. Eating alone in the dining room also allowed him to listen to his music and, when not indulging in that, he would want absolute silence when he decided to read a book over his lunch.

For most of the day I lingered about the castle grounds or sat on the wall down by the front gate, talking to the odd person who drove up in a car and wanted to know what went on inside the gates and if the castle was really haunted. My response was always the same. I told the curiosity-seekers that Dracula and Frankenstein lived in the castle and they were not available to visitors. This misinformation always got a laugh. It also encouraged the curious to depart in a hurry.

Whether it was spontaneous or planned I didn't know but Mrs. Axe, becoming concerned that I wasn't using my time in a productive way, suggested I spend time in the office where I could occupy myself and maybe even learn a bit about the business. She suggested I visit the office during the week which I did about ten o'clock every morning after I had finished serving Maggie her breakfast. For several weeks the men and women who worked in the office got used to me arriving hours after they had come to work and hanging around. They had been filled in on my connection to Maggie Sheridan and Mrs. Axe. Most office employees were friendly and welcoming. For weeks on end I sat and chatted with the executives who spent most of their time on the phone while scribbling numbers on charts and sheets. I learned how to use an adding machine but I remained a blank page when it came to understanding anything about mutual funds and the world of Wall Street. My knowledge and absorption of sums and numbers and charts was essentially nil.

Half the time I didn't know what to do with myself. At coffee breaks I was asked about my family and Ireland but lately the connection to both seemed to have receded and was less intense. Instead I talked about American movies and the employees were surprised, even mystified, by my interest in them. I had no knowledge of any other subject that I could impress them with.

Mrs. Axe's secretary reported back to Mrs. Axe on my progress in business studies but by the way she greeted me every morning I sensed she wasn't too impressed with me. She moved me from one department to another. Each department had its own function and purpose. All of them had to do with how the stock market was behaving. Not having any visceral sense of what it all meant, I displayed no great interest and was moved from one individual to another. Each made an effort to inform me of their responsibilities and duties but the greater dimension and area of my mind didn't gravitate towards their vocational ambitions and instruction. My inability to focus on what I was being told didn't impress many of the executives and for the most part they reached the conclusion that they didn't know what to do with me.

Mrs. Axe didn't seem to know what to do with me either. She appeared to have as much knowledge of what do with me as I had of myself.

Eventually I drifted away from sitting at an empty desk and volunteered to help in the mail room, a place where hundreds of envelopes were stamped, addressed and readied for posting by a big machine. Working there didn't require too much brain power.

When I wasn't in the mail room I was on occasion driving back and forth to the post office with Tom Walton, who was in charge of the post coming and going to the Axe Corporation. Tom was in his mid-thirties and had lived in Tarrytown all his life. In the course of his driving trips to and from Tarrytown he showed me the town from a local's point of view. I spent quite a bit of time with him in coffee shops and bars where he stretched his time out between the post office and the castle. Tom liked to drop off at the local tavern and have a beer with friends he had gone to high school with. On my first visit, by the time Tom had finished his second beer I was introduced to many of his friends. Most of them wanted to know how I came to be living up in the castle but rather than go into details I told them I was a friend of a guest who stayed there every so often. The castle was well known by the locals but few knew much about it. Some joked that it was haunted and almost to a man none of them had ever visited the place.

Frank Dillon, a man in his mid-thirties and a permanent patron at the bar, had a talent for mimicking famous people.

In particular he was good at pretending he was James Cagney and Humphrey Bogart and had an obsession with talking about his time in Hollywood when he was younger. Frank's talk of Hollywood had a ring to it that suggested he had only read about the place in magazines but nobody questioned the veracity of his Hollywood reminiscences, mainly because he was an attraction for those who came into the watering hole to drink and forget the reality of their own everyday existences. I listened to Frank because in some ways he nourished in me the fantasies of my own childhood. Trivia passed for intelligent conversation with Frank Dillon and his fellow imbibers.

The first time I met him Frank started to wax on about *On the Waterfront*, a movie he had seen at the local cinema sometime during the week. He talked about the actor, Marlon Brando, as if he had discovered a new brand of whiskey. Frank identified with Brando's character in the movie so much he swore to give up drinking and, very much under the influence of the brew, he proclaimed that he would in the not too far-off future offer his acting *talent* to the world. After consuming two beers I sat next to him at the bar and bragged that I would do the same thing. This proclamation of mine nearly sobered Frank and everybody up. The silence that followed was quickly broken by a loud burst of laughter and I timidly withdrew my assertion and declared that I would more than likely become a banker instead.

* * *

One weekend Tom took me to a football game in Tarrytown at Washington Irving High School, the school he graduated from. It was not only the first time I had seen American football but, more importantly (at least to me at the time), I witnessed cheerleaders. Half a dozen beautiful girls dressed in colourful costumes were dancing, twisting and cheering on the local team. Tom at an earlier time in his life had played for the high-school football team and he was somewhat hypnotised by the game he was watching. I was mesmerised by the cheerleaders and for the first time my body, as opposed to my mind, realised it was in America.

When Tom drove me back to the castle that evening I knew I could no longer live isolated on the estate. It was too far from town and the bus that passed the gates came by only every two hours. The experience of the football game at the high school and the cheerleaders was for me a bit like going to a happy movie that I didn't want to end.

That Sunday, after Pat and Jim brought me back from Mass, I approached Mrs. Axe and asked her if I could get driving lessons and learn how to drive. There were several old cars that belonged to the Axes parked in different areas of the grounds and nobody seemed ever to use them. I asked Jim about the cars and he told me they used to belong to people who were no longer employed by the Axes. Mrs. Axe would provide an employee with a car when they came to work at the castle. The place was so far away from the town that anyone who worked for her had to have transportation. I knew if I could get my driving licence I would be able to borrow one of them.

The following Monday Mrs. Axe arranged for me to take driving lessons every day for three weeks. When I got my driver's licence she let me have one of the old cars: a 1948 Ford Convertible. It was yellow with a black top and I couldn't tell whether it was made for me or I was made for it. I fell in love with the damn thing and would have slept in it if it had a mattress and a bathroom. Getting my driver's licence and having my own wheels opened up a path for me to get out and away from the castle.

* * *

One day as I drove up the driveway I passed another car coming in the opposite direction. I had slowed down to give the right of way when I saw Father Leo Clifford sitting in the back seat. I waved to him but his driver was driving too fast and I don't think he noticed me. When I got back to the castle Mrs. Axe told me that Miss Sheridan wasn't feeling well and had asked for the priest to come and visit her. She also asked me to go and say hello.

I made my way up to Maggie's quarters, knocked on the door and, like so many times before, Maggie's voice called out, "Come in!" When I entered her room she was standing at the window looking outwards and appeared to be just staring into space. One of her old recordings was playing softly on the portable record player and I was reminded of the first day I met her. The same record was playing now and, even though she wasn't on the floor looking for a lipstick tube as she had been that day, she did look as if she was looking for something. When she sensed I was close to her she turned around, silenced the record player and told me to sit down, which I obediently did.

"What's going on with you now?" she asked.

I answered, "Nothing."

Maggie then walked to her huge travelling trunk that was wide open in the centre of the room. It hadn't been moved since the day she arrived. With the exception of the clothes she was wearing all her belongings now seemed to be in the massive travelling piece of luggage. She fussed about with the old trunk and rearranged a few items of clothing.

"I'm going to Long Island to visit the nuns at the convent. I'll be there for a week maybe."

I had never questioned why she visited with the nuns on Long Island and didn't ask now. Maggie had a history of being connected to the nuns' way of life. She spent her childhood in a convent in Dublin and it was a nun who got her started in her singing career. In many ways Maggie was almost a nun herself. Had she not become a singer she might well have taken religious vows and lived a life opposite to the one she was living. She lived a life as a single woman and for the most part embraced being alone as a religious expression.

"When I come back here I'm going back to Ireland," she then said very matter-of-factly. Intentional or not, the absence of emotion in her words pained me. I felt a shiver in my body. As I heard her words ring in my ear I thought she had purposely underlined the implication of them. For the first time since the day I arrived I wondered what my life would be like without her being in it and close by. The freedom of having my own car was suddenly relegated to a meaningless reality. The thought of living in the castle without Maggie was not a good feeling. In fact it was not unlike the sense of detachment I had with my mother when I was packing my suitcase the morning I left home. Here I was again, only a few months but thousands of miles away from home, feeling another emotional trapdoor opening under me. The sense of falling and floating and the feeling that I couldn't grip or hold onto anything became pervasive all over again in my mind. At the same time I knew the only option I had was to wait and witness what was gradually unfolding in front of me. My mother Molly was home in Dublin and that link had snapped insofar as I could emotionally comprehend. Today, standing in Maggie's room, I was doing my best to ignore and deny in my mind that I was once again vulnerable to the thought and feeling of abandonment. To fend off the rush of fear and pain, I thought of the car I was now in possession of. I imagined myself driving up and down the entire State of New York. Or even America for that matter. Knowing I could jump in the car and speed away helped me somewhat but Maggie's reaching out to me in the hotel in Dublin was a big part of my life. Even though it was a near-silent relationship, my life and welfare was still very much determined by her.

Whenever Maggie came down from her apartment for dinner she sat at the table as if an opera was about to begin. Maggie's biting wit and humour always electrified those who sat with her. Her personality and fame as an opera singer added an element of fun and culture to the life of the Axes. Ruth and Maggie complemented each other in ways that either might not have thought about or imagined. Maggie's presence kept Ruth's artistic impulse alive and Ruth's business success and wealth afforded Maggie a lifestyle she might not otherwise have had. Emerson's passion for opera embraced both realities.

In the world of opera, particularly in the late thirties, Margaret Burke Sheridan had a glorious history and career as a first-class diva and prima donna. Her suggestion that I be brought to America might have had something to do with her own disappointments in life. She was essentially alone and not financially secure. Her voice had failed earlier than she would have wished. It was rumoured that the failure had coincided with the failure of a love affair she'd had with a married man in Italy when she was both young and in her prime as a singer.

Maggie in her floating retirement was accepted by both the Axes as if she was part of the family. The thought and inspiration of having me leave Dublin and serve her breakfast in Tarrytown, New York, may well have resonated in Maggie's mind as part of an operatic plot line by Verdi or Puccini. Mr. and Mrs. Axe may well have seen it in the same context.

The impending reality of Maggie returning to Ireland left me with the impression that I was now in an opera of uncertainty.

As I stood now in front of Maggie I could feel a change coming over my life and I was immediately saddened and even a bit frightened. Before I could fully digest the implications of her pending departure, she broke into my thoughts again.

"What will you do with yourself? You'll have more time on your hands if I'm not here."

I could feel a tone of concern in her voice but I didn't know how to respond. I'd no complaints and for the most part everything had gone quite well since I'd arrived. The Axes were supportive and considerate.

Maggie walked to the armchair and sat down on it. I sat on the chair that was in front of her small desk. I simply didn't know what I was going to do if and when she returned to Ireland. I got the feeling she wasn't truly anxious to go but I also sensed that she felt she had to. Why that was she didn't relate to me. As we both sat in a sad kind of silence Maggie began to talk again.

"Think about going to school while you're here, Gabriel. Mrs. Axe is in favour of that. Mr. Axe might have little input on the matter at the moment but Mrs. Axe thinks you can improve upon yourself by going to school. Would you like to go to school? I know you're a bit older now, but you can still go to school if you want to. With all the tutoring Mr. Axe has been heaping on you," she was referring to our 'chats', "you should have no problem getting into school here in Tarrytown."

* * *

The ritual of family dining was essentially non-existent at the castle. More often than not Mrs. Axe either had a meeting in Manhattan that ran late or she got tied up in traffic on her way home. Sometimes she'd stay in the city if her meetings went past a certain hour. Mr. Axe would then eat alone at the dinner table while reading a book or listening to an opera. When he was in a good mood and wasn't overtly annoyed at his wife's absence, he'd share some of his thoughts with me about the opera or the classical music he was listening to. If his business day had gone well he would give me a lesson in chess. One day he'd explain the function of one chess piece, the next day he'd spend time explaining another. By the end of that month I knew where all the chess pieces on the board were placed and what purpose they served.

I learned to play chess but it didn't take long for me to come to the conclusion that my life in the castle was a bit like a chess game itself. I was never sure of which direction to move. Some days I could move forward. Other days I could move sideways. On days when Mr. and Mrs. Axe were entertaining guests I could even leap out the door and jump into my car and speed away.

When I'd meet up with Mrs. Axe she'd inform me about Maggie's whereabouts. At one point she related to me that Maggie had gone into hospital in Dublin but was out again and staying in a special nursing home. Mrs. Axe didn't tell me and I didn't feel it my place to ask why Maggie was in a nursing home instead of the Shelbourne Hotel.

After Maggie's departure I was less inclined to stay at

home. Without her presence and indirect supervision I was free to drift about in my car. I didn't hesitate to take the opportunity to get behind the wheel of the Ford Convertible and drive to town to listen to Frank Dillon talk about his non-existent time in Hollywood. After an hour or two of heavy drinking Frank would announce that he was leaving for Tinseltown to seek fame and fortune, only to be back sitting on the same bar stool the next night and the night after that.

The stories I brought back to Pat and Jim prompted them to warn me about spending too much of my time in the bar. Whether it was on purpose or not, Pat and Jim found a way to keep me home at night. They asked me to help in the kitchen when Pat was under stress and in need of assistance. I agreed that I would forgo my trips into town and oblige, particularly when Pat informed me that Mrs. Axe had expressed concern about my visits to the local watering hole at night.

Because of its isolation my apartment was a place I only wanted to be in when I was asleep. Once I had climbed the marble staircase and entered the quarters I felt I had entered a lock-up. As comfortable as it was with its big bathtub and hot water, clean bed sheets and great view of the Hudson River, I felt as soon as I lay down on the bed that I was lost to the world at large. There wasn't a phone or any way of contacting anyone. To get attention or to let anybody know I was home or even alive I'd either have to step out on the landing and yell or run all the way back down to the kitchen or knock on Pat's apartment door.

The kitchen had become my favourite room in the castle. I ate there most of the time and it was where I met up with Mrs. Axe when she wanted to talk to me or when she was giving Pat orders for the week's menu.

Sometimes the Axes entertained guests. I avoided so many parties and functions at the castle that Mrs. Axe gave up on inviting me to them. Most of her guests were business associates and elderly folk. I didn't fit in and I didn't want to either. My life with the Axes since Maggie's departure had fallen into a void and a limbo. The daily routine of living in the castle with them was something akin to being a pendulum. One day I'd be talking to Mr. Axe, another day I'd be talking to Mrs. Axe. Without prior notice I'd drive with them when both went into New York City. In Manhattan they would stop off at the Metropolitan Club on Fifth Avenue. The club was an exclusive address for wealthy patrons. In the course of two or three months I had dinner several times in the dining room and sat next to the big window that faced Fifth Avenue. The view from the window opened up to Central Park. Between dessert and coffee I saw half of America walking by outside. At such times I was always alert to be on my best behaviour and to display my table manners and all the facets of upper-class living that I had observed at the Shelbourne and that Maggie and Mrs. Axe had instructed me in.

But whether I was dining at the Metropolitan Club on Fifth Avenue or sitting in a rundown bar in Tarrytown with Frank Dillon and his cabal of disillusioned mates, I sensed a feeling growing in me that was telling me I wasn't comfortable in either reality. I wanted to be on the road and highway hearing the blast from the dual exhaust pipes I'd had put onto the old Ford I drove. The feeling of being alone and moving fast at the same time was, if nothing else, intoxicating.

* * *

Sitting in the office one day I got a call from Mrs. Axe. She told me she was driving into Manhattan and suggested I go along with her and that I could drive her car if I was up to it.

An hour later I was behind the wheel of her Cadillac driving down the Saw Mill River Parkway and heading for New York City. The journey to Manhattan took about forty minutes and, by the time I'd parked the car in a garage on West 56th Street, Mrs. Axe and I had talked to each other more than we had since we first met in Dublin. I learned how the business she and Mr. Axe founded had become so successful. Both of them had a passion for finance and each was a highly respected financial adviser in different fields of expertise. The Axes had established a very successful mutual funds corporation that enhanced their reputation in the world of Wall Street. Even though I had been living in the same residence as Mrs. Axe and frequently meeting up with her for many months, the one-on-one conversation in the car was like two people meeting for the first time. It was my sense that when Maggie was around Mrs. Axe kept her distance. For a time I actually believed she was a bit cold and icy: always nice but somewhat indifferent and distant. Prior to today there was always another individual, such as Maggie, Pat or Mr. Axe in our company. As I drove along the highway Mrs. Axe heard more about my life than she had ever heard before. Most of her knowledge of me had come from Maggie, though she and Maggie had also met my mother in Dublin – a meeting I still cringed to think about. When she asked in detail about my schooling I, with some embarrassment, told her I had very little of it in Dublin. I had assumed she knew but by her reaction I realised she didn't. That put a new light on her efforts to mould me into a financial whizz kid. She simply had no idea I could barely compute.

As I drove closer to Manhattan Mrs. Axe got around to talking about her love of music and the opera, and her own life. Her childhood ambition was to be a violinist but when she met and married she neglected to pursue her creative impulse. I sensed, if only vaguely, that at some level or in some part of her brain her attachment to Maggie substituted for the lack of her own artistic expression.

She talked on, telling me how she had contemplated going professional and joining an orchestra. Had she not embarked on a weekend trip to Boston where she met Emerson Axe, the captain of the Harvard fencing team, a gifted student in economics and a descendant of the ninth Attorney General of the United States, she might be playing in some orchestra pit in a major American city. Whether it was his rapier, his mind or a combination of the two, Emerson Axe persuaded Ruth Houghton to abandon her musical ambitions and throw her lot in with him. Both graduated in the same year and shortly thereafter got married. Not long after that they formed their own financial advisory company and set up offices in New York City. For some thirty years they worked in tandem with each other and shared just about everything in life except children. Over the years, as they became more and more successful in the world of finance they became less personal in their marriage and relationship. When they moved from New York City to the castle in Tarrytown they had decided on separate living quarters and a sharing of professional responsibilities.

She told me how she was so attached to Maggie and how much she missed her. I expressed the same sentiment. We both laughed when we innocently remarked on Maggie's temperament. Mrs. Axe laughed out loud when I told her about Maggie's reputation at the Shelbourne Hotel. What made the conversation about Maggie humorous was that Mrs. Axe always paid Maggie's hotel bills and she jokingly apologised for causing the ruckus that seemed always to take place when Maggie registered in the hotel.

Since the time she had become my legal guardian via Maggie's influence, this was the first long and uninterrupted opportunity for Mrs. Axe and me to talk and exchange thoughts, ideas and perceptions.

She inquired about how I was getting along with the people I sometimes worked with in the office and if I was receiving my pay cheque of forty dollars per week. She queried me about my relationship with Pat and Jim. She mentioned that she was aware of the time I was spending driving about town in the car she had allowed me to have and the amount of time I was using up in the local bar with some of the town drunks. When I explained that I only went to the bar for a bit of company and amusement she laughed.

Mrs. Axe appeared to be pleased with how I had integrated into her home, her life and the area in general. For a part of the drive she talked about my family in Dublin and wanted to know if I had kept in touch with them, mainly my mother Molly, and asked if she should send Molly the dress she'd promised. I told her I hadn't written home since I arrived and, with the exception of two small one-page letters I received from my mother when I first left Ireland, I hadn't heard from her or anybody else in the family. As for sending my mother a dress, I submitted that Molly, because of her obsession with pain, suffering and penitence, would in all likelihood not wear it. Transforming my mother from her self-imposed image of a sixth-century martyr would take a miracle. The first thing she would do with the dress would be to take it to the pawn shop and get whatever she could for it.

She would rather be seen wearing an old and tattered dress and a crown of thorns. The latest fashion in clothing, particularly if it had come from America, would in Molly's eyes be an attack on her devotion to her religion and an obstacle in the way of her journey to Heaven. I didn't want to deny my mother a new dress nor did I want to influence Mrs. Axe in her proposal of sending one to her, but I was convinced that it would be better for both of them if the gift of a dress was postponed indefinitely. The existence of a new dress in Molly's life, were she to accept and wear it, would be a life-changing experience not only for her but for those who knew her. It wasn't the Way of the Cross and no saint ever got to Heaven wearing a new dress. Also the presence of a new dress would probably have a traumatic effect on my father. If, by way of a miracle, Molly wore the dress, he'd be obliged to change his lifelong opinion of her and the consequence of that would impact on both of them and force them to reassess their marriage and relationship.

In the course of the drive Mrs. Axe also told me how I might rethink my own life. Essentially she said she had talked to Maggie prior to her departure and both agreed that I should go to high school in Tarrytown. I was happy to hear this and felt very positive about my future at the castle. As Mrs. Axe related it, I was to go to the school the next week with a Mr. Dolan, a man from the office designated by her, and enrol in the school. The thought of jumping into my hot-rod car every morning was as exciting as it could get for me. Washington Irving High was about a five or ten-minute drive from the castle. For days, weeks, and months I had observed students entering and exiting the building on the main road that went through Tarrytown.

Tom Walton and I had gone to see the school play soccer

on a few occasions and I looked forward to being not only a student at Washington Irving but a member of its soccer team as well. Nor had I forgotten the cheerleaders.

* * *

On the way back from New York City that evening, as I drove through the main gate of the castle, Mrs. Axe asked me if I would prepare and serve her breakfast every morning before I attended school. She required her breakfast brought to her room about seven forty-five. She also requested that I bring it to her by the back door to her office and living quarters. This directed me away from passing by Mr. Axe's quarters so early in the morning. Part of the fascination of the castle was that it had so many doors and staircases and passageways that one could almost live an entire life in one part of the castle and not be seen or even noticed by those residing in another part.

The schedule we discussed before getting out of the car allowed me enough time to get myself ready for school which started at about eight thirty. After the early-morning chore I'd be free the rest of the day to attend school as well as being out of the castle and inhabiting a new world that I very much looked forward to.

* * *

With the beginning of the new school year I enrolled in Washington Irving High as a junior. The admissions officer tested me on several subjects and it was clear by the look on his face he wasn't impressed with my score. I had only the bare rudiments of maths and English and almost no knowledge of history. Subjects such as geometry and algebra were foreign to me. There was nothing on the aptitude test about opera, chess or Mozart – or Churchill for that matter. I was placed in the junior grade mainly because the admissions officer was willing to accommodate my enthusiasm rather than my sagacity. Putting me in a class with students a year or two younger was more practical, at least in his mind, than placing me in a lower or higher grade. I was about two years older than the average junior grader. The junior grade seemed like a perfect placement for me. I could fumble and fail there, more than in any other grade, before it became obvious and apparent that my previous academic background was lacking in just about every department.

My brain had been so conditioned to getting up early since I was thirteen when I started working that getting up at seven every morning in the castle to prepare and serve Mrs. Axe her breakfast in her bedroom was as routine an experience as any I'd had in life.

Business began and ended Mrs. Axe's day. Every morning when I entered her bedroom she was inevitably on the phone conducting business. When she put the phone down she engaged me in talking about how I was adjusting to life in high school. Every conversation I had with Mrs. Axe had the element of teacher and pupil. She, like Maggie, had a compulsion to correct my English: so much so I became very self-conscious and often when delivering her breakfast kept my mouth shut. My retreat into silence, however, only made her suspicious and she didn't hesitate to ask how I was doing in the classroom. I told her I was happy with the entire world of high school. She seemed impressed that I had classes in several subjects she had recommended.

Because of high school most of my time was now spent outside the walls of the castle. When I came home from school in the late afternoon I'd help Pat and Jim in the kitchen. Every so often the Axes entertained guests and Pat would recruit me to assist her. Because of my new schedule of being up early every morning and spending the day in school I was not expected to be in the company of the Axes or their dinner guests. On the rare occasions when the Axes entertained, I'd walk into the main dining room and meet a few guests but that was not something I did often. Mornings, after serving Mrs. Axe her breakfast, on my way down the marble staircase I'd bump into employees who worked at the office. When asked if I was going to join them at work I'd remind them that I was now a full-time high-school student.

When questioned by Mr. Axe about my scholastic progress I would purposely divert the conversation to how well I was doing on the soccer team. He, in his usual mode of indifference, would just shake his head and talk about history or opera as if I knew what he was talking about.

The fact that I had been recruited by the soccer coach to play on the school team actually made Mrs. Axe laugh.

* * *

For once something about my childhood in Dublin had come in handy. On the streets in Dublin I picked up the ability to dribble and move the soccer ball without much opposition from opposing players. When Washington Irving played other schools I displayed dexterity with the soccer ball that, at least to some of my teammates, was special and unique. For me it was simply a matter of recalling a routine I had been used to since childhood. Most of the time and in most of the matches I managed to score the winning goals for the high school. After a short time I became popular with those who cheered the team on and when I arrived in school the morning after a game I was greeted by just about every student in my junior class with a smile and a greeting. Some of the boys referred to me as 'Irish' while several of the girls in class took it upon themselves to name me 'Foreign Intrigue'. The 'foreign' appellation probably came from the fact that I spoke with an Irish accent.

One morning, while I was withdrawing my books from my school locker I found a note in it. The note was written in Spanish and it said: "*Yo te amo.*" It wasn't signed and I didn't know what it meant so I took it to a schoolmate, Jerry DiCicco. Jerry had spent time in Spain and was chairman of the Spanish Club at school and he was close to being fluent in Spanish.

"This says 'I love you'!" he said to me as he handed the note back to me.

"It says what?" I asked.

"It says, 'I love you'. Who wrote it?"

I had no idea. I was happily shocked.

"Someone said they love you in Spanish. Who are you seeing?" Jerry asked me.

"Nobody," I answered with a tinge of self-consciousness in my demeanour. I was flustered that someone would put a note in my locker and not sign it. A note that said they loved me.

"I've had a few put in my locker too," Jerry volunteered.

"Hey, thanks, Jerry," I said gratefully and took the note from his hand and put it in one of my school books.

For the next week, whenever I opened my history book, I'd read the note over and over in English. "I love you. I love you." The more I read the note the more I wanted to know who wrote it. I assumed it was one of the girls in my history class but I had no idea which one. All of the girls were warm and friendly towards me and I just couldn't figure out which one had taken the bold step to write me a note in Spanish. When I entered the classroom the next few days I walked around the room hoping I'd spot a Spanish text book. I spotted one then another. It seemed all the girls in my junior-grade class were students of Spanish. I gave up trying to solve the mystery of the Spanish Note.

* * *

As I sat in class an announcement came over the public-address system that a school dance would be held the following Saturday night. I couldn't wait. Seniors, juniors and freshmen were invited to attend and, even though I was a year or two older than my classmates, I felt comfortable about the prospect of attending the dance.

The next morning when I brought Mrs. Axe her breakfast I told her about the dance. She wasn't impressed with a low-grade report card I had received recently but in spite of my slow academic progress she appeared to be in favour of my going to the dance. She immediately warned me about alcohol consumption and to be careful behind the wheel of the car. So, with my car on standby and no obligations in the evening at the castle, I looked forward to attending my first high-school dance.

* * *

The dance was held in the school gymnasium and popular songs of the day were played over the public-address system. Listening to some of my favourite songs brought back memories of Sunday nights in Dublin when I used to listen to Radio Luxemburg playing the Top Ten hits of the week. Only this time I didn't have to be sitting outside a neighbour's house listening to someone else's radio. The gymnasium was packed to the rafters and just about every student in the entire high school was in attendance. I entered the building wearing new trousers and sports jacket as well as a shirt Mrs. Axe had bought for me recently. After wandering about in a circle I settled and sat on one of the bleachers where I watched couples dance. Several of my school and soccer mates greeted me with warmth that made me feel very much at ease and at home. After the four months since I started at the school, I was getting used to being accepted as one of the gang. My prowess on the soccer field had elevated me in the eyes of some of the other boys in the school and I was welcomed into their circles as if I had lived all my life in Tarrytown.

When the record of Marty Robbins singing "A White Sports Coat and a Pink Carnation" stopped, someone made an announcement over the address system.

"And lucky students, boys and girls, the next dance is a Sadie Hawkins!"

I'd no idea what a Sadie Hawkins meant. A friend on the soccer team told me it was when the girls got to choose what boy they wanted to dance with. The prerogative came only once during the course of the evening. How would this be done, I wondered. The mystery was solved when I noticed almost every girl in attendance crossing the floor in unison and inviting the boys to dance. The expressions on some of the boys' faces reflected disappointment and displeasure because they were being invited to dance by the wrong girl.

As I sat, amazed and amused, listening to Kay Starr's voice singing "The Wheel of Fortune", a girl approached me. She held out her hand and unhesitatingly led me to the centre of the floor. I hadn't danced since I'd left Dublin and I was about to drown in self-consciousness. The girl, however, was smiling, radiant and looking very confident. If she wasn't the most beautiful girl at the dance she was certainly in the top five.

As I held my newly found dance partner at arm's length she blurted out, without looking at me, "My name is Muriel."

I attempted to mumble something interesting to her but I could only say: "I'm Gabriel."

Muriel, with her head partly leaning on my shoulder, looked at me and said, "*Sí*. I know your name."

I was so shocked my ears began to heat up. I knew what the word '*sí*' meant and I instantly stopped dancing.

"What's the matter?" Muriel asked.

"Nothing," I replied.

"It's not nothing! You're shy. I know you are."

It struck me like a bolt of lightning. I assumed my shyness was a secret known only to me. For as long as I could remember the feeling of withdrawal and retreat, brought on by the silent shower of personal exposure, kept me from indulging in personal confrontations. Inwardly and secretly I wanted to battle the feelings that were pulling me back from my impulses. The feelings I had were attached to my days and years and life in Ireland, and for the most part they were to be denied or at the very least ignored.

What my impulses were exactly at that moment I wasn't sure because I felt as if my entire body was melting and breaking down and running away from me. I was, to say the least, simply out of control. Anything that heretofore seemed strong and solid about my sense of self had suddenly crumbled away from me. It was as if something in me had exploded and reshaped the definition I had of myself. I wasn't confident that every particle of my existence would regroup and reshape itself.

I was standing in the middle of the dance floor when another record with the voice of Eddie Fisher singing "Oh My Papa" was put on and hung in the very air I was breathing. The song reminded me so strongly of how my own papa was different to the one Eddie Fisher was singing about that I was about to choke on fatherly comparisons.

Despite my engulfing emotions I managed to continue dancing with the beautiful girl who had chosen to dance with me.

"I love this song," I said.

"I do too," my dancing partner replied.

"You do?" I asked her.

She hesitated but, just as I was about to query her on why she liked the song, she answered in a loud and clear voice: "*Sí! Sí! Mucho!*"

I immediately stopped dancing and stared at her.

"What's the matter?" she asked as if she didn't know why I had stopped dancing so abruptly.

"You? The note in my locker!"

Muriel put her hand on my shoulder as if she had known me for a hundred years. "You understood it?" she asked.

"No, but Jerry DiCicco translated it."

"Jerry's in my Spanish class," she said with a smile that was as red as ketchup.

The music stopped and we both looked at each other and, after what seemed like an eternity of silence, we walked back to one of the small tables that were lined against the wall. A small vase filled with flowers was in the middle of the table and the first thing I did, without much thought, was to take a flower out of the vase and hand it to Muriel. She smiled and seemed pleased with the gesture. We then sat down opposite each other just as another song started up. This time it was "Rock around the Clock" with Billy Haley at his best.

The music was fast for me but I took the chance and asked Muriel if she wanted to take a go at it. "Want to dance?"

"I'm taking a rest," she responded.

I was glad she declined.

A silence that seemed longer than my entire existence followed as I sat at the table facing the lovely stranger who appeared to be so relaxed she might well have known me all of my life. As the rock and roll sound blasted in my eardrums and the floor under my feet shook from the crowd on the dance floor, I wondered who Muriel was and why she had the confidence to put a note in my school locker and why she had come over and invited me to dance. I was so transfixed by her I could actually hear my heart moving to the beat of the music that was blaring all over the gymnasium. I began to shake my head to impress Muriel with my sense of rhythm but I quickly stopped when I noticed she wasn't paying any attention to me. With what I can only describe as an onslaught of Irish insecurity I accepted I was making a fool of myself and retreated by leaning back in my chair. Muriel then reached to the back of her head and pulled out a large hairclip that was apparently holding up her hair. Within a second or two her beautiful blonde hair was touching her shoulders and I became even more transfixed. Before I could fully embrace my lucky predicament, several schoolmates from the soccer team came by the table to say hello. I hardly heard their voices speaking to me because I couldn't take my eyes off Muriel. She was as beautiful as any movie star I had ever seen in the films in Dublin and I was feeling an intensity I hadn't felt before.

Then a soft romantic ballad began to fill the air and caressed everyone in attendance. With the implosion of my new-found energy I reached out to Muriel and led her to the dance floor.

* * *

For the next month I met Muriel every day in school and after school and drove her home after we toured the area and parked by the local lake that supplied the water to Tarrytown. The lake was a favourite spot for young couples. Those of us in school who had a car and a girlfriend drove to it immediately after school and began our "make-out sessions". I had my first kiss by the lake and experienced the heat, passion and power of embracing my new and first beautiful girlfriend. When word got out in school that Muriel and I were an item I was told and encouraged by other schoolmates that if I really, really liked her I was to offer her my high-school ring, which she in turn was to wear around her neck on a small chain. It signalled to other boys that Muriel was spoken for and was going steady with me. I secured a high-school ring and offered it to Muriel. Without hesitation she accepted it and sealed it with a kiss like no other I had ever imagined.

However, wearing the ring around her neck also caught the attention of Muriel's father. One day he spotted me dropping her off at their house and he called me in. Mr. Robert Anderson wanted to meet the boy who was seeing his daughter on such a steady basis. My introduction to Muriel's family – her parents and younger sister Kim – took place over dinner. Mr. Anderson asked me lots of questions. Mainly they were about Dublin and Ireland. When I had related to him what I thought I knew about that, he moved on to questioning me about my father. I don't think I impressed him when I related my father's history. I wasn't sure what he thought of my parents' marriage when I told him about my mother Molly and how she went about life in search of sainthood. Molly's obsession with suffering did interest him however. He smiled and then laughed when I related her need to embrace pain. Mr. Anderson was Protestant and, when I spoke of the ritual of the Rosary and how it hurt my knees each time I and other family members knelt down to pray, he laughed out loud. Explaining the Catholic rituals to Muriel's father was like describing a movie I had seen over and over. Judging by their constant interruptions and questions, Muriel's mother and sister appeared to be genuinely interested in my youthful Irish Catholic tales. This reception emboldened me even more to go on and on about what it was like to grow up in Dublin. At times, however, I became overcome by embarrassment under Mr. Anderson's grilling and then Muriel's mother diplomatically intervened. She mainly did it to keep me from burning up like the roast beef that was on our dinner plates. Muriel also did her best to ameliorate my embarrassment by telling her father about the circumstances under which I happened to come to America.

It seemed to me that Muriel accepted that my presence in New York and now in her house was something of a romantic adventure she herself might have conjured up. Muriel was as spontaneous and free as she was beautiful. Her curriculum in high school had the profile of a European one. Muriel liked all things foreign. I wasn't totally confident that being Irish was foreign but I kept that sentiment to myself. Muriel's passion was art and languages, Spanish being her major interest. She told her family how she had first spotted me walking along the school corridor wearing clothes that stood out from the other students and that I definitely looked like a foreign student who had just arrived from somewhere other than the neighbourhood. I was wearing the clothes that Mrs. Axe had bought me and I had left that choice, even though I didn't have one, to Mrs. Axe. As a consequence I was wearing clothes that were more businesslike than student-casual. The good news was that the clothes – pants, shirts, jackets –

actually fitted me. I also had a tendency to wear a cravat around my neck and that more than any other piece of apparel intrigued Muriel. The colourful cravat was something I had seen worn over and over again in films. If it wasn't Errol Flynn wearing one it was Tyrone Power or Clark Gable. The cravat I wrapped around my neck every morning before I went to school may well have been the cause and the reason why I found myself in love with a beautiful American girl sitting with an all-American family in an all-American household.

* * *

Mr. Axe was as particular about his diet as Mrs. Axe wasn't about hers. He swallowed vitamins every morning and insisted on freshly squeezed juice. Mrs. Axe basically ate what was in front of her and would drink orange juice out of a can. It was the same with just about everything else in their lives and relationship. Mrs. Axe was impulsive and spontaneous whereas Mr. Axe was studied and reserved. Mrs. Axe laughed and smiled more and seemed to have a more adventurous spirit than her husband. On weekends her clothes would be almost the opposite to what she wore during the week. Her fitted two-piece suits were shed and colourful oriental kimono-like gowns were her choice of attire. It was as if she made a determined decision that on weekends she would be free and unattached to the activities that absorbed her time while conducting business at the office in New York City during the week. Earrings of an antique nature hung from her ears and a noticeable scent was also obvious. Had the Axes' personalities been reversed I probably would not have been in their lives.

The kitchen in the castle was huge and contained freezers that were the size of small living rooms and sometimes it was an easy place to hide or get lost in when the three of us happened to be in it together. At times we'd unavoidably bump into each other and exchange niceties and talk about the past week.

Sometimes both Mr. and Mrs. Axe would ask me if I was coming or going and I'd invariably say I was going to town to meet friends or to participate in soccer practice for the high-school team. I purposely didn't mention Muriel because I wasn't sure they'd take to it in a friendly way. I also didn't want to alert them to the fact that I had something of an independent life going for me outside of the castle. But, in any case, personal things were rarely talked about.

I didn't spend any time talking about my social life in town. Time in the pub with Frank Dillon and others who were almost constantly drunk, more so on Friday nights, was not something I thought the Axes would appreciate. Most holidays, both religious and national, I'd meet up with Frank Dillon at the watering hole. At the back of the bar Frank would recount and recall his fantasies from his previous inebriated night, and continue his rants about how he was going to give up his life as a tile-setter and relocate to New York City or Los Angeles to pursue a career as an actor. Frank had a sidekick called Wayne. Whenever Frank worked on a construction site, Wayne was the one who got the chore of mixing the cement. He was also the person who kept cheering on Frank to show off his acting talents. For this support he was handsomely rewarded. Frank supplied him with a constant flow of booze every night they sat at the bar. Frank's performances were always more real and believable when he was intoxicated. To witness this in its full dimension, however, required drinking with him. Frank on more than one occasion asked me to invite him to the castle but it was not a request I seriously entertained. A drunken tile-setter spewing Shakespearean sonnets would not have been welcomed by Mr. and Mrs. Axe. His ranting might easily have been a setback both for them and me.

* * *

Saturday mornings allowed Mr. and Mrs. Axe to vent some of their personal frustrations and annoyances towards each other. What they couldn't express during the regular workday came out on Saturday mornings. Whatever disagreements they had with regard to business decisions during the course of the week they let fly toward each other in the kitchen on Saturdays. Most of their arguments had to do with who should be hired and who should be fired in the New York office and the Tarrytown office. Sometimes they argued about financial decisions that hadn't worked out to their satisfaction. Occasionally it came down to personality differences. Each had favourites they argued for. Certain individuals were liked and disliked by both Mr. and Mrs. Axe. Because Mrs. Axe had responsibility not only for both offices but the running of the castle she would most likely win out. Mr. Axe had a tendency to retreat from her after a quick burst of anger. Once he'd expressed himself he retired and returned to the dining room to his music and books. The tranquillity and silence of Mrs. Axe sitting by the kitchen window immersed in her newspaper would soon be assaulted by a blast of a Beethoven symphony, usually the Ninth, thundering from the dining room. The loud music was Mr. Axe's way of showing his displeasure and frustration.

Apart from this Saturday-morning confrontation, only occasionally did Mr. and Mrs. Axe venture out of their own private suites on weekends. In the early evening, for exercise,

Mr. Axe would take a walking stick and walk up and down the driveway several times. At times I'd walk with him. Sometimes on a Saturday and Sunday I'd accompany Mrs. Axe in her car when she drove around the estate inspecting the work that had been carried out in the garden during the week. Periodically she'd stop when she observed something she wasn't satisfied with. "Remind me to check with Jim and Arthur about this tree," she'd say as if she was dictating to her secretary. It wasn't out of the question for her to use a few expletives when she referred to some of the groundsmen by name.

Most of the food and house supplies were purchased by Pat and Jim during the week but Mrs. Axe enjoyed doing her own shopping and on the odd Saturday I would accompany her when she drove into Tarrytown to buy food and household items in the supermarket. These drives often extended into different parts of the county. I sat in the big car while Mrs. Axe drove around the town of Tarrytown and its adjacent township Sleepy Hollow.

Tarrytown and Sleepy Hollow were once Dutch settlements even before America was America. Mrs. Axe, in the role of tour guide, pointed out places of interest and recounted local history.

Tarrytown was a favourite residence for many rich New Yorkers, including John D Rockefeller. His elaborate family mansion Kykuit was on the far side of the town and only minutes away from the Axe Castle.

Mrs. Axe clearly enjoyed telling me about "The Legend of Sleepy Hollow". The story, written by New Yorker Washington Irving, tells of Ichabod Crane, a superstitious schoolmaster, who competes with Abraham "Brom Bones" Van Brunt for the hand of Katrina Van Tassel, the sole child of a wealthy farmer. The story goes that one autumn night Crane left a harvest party at the Van Tassel home and was pursued by the Headless Horseman, supposedly the ghost of a Hessian trooper who'd had his head shot off by a cannonball during the American Revolutionary War, who "rides forth to the scene of battle in nightly quest of his head". That night Ichabod mysteriously disappears, leaving Katrina to marry Brom Bones. The story implies that the Horseman was really Brom in disguise but the locals believed that Ichabod was "spirited away by supernatural means". By the glint in her eyes and the smile on her face it was obvious Mrs. Axe liked to tell this story.

* * *

More than a few times Mrs. Axe found out-of-the-way places to have lunch or, if it was late in the afternoon, she would find a coffee shop and we'd sit and have an espresso. The relaxed atmosphere and visits to country restaurants on weekends afforded both of us the opportunity to get to know each other on a more personal basis. I got to the point where I looked forward to the Saturdays and Sundays when she would ask me to get into the car and drive way from the castle for a few hours.

Whenever she was away from the castle and the demands of her business, especially while we were marooned in some country café, Mrs. Axe talked about another part of her life and personality. The undemanding hours of a Saturday and Sunday afforded her the opportunity to be in touch with what she often called the artist within her. When she talked about art, music and her early ambition to be a violinist, the subject of what she might have been, had she not married Emerson and joined him in business, came up. It was during these outings that I sensed she had become more and more attached to me and I also found myself thinking about her in a very different way than I had when we'd first met in Dublin eighteen months earlier.

Mrs. Axe enjoyed going to coffee shops and outdoor markets and buying things she wouldn't admit to liking during the week. She purchased items like colourful throw rugs, small paintings by unknown artists, large-brimmed hats and objects that appealed to her Bohemian taste. On her return home she would quickly and even secretly store everything she bought in a big room off the foyer to which only she held the keys. It was unlikely the items she purchased would ever be used, nor were they even seen again until she opened the door the next time to add more. It appeared Mr. Axe remained totally oblivious to what was stockpiled in the massive "closet" that was off the foyer.

Mrs. Axe's personality was such that she seemed capable of accomplishing anything. She was a brilliant economist and was highly regarded by the elite of the business world on Wall Street. She certainly gave the appearance that she could manage and conquer anything. On the other hand, and perhaps more awkwardly, my presence in the castle didn't seem as conquerable. Our friendship and relationship had evolved into one of private emotion and it presented a set of problems and, in some cases, responsibilities for Mrs. Axe that she was not prepared for. After all, waking up one morning to find a seventeen-year-old boy roaming about her cavernous residence was something she might not have taken into consideration when she acquiesced to Maggie's wish of transporting me to New York.

* * *

One Sunday while driving about Westchester County with

Mrs. Axe and looking for a new watering hole that served espresso, her attitude changed somewhat. She was not in her usual free-floating mood and there was no talk of art, artists or chasing creative dreams. After driving about for an hour or so she decided to return to one of the small country restaurants we had frequented on previous trips. Once inside the place she immediately inquired about my progress in high school and went so far as to suggest that I was spending an inordinate amount of time with Muriel after school. I had eventually, perhaps foolishly, confessed to the fact I was going steady with a girl. Mrs. Axe had taken the news coolly and without much comment at the time, but now it seemed I had given her rope to hang me with. Apart from the issue of Muriel, the whole afternoon was taken up with arguments and discussions on just about everything. Some had to do with the loud sound of the dual exhaust pipes I had put on my car that sped around the lakes and streets of Tarrytown. She told me the local police sergeant John Gilroy had called her and informed her about the change I had made to the car.

As we drove back to the castle I did my best to assure Mrs. Axe that Muriel's parents were very strict about their daughter's focus on her school subjects and insisted she pay attention to her homework as soon as she came in the door. Mrs. Axe remained silent.

* * *

The luncheonette was crowded with juniors and seniors and the word was out that the school districts of Tarrytown and North Tarrytown had completed their consolidation into one high-school jurisdiction. The new school, Sleepy Hollow High, located closer to North Tarrytown, was built on land donated by the Rockefeller family and its glass and concrete architecture reflected the modernity of the building. Juniors at Washington Irving would be the first seniors and graduates at Sleepy Hollow High. But not every student at Washington Irving looked forward to attending it. The old school, Washington Irving, on the main highway, was the heart and soul of Tarrytown and there were some parents and students who didn't want to become part of North Tarrytown. North Tarrytown's image and reputation was considered a bit more working-class and somewhat less trendy than Tarrytown. The school's football home games, normally played in Tarrytown, would be a thing of the past. However, many of the soon-to-be-seniors at Washington Irving, including me, looked forward to attending the newly built school. It had its own parking lot and those of us with cars relished that fact. There would be no more time spent driving up and down the main thoroughfare looking for a place to park.

Muriel was more inclined to take the position that the combining of the school district was in the best interest of most of the citizens of both Tarrytown and North Tarrytown. I wasn't versed enough in the politics of either township and I abstained from even having an opinion on that. This neutral stand annoyed Muriel and she let me know about it. When Muriel and I couldn't resolve some of the social issues floating about in the luncheonette we'd get in my car and drive all over Tarrytown and North Tarrytown to see if we could see any obvious distinction between the two townships. When we finished our limited inspection we'd return to the luncheonette where we made out with each other in a booth in the back while the jukebox transported us away from any kind of responsibility, academic or otherwise.

Muriel's affection for me may well have been influenced by my display of innocent ignorance when we attended class together. A certain kind of humour mingled with physical attraction certainly defined us as a young couple going very steady.

When I was at her house, her father wouldn't hesitate to inform me of my school responsibilities. Mr. Anderson was so involved with social issues and politics that I sometimes thought he looked upon me as some kind of vote. Every time I came to his house to take his daughter out he'd belabour me with questions. Mostly they had to do with where I was going and when I'd be back.

Unsurprisingly, my discipline for doing homework was negligible and I found it difficult to complete it each evening.

* * *

Father Leo Clifford came by the castle to visit Mrs. Axe and fill her in on Maggie's condition in Dublin. On this visit he waited for me to return from high school and we sat in the kitchen and talked about Dublin but more importantly about Maggie. I wanted to believe that her poor health kept her away from Tarrytown and from writing to me directly. Had we communicated I would have told her about my life since she'd left the castle and would definitely have informed her about my time in high school and the kind of life I was living now. I probably wouldn't have told her much about my girlfriend Muriel. I assumed Mrs. Axe had passed along that information. Without going into specifics Father Leo told me more about Maggie's health, in both mind and body, than I had known previously. He described her behaviour as something akin to her operatic roles wherein one wasn't fully sure if she was performing a bit even in her present physical condition. He mentioned that Maggie had asked him to inquire about my religious observance and wanted him to remind me that

I was a Catholic and that she hoped I was paying attention to that fact. Specifically she meant that I was to attend Mass on Sundays and receive the Sacrament of Communion. Receiving Communion carried with it the obligation of going to Confession. Father Clifford related that Maggie hoped I hadn't been up to anything that required me to confess. He said she felt obligated and responsible for me, particularly with regard to keeping my religion. When the Reverend queried me on my going to Mass I told him I had "minimised" my attendance since Maggie had left for Ireland and it didn't appear to surprise him. The word 'minimised' had brought a smile to his face. Whether it was my usage of it or the fact that it wasn't a definition of a total break from going to Mass I wasn't sure. His reaction might have had something to do with the way he was trained to handle apostates and sinners. Certain orders in the priesthood had special training with regard to dealing with the various strains of a wandering flock and this may well have been the reason he seemed to ignore my response to his answer. For a few minutes he talked about other things. He told me how much he enjoyed his station in America and seemed very happy with his life in New Jersey. Then, after we shared a few laughs about Dublin, he abruptly reverted to the subject of Mass. I told him it did not seem as important to me in America as it was when I was in Ireland. When pressed to be more specific I wasn't really able to explain it in clear terms. Father Clifford was very much the missionary and perhaps even more so when he was dealing with his own flock from Ireland. It might have been harder for him to accept that a young Irishman was unhinging from his religious practice than someone who had never been exposed to orthodoxy before.

I could sense that he was very concerned with being

something of a bridge between me and Maggie. I didn't want him to return to Dublin and report to her that I had fallen by the wayside when it came to my religious observance. I tried to change the subject by informing him of my success on the soccer field and my difficulties with my academic subjects in school. I thought he'd like to hear about my social transition from almost no schooling in Dublin to almost too much of it in Tarrytown, but he only paused and asked me again why I was not concerned about attending Mass. He also asked me if I could pinpoint the moment when I'd had a change of feeling in this regard.

As I pondered his question he quickly reframed it. "When did the Devil take hold of you, Gabriel?" He did have a bit of a smirk and smile on his face when he looked directly at me.

I told him that I had been going to church every Sunday since I'd arrived up until a few months ago. In my confessional state, I told him I got out of bed as usual one Sunday morning and proceeded in my car to the church. On my way I got a flat tyre. For a moment or two I thought that event was the work of the Devil. Following that, the tyre-changing contraption, normally in the trunk, was missing. It was at that point that I truly felt the Devil had me checkmated. While I wrestled with the dilemma of being stuck on a back road with a flat tyre and time running out for me to get to Mass, an onslaught of guilt and fear flooded my mind. I had religiously and mechanically attended Sunday Mass most of my life in Ireland and had developed a fear that if I missed it on the Sabbath I would fall into hell, as I had been told all of my life. Then I remembered that Jim would be heading home from Mass on the back road I was stranded on. I decided to sit and wait for him to come by and rescue me. As I waited I turned on the car radio and got a station that was playing some of my favourite songs. The long wait for Jim seemed to go by in seconds. I opened my eyes after he tapped me on the shoulder and asked me what I was doing. After a little explanation Jim got to work on changing the tyre.

On my way back to the castle I felt that even though I had missed Mass I had found something else. I had discovered that I wasn't struck by lightning or grabbed by the toes and pulled into hell. The feeling was as if I had come out of something rather than having gone into it.

When I finished telling Father Clifford the story of my flat tyre he told me that I really hadn't committed a sin by not being able to attend Mass. He said it was the fault of the tyre and that I wasn't to be blamed for its malfunction. He also said that because I was willing to wait for Jim to come and rescue me it showed that I was still a person with a strong faith.

Father Clifford had an easy and warm way about him that made me want to continue talking to him. I knew if I wanted to get his attention I'd have to talk as if I missed the culture and practice of going to Mass in Dublin and the ritual of kneeling down in the confession box. A part of the connection with the priest was something like having played for the same football team in another time in another place. Conversing about the Mother Church in the Mother Country resonated with an authenticity and familiarity that was at the very least comforting if not downright fraternal.

"Can I confess, Father?" I asked in a foolhardy moment.

"Sure you can. I can hear a confession anytime, anywhere from anyone. Have you committed any sins? Are there sins you want to confess, son?"

I admitted to Father Leo, as if he was my confessor, that because I wasn't in an environment where everybody around me marched off to church every Sunday I didn't feel the same compulsion to attend. I told him there was no one keeping score or adding up and subtracting the amount of times I attended and didn't attend Mass. I related to him that I had a girlfriend who was Protestant and I wasn't sure if she would like or understand my running off to Mass every Sunday and every religious holiday, particularly if we partied late on a Saturday night. I knew for sure that Muriel's father wouldn't be in the stands cheering me on when I dressed up in a clean shirt and marched off to church.

Father Leo responded by asking me if I had shared any part of my religion with Muriel and I told him I took Muriel to Mass one Sunday and showed her what went on inside a Catholic church. The event, or more precisely the experience, didn't impress her parents. When I sat round the dinner table with Mr. and Mrs. Anderson they looked at me as if they weren't sure what to make of me. I began to sense an unwelcome and unwanted crusade falling upon me. The ignorance of my action, coupled with an insensitivity that I wasn't yet mature enough to acknowledge or apologise for, kept my brain twitching awkwardly for at least a week. It was at least two weeks before Muriel's father smiled in my presence again. It might have been because he and her mother believed I was a devout dedicated Catholic who was trying to convert Muriel.

"You took her to Mass?" Father Clifford asked with great incredulity.

"I did, Father." I was still behaving in front of the priest as if I was in the confession box and for a moment or two I accepted that I had committed sin and would be obliged to do penance for it.

Father Clifford went silent and looked up at the ceiling. I thought he was contemplating an instruction, as per his vocation, for me to say a hundred prayers and ask for forgiveness. He brought his head back and rubbed his chin with his right hand.

"What happened? What happened?" he asked.

"What happened where, Father?"

"What happened with the girl?"

"Muriel?"

"Yes – Muriel!"

"Muriel had no problem with coming to Mass with me, Father. It was when I took her home her father asked us where we'd been."

"Did you tell him?"

This question I didn't want to answer but Father Clifford pursued me.

"Did she tell her father that you took her to Mass, Gabriel?"

I leaned back and felt that my confession was coming to an end. "Yes, I told her dad that I took her to Mass, Father."

Father Clifford laughed. "What did this child's father say to you, Gabriel, when you told him that?"

This question I definitely didn't want to answer.

"What did her father say, Gabriel?"

"Muriel's father got annoyed. He suggested that Muriel had a lot of homework to do and that I should go home."

"You left his house?"

"Yes."

"And?"

"And on my way back to the castle that day I thought I really had committed a serious sin, Father."

Father Clifford was very sympathetic. He said something

to the effect that my faith was being tested and that it is much easier to go to church with the entire flock than it is to go on one's own. He also said that when he got back to Dublin he would tell Maggie that I was growing stronger in my religious beliefs but it would be another matter if she believed it.

* * *

Mrs. Axe gave a party for the executives who were on the board of the firm. I was told I could attend if I wanted to. Sometimes it seemed that Mrs. Axe didn't know what to do with me or how to make me feel at home. Of the social functions I attended at the castle there was never a visitor who was even close to my age. Not once did I ever encounter a family with children, young or old, and definitely none in my age bracket. Essentially just about everyone who came to Axe Castle was a work colleague or a distant and older relative. Mrs. Axe had an older sister who was a professor at a mid-western college. Mr. Axe, as far as I could ascertain had absolutely no living relatives. He was himself a very private person and outside of his relationship with Mrs. Axe and the odd walk I took with him once or twice a week he rarely showed any need for real live human company. There were even times when I thought he was as lonely as I was. However, although his penchant was for spending most of his time in his palatial home he, every so often, reached out to his wife to provide him with company. Parties and social functions took place in the castle only when Mrs. Axe arranged them. On many occasions I heard Mr. Axe inquiring about the social calendar for the castle. When he was informed about persons and dates by Mrs. Axe he'd react like a happy young boy who was given a toy or a present.

Mrs. Axe spared no expense when she gave a dinner party. When the Axes had just a few guests I helped Pat out, but for a larger event Mrs. Axe brought in temporary help to assist Pat and she oversaw every aspect of the evening. Mr. Axe would choose the wine from his wine collection and there would be plenty of it. When the guests arrived, a woman from the temporary agency, dressed in black with a white apron, would take their coats. Mr. and Mrs. Axe would greet them and show them into the living room where they would be served the most expensive wine in Mr. Axe's collection. Such events allowed Mr. Axe the opportunity to wax on about his wine collection. He presented five or six types of wine and he explained the history of them from the grape to the glass it was poured in. Acting as his informal assistant I would line up the wineglasses for each guest and make sure their glasses were instantly replenished and would sometimes indulge in a little wine-tasting myself. If Mrs. Axe noticed me imbibing she would quietly suggest I go into the kitchen and help Pat with the task of preparing the food for the buffet table.

At this particular party one of the guests was Mr. Art Linkletter, the host of the famous and popular television show *Kids Say the Darndest Things*. His presence must have had something to do with the financial world of the Axes. He might have been a candidate for the board of directors or someone who wanted to invest his money with the Axe financial-management firm. Whatever the reason for him being present he was the life of the party. He joked, laughed and told stories about his television show and about how children are spontaneous and innocent when asked questions by an adult.

I ambled about the big dining room as if I was the house

cat. With the guests mostly involved in business talk I might as well have been at a silent movie. I was too shy to introduce myself to anyone in case they'd ask me a question about the Axes' business. In one corner of the room as I was replacing a bottle of wine on a small table, one gentleman asked me my name and who I was and what I was doing at the party. He jokingly said I was too young to be drinking and I agreed with him. When I offered him the first of the wine from the bottle he nicely asked about my presence at the party. I was able to avoid going into details by telling him he'd have to drink a lot more to understand the reason why I was talking to him. He seemed to get a laugh out of it and introduced himself as Albert Wedemeyer. He looked a bit like Father Clifford, but with a bit more grey in his hair, and he told me he had recently joined the board of directors at the Axe Corporation. After spending a few minutes in his company I learned from Justin Dunn, a vice president of the company who sometimes supervised me in the office on the odd school holiday that I worked there, that the man I had been talking to was General Albert Wedemeyer, the man who replaced General 'Vinegar' Joe Stilwell in the battle of the South China Seas during World War II. The General, Mr. Dunn informed me, was a very important American hero. For a second or two I wondered if I had seen him in the movies. He did look a bit like the actor John Payne. Justin Dunn couldn't hold back his admiration for the man whose presence dominated the room.

Stepping back and taking a professorial posture, Mr. Dunn elaborated: "During the Second World War, young fella!"

Mr. Dunn always called me "young fella" when I sat at a desk near him in the office.

He continued: "General Albert Wedemeyer was a staff officer to the war-plans division of the United States War Department and was the number one author of the Victory Program that advocated the defeat of Germany's armies in Europe. He said, or he informed his political bosses in Washington, that this should be America's first war objective. General Wedemeyer's plan was endorsed and expanded as the war progressed. Added to that, Wedemeyer helped to plan the Normandy invasion."

I thought I was listening to the radio for a minute. Mr. Dunn then went back to his glass of wine and drank its contents as if he was congratulating himself on giving me a lesson in American history.

I finally noticed Mrs. Axe walking about the room, perfunctorily acknowledging her guests and introducing them to Father Clifford. She seemed happy and cheerful. Father Clifford greeted everyone as if he was standing in front of the church welcoming his observant flock.

Mrs. Axe spotted me as I was heading for the kitchen. "Gabriel! Gabriel!" she called.

I stopped in my tracks and saw Father Clifford looking at me with a confused look on his face. I wondered if he had said anything to Mrs. Axe about my flat tyre and my taking Muriel to Mass, or if she had told him about the struggle I was having with my school subjects. I had recently failed Intermediate Algebra and was barely hanging on with Latin. When she caught up with me in the kitchen she didn't mention anything about school. She was in a good mood and wanted to know if I would do her a favour by driving one of her guests home. I of course agreed and went back to the dining room to meet the guest who had to unexpectedly leave the party. The man was as nice as could be and apologised both to Mr. and Mrs. Axe for having to leave. Mrs. Axe assured him that I was not only a very good driver but I knew exactly where he lived and was very familiar with the route to his place of residence. With a touch of humour, befitting the night, Mrs. Axe reassured the gentleman that I was not a "drinker" and was sober. The man instantly displayed a broad smile of relief.

Ten minutes later, in Mrs. Axe's Cadillac, I was on my way to my destination, Tuxedo Park. Tuxedo Park was a recently developed upscale housing estate slightly north of Tarrytown. My passenger, sitting next to me, was a Scotsman with a biting sense of humour who jokingly remarked that one had to be always wearing a tuxedo to live there. When I commented that he wasn't wearing one he laughingly replied that his was still in the cleaner's and had been there for the last month. During the course of the drive he asked me about my life and times at the castle and I did my best to tell him about the circumstances that had me there. He said he knew Dublin well and had been to Trinity College a number of times. His voice and tone was very precise and a bit like that of Mr. Axe. He mentioned that Mr. Axe was of Scottish descent but that he himself was an actual born-and-bred Scotsman. He talked about how bright and industrious Mrs. Axe was and how she and Mr. Axe had succeeded in being top in their business.

As I was about halfway across the Tappan Zee Bridge a news bulletin came over the radio and referred to a plane crash that had taken place somewhere on the east coast of the United States. My engaged passenger reached for the radio volume and turned it up. He seemed to pay an unusual amount of attention to the radio bulletin. As he listened he commented that he thought the pilot of the said plane might not have used his weather instrumentation panel properly. Why he mentioned this was beyond me. It was the next morning when I brought Mrs. Axe her breakfast that she told me the man I had driven home from the party the previous night was Robert Watson-Watt, the inventor of radar.

* * *

Sundays more often than not underlined the loneliness and isolation of life at the castle. Apart from the many squirrels and birds that were living in the woods it was rare that anything else moved inside the castle or on the grounds of the estate. There had been Sundays in the past, although not too many, that I actually went to Mass to avoid the emptiness of the Sabbath at the castle.

A weekend at the castle was like being a resident in an abandoned church that nobody attended or prayed in. The size of the place seemed even bigger when it wasn't occupied by office workers and functioning as a financial institution. Only the odd sparrow from the garden that had lost its way and entered through one of the large windows gave the place a bit of life. More than once I felt as if I too was a sparrow looking for an open window to fly out of. Outside on the grounds the birds and animals, mainly rabbits and a few deer, were at play as if they were taking advantage of the lack of traffic on the driveway and the absence of cars in the parking lot. In the dark of night or the early hours of the morning I imagined ghosts and spectres walking up and down the stairs wailing and weeping and looking for a place to deposit their undying souls. I envisioned other unearthly and shadow-like creatures carrying their own heads up and down the marble staircase. The interior of the castle on weekends seemed very suited for goblins and fairies. Even the silence of the place had an echo that increased with the passing of time. Books, papers and large files of documents rested on the desks of the absent employees waiting for them to return on Monday morning.

* * *

With little to do and no place to go, on what I accepted as the day of emptiness, one Sunday I was standing on the hill in front of the castle when I noticed a car coming through the front gate. Normally Mrs. Axe would have told me if she was expecting visitors on a Sunday and, given that she hadn't mentioned anything to me, I was intrigued all the more by the sight of a car moving up the driveway. The car was big and black and looked a bit like a hearse, although it wasn't.

When the car turned towards the direction of the front entrance I decided to investigate and see who was in it. As it approached the main door a few seconds ahead of me I saw Mrs. Axe standing on the front steps. She had a smile on her face and seemed happy. The driver stepped out of the car, opened the back door and a little woman wearing a black hat and a black dress stepped out of it. Mrs. Axe greeted the woman and led her into the castle. I stood and waited till the car departed before I decided to investigate the surprise Sunday visitor. After waiting a few minutes and not wanting to be noticed, I made my way back to the castle through the back door that led directly to my apartment – when I didn't want to be seen or noticed by Mr. or Mrs. Axe, or anybody else who might have wondered why I was walking about on my own, it was my way out of and into the house. No more than ten minutes had passed when I walked into the living room and encountered Mrs. Axe with the little woman in black. They were sitting in front of the fireplace drinking cups of tea. Mrs. Axe had apparently prepared the tea in advance of her guest's arrival. At first sight the diminutive woman looked to me like a hen dressed in black.

When I approached, both Mrs. Axe and the tiny lady stood up.

"Oh, this is Gabriel," Mrs. Axe said but before she got a chance to introduce her guest the petite woman extended her hand and greeted me with a gentle squeak-like voice.

"I am pleased to meet you," she said with an accent that I couldn't immediately identify.

For a moment I thought it was French but I wasn't sure. Also the little woman let out a giggle and sat back down on the chair closest to the fireplace.

"Countess, you should chat with Gabriel sometime but not now," Mrs. Axe added and returned to her chair as well.

I took the words "not now" as a signal for me to move on. It didn't take more than five seconds for me to realise that I was in the middle of a meeting that I wasn't invited to. Feeling awkward, I excused myself and beat a retreat.

As I was about to vanish out the door Mrs. Axe called to me. "Gabriel, take this teapot and heat up some more water, please!" I went back and picked up the teapot from the table.

Mr. Axe then entered the room.

Mrs. Axe greeted him with: "You've read the stories, Emerson?"

He instantly responded, "I did indeed."

Inside the kitchen I filled the kettle with water and put it on the stove. As I waited for the water to boil Mr. Axe entered and retrieved a bottle of wine from the refrigerator. He had apparently left it there for the occasion that was now taking place in the dining room.

As he uncorked the bottle he asked me what I thought of the petite woman who was dressed as if she was in mourning.

I responded by saying she reminded me of a hen. He laughed and said that she was a writer of children's stories and one or two of her tales had to do with how hens ate their food, and added that the reason for her visit was that a collection of her stories was being published the following week and that the publisher of her books was a client of the Axes. While sitting at the kitchen table I asked Mr. Axe about the name "Countess". For some reason or other he thought my question bordered on being humorous and, as was his custom and practice, he went on to relate to me in his usual instructive way that the lady liked to be known to anyone and everyone she talked to as "Countess". The noble appellation applied because in reality she was Count Leo Tolstoy's last living granddaughter. With a predictable ignorance that Mr. Axe was very used to by now I asked who Count Leo Tolstoy was.

After pouring a drop of wine into his glass and tasting it Mr. Axe paused and told me that Leo Tolstoy wrote *Anna Karenina* and *War and Peace*. He said that he would tell me all about those books at a later date if I was interested. He then added that the Countess was also known to some as Vera: a name she relied on for political reason when she fled to Paris from Russia many years ago.

Before the water in the kettle had come to a boil I was filled in on many facts about the woman sometimes known as Vera and sometimes known as Countess Tolstoy. She had been seven years old when her grandfather, the great literary master Count Leo Tolstoy, died in 1910.

* * *

Since Maggie departed my relationship with Mrs. Axe had grown more and more ambiguous if not outright confusing.

In its own odd and unusual way my relationship with Mr. Axe was a much more direct and easy one. Sometimes, particularly during the week, Mrs. Axe would not look directly at me when she bid me good morning. When we did exchange niceties she would speak so fast she was gone from my presence before my ears had finished listening to her. Weekends were a different matter. In many ways it was as if the roles were reversed. She asked how I spent my week and went about suggesting recreational and artistic activities. Mr. Axe seemed to have neither the desire nor the patience to go driving about on a Saturday and as far as I could discern Mrs. Axe more than appreciated that reality.

For my part, I was in a state of constant hope and anxiety. I nervously waited to be invited to accompany her on her drives about the county. Weekends defined and even underlined my personal domestic insecurity and emotional condition at the castle. Half the time I was, or at least appeared to be, a member of the family and participated in many of the social activities and functions that took place in the mansion. Other times my presence in the castle was a bit like being a fly in a glass of milk.

I drifted towards Pat in the kitchen when I wasn't given a clear signal as to where I should or could be on any given day. In keeping with not having a clear and tangible compass applicable to our relationship, Mrs. Axe seemed to wrestle with my presence and often, when she discovered me in the kitchen or helping Pat with some of her domestic chores, she'd remind me about the upcoming weekend and her plans to drive about Connecticut for some purpose or other – for example, to visit the antique furniture markets that were reliably held on Saturdays and Sundays.

If a much-talked-about artistic event took place in New

York City the Axes would invite me to go with them. My first opera was *Der Rosenkavalier* by Richard Strauss, in the opera house on Broadway. On evenings such as that we'd stop off first at the Metropolitan Club on Fifth Avenue and have dinner and we'd likely stop off for a late snack before driving back to Tarrytown. Most of the time I volunteered to take the wheel of the car. Mrs. Axe always sat in the front passenger seat and she seemed to relax when she was able to talk without having to concentrate on driving. Mr. Axe liked to pontificate on the opera or the play he had seen and more often than not he exhibited a sense of humour not often witnessed when he was home or working at his desk. He wasn't shy about comparing the voices of the performers either. Mrs. Axe would sometimes argue and debate him on what tenor or soprano had achieved near-perfection in productions they had seen previously. I would listen attentively and with interest although I had no opinion or knowledge on the subject matter. Nor was I ever asked for it. Only rarely did I mention the world of cinema and that was mainly when I was asked if I missed Dublin or my family back there.

When we found ourselves in the same quarters in the castle Mrs. Axe would sometimes change her attitude towards my presence. It seemed at times that she would go from having the concerns of Maggie Sheridan towards me and other times not know how to communicate with me with regard to activities I should or could be involved in during the course of the day.

I felt more comfortable when I sat with Pat in the kitchen. Pat may well have been a better talker than a housekeeper. She seemed more interested in filling me in on the entire history of Axe Castle – its past, present and its personal existence – than getting things done. I learned that the castle was built around 1900 by an American army general named Carroll. Pat didn't know what war General Carroll had fired a few bullets in but it must have been the Spanish-American War. She informed me that for years the castle was occupied by the General's family until twenty-five years after his death in 1916 when it was sold to Emerson Axe. Emerson was an expert on financial matters and had a client list of successful American companies. He predicted the fall of the stock market just prior to the great depression in 1929. It was around that time that he met and married Ruth Houghton. Both were starting out on Wall Street and each found in the other the perfect vocational partner. Their careers began in New York City but as they became more and more successful they and their newly acquired research team used a large part of the castle for business purposes.

* * *

The next time I saw Muriel was in the school corridor at lunch break. She had missed the first two days of the school week and I thought she was avoiding me. It turned out she was not feeling well and her mother had kept her home. Before I could inquire about her father's state of mind after I left her house the previous week she told me her dad wanted to see me at the weekend. She reassured me that there were no hard feelings in her house towards me, but hearing that her dad wanted to see me sent a shiver down my spine. I was still somewhat terrified about the 'Mass Incident' and I wanted to apologise. Muriel's father had appeared to be seriously angry at me for taking his beloved daughter to Mass and I hadn't had a chance to explain to him that it was only to show her a part of my life and culture as it was before I arrived in America.

Had it not been for Muriel's calm demeanour and her

display of affection as we walked along the corridor I might easily have run away from her that very day! She didn't seem as concerned as I thought she should have been and for a moment I was tempted to say I didn't want to go to her house and see her father again. It would have been a different thing had it been her mother who asked me to come to the house but Muriel emphasised that it was her father who was looking forward to me coming to the house on Saturday.

* * *

For the next three days I got up early, served Mrs. Axe her breakfast, had my routine and regular chat about my studies and my social life and made my way to school each morning.

The sense of freedom and the secure feeling I felt when I got behind the wheel of my car was palpable. Inside the castle I felt lost and detached most of the time. Waiting for Mrs. Axe to show and give approval to what I was doing, and even how I was thinking about my life, was like betting on a horse in a crowded race. Some days she'd seem to be supportive and encouraging, other days I felt like I was at the point where I was begging for her approval. My bad grades in algebra didn't impress her and she didn't hesitate to point out to me that I might be spending too much time driving about in my car when I should be studying. I had also fallen behind on reading books that Mr. Axe periodically gave me to read. That situation led me to avoid him whenever I sensed he was going to ask me about a certain subject, but the activity and chore of serving Mrs. Axe her breakfast every weekday morning put me in the position of having to explain myself and face her criticism on a daily basis. Without wishing it, knowing it or even understanding it, my daily contact with Mrs. Axe and her concern about me was slowly turning into something like the relationship I had with Maggie. I was falling into the habit of wanting to please her with everything I said, thought and did.

On Friday she told me that Father Clifford had related to her the story of my taking Muriel to Mass one Sunday. She also informed me that she'd be going to Dublin the next day and would be seeing Maggie. I got the impression that all might not be well with Maggie. It had been months and months since her departure and we'd had no communication. Whenever I heard about her it was either through Mrs. Axe or, on the rare occasion I met him, Father Clifford. According to Mrs. Axe, Maggie was disappointed that I didn't write home and let people back in Dublin know how I was and what I was doing. My defence was that I had not had any communication from the other side either. Alienation had been bred into my immediate family as if it was a virtue. Affection and concern were emotions that were rarely if ever practised by my parents or by my siblings.

* * *

Saturday afternoon arrived. Mrs. Axe had gone to Dublin, Mr. Axe was in the city and Pat and Jim were off duty. I readied myself to face Muriel's father.

I got to Muriel's house just after lunch and her parents greeted me as if I was a long-lost child. Her mother was a very attractive suburban woman who always appeared gentle and easy and welcoming whenever I entered the house and today was no different. In fact this day she seemed even more delighted than usual that I had dropped by. Kim was also home and she greeted me as if I was a member of the family. It was clear to me from the warm hug she gave me that she had not paid any attention to her sister going to Mass with me a few Sundays ago. Muriel's father was in a good mood as he greeted me and led me into the living room. I sat on the large sofa in the living room and listened to him ramble on about politics and various social issues that I not only didn't understand but didn't even want to.

Mr. Anderson approached me with a copy of the *New York Daily News*. As he opened the paper he talked to me.

"I hear great things about your goal-scoring for the soccer team, Gabriel," he said without looking directly at me.

Muriel was in the kitchen helping her mother clean up after lunch and I felt a little lost sitting alone on the sofa while her father stood next to me browsing through the newspaper.

"Soccer is not very popular in school, is it, Gabriel?" he asked me.

"It's getting there," I said with a shrug of my shoulders.

"You're the best on the team. I'm told that anyway. I hope I get a chance to see a match one of these days. Muriel says you're very good."

I wasn't sure how to respond to his compliment but I decided that because his tone of voice was friendly I'd go along with him. "Yeah, I scored two goals last week when we played Nyack High," I answered.

"You got to be in great physical shape for that game, don't you?" he asked me.

I continued on the same friendly course. "When school's out I run the track every afternoon," I answered.

He went silent for a bit and I could hear Muriel's voice calling from the kitchen asking if anyone wanted coffee. Mr. Anderson responded that he did. I wasn't sure what I wanted at that point. I wanted Muriel to come out of the kitchen and ask me to go downtown with her: anything that would get me out of the living room and away from her father. A few seconds passed and Mrs. Anderson came into the living room with a tray and four cups of coffee on it. Mr. Anderson sat next to me on the sofa and reached for his cup first. I wanted to see if Muriel and her sister would come out of the kitchen and change the air and the atmosphere that I felt I was drowning in. Muriel's mother went and opened the living-room curtains further and I could see my old car parked outside on the street and I began to wish I was speeding away in it. Then she came and sat with us.

We had settled into drinking our coffee when Mr. Anderson asked me if I ever read the *Daily News*. I told him I had but not too often. I didn't tell him that the only time I came across the *Daily News* was when I was visiting Frank Dillon and his friends at the bar on the odd Friday night.

"Gabriel, there's something in the *Daily News* that I wanted to ask you about . . ."

Before I could ask him what he was talking about or what he meant, he continued, "Remember you told me that you used to be in a boxing club in Dublin?"

I had forgotten I had told Mr. Anderson anything about that. In fact, I normally made an effort not to talk too much about Dublin, my family and what I did when I lived there. Dublin was even more foreign to Muriel's family than Tarrytown was to me when I first arrived.

"I told my dad you used to be in a boxing club, Gabriel, when you were about nine or ten!" Muriel called as she stuck her head out of the kitchen.

I wasn't sure where the conversation was going so I decided to go along with it. "I was about twelve, Muriel," I responded with a bit of pride.

"And you boxed for the club every week?" Mr. Anderson queried.

"I think it was once a month. I was only in the club for about six months. I joined it because they had great dinners every Friday night before the fights. Every neighbourhood in Dublin had a parish club and once a month we'd play a football match against each other and sometimes we'd fight on a Friday."

Mr. Anderson leaned towards me and showed me a page in the *Daily News*. "See that," he said as he circled the print with his finger.

I wasn't sure what he was referring to. He then pointed his finger and tapped it a few times on what appeared to be a drawing of two boxers with an application form of some sort under the image.

"What?" I asked him.

"*The Daily News* is sponsoring the Golden Gloves and that's an application for anyone who wants to participate. Have you given that any consideration?"

The Daily News and the Golden Gloves were as foreign to me as Santa Claus was in Dublin. Before I could determine or figure out what Mr. Anderson was getting at, he blurted out, "You're over eighteen now. Give that a shot, Gabriel."

Not being sure what he meant I answered, "Give what a shot?"

There was a silence. He looked back at his wife and then at me. I looked at him and Mrs. Anderson looked at both of us.

"Tell him, Rob, what you have in mind," she said. She seemed to be enjoying what I was considering to be mysterious.

Mr. Anderson was definitely acting in a very nice way and I was feeling more and more comfortable. It looked as if he had completely forgotten the incident of my taking Muriel to church.

"Given that you're in such good physical condition, Gabriel," he said, "I figured you wouldn't even have to train or work out. It's mainly an amateur contest. All kinds enter it every year. When I was growing up in the Bronx I had visions of competing in the Golden Gloves. That, of course, was many years go and needless to say I didn't. I think it was because my parents moved from the neighbourhood I was born in. This is the kind of experience that can make a man out of you."

I couldn't believe it: Mr. Anderson wanted me to participate in the Golden Gloves contest that was being sponsored by The *New York Daily News*.

"What weight were you when you boxed?" he queried me further.

"I don't know how much I weigh now, much less seven or eight years ago." I thought I had put it to rest but then Muriel entered the room looking as beautiful as always.

She appeared to be happy, even excited, that her father and I were sitting on the same sofa having a conversation.

"Are you going to do it, Gabriel?" she asked me.

For a second or two I felt outnumbered but I didn't want to commit to something I wasn't interested in or prepared for. Before I could muster up the courage to decline Mr. Anderson's ambition of having me sign up for the boxing contest, he looked over at his daughter.

"I think you're either a featherweight or a lightweight," he said, smothering my impulse to retreat from the conversation, and added with a deepening sense of interest in my life as a boxer: "You'll have three two-minute rounds to do the job, Gabriel. I think you've got what it takes to win."

* * *

The following Monday after school Mr. Anderson in his red-and-white 1956 Chevrolet drove from Tarrytown to the Bronx. The drive to the boxing arena took about forty minutes. I was extremely apprehensive but I did my very best not to show it. I didn't want Muriel's father to think I was not brave, proud and fearless.

After parking on a side street, Mr. Anderson and I walked a few blocks and entered a huge public area. The building looked as if it was a cattle market in a previous incarnation. We entered the building with a crowd that seemed to be in a serious rush. In no time I found myself in a dressing room somewhere in the bowels of the building. The place was saturated with voices in languages that sounded like hungry animals fighting and howling to be let out of a cage. There were screams, and bells ringing every minute. If it wasn't a Roman Circus it was easily a place for a PT Barnum. The public-address system was bellowing out names of individuals, young contestants like me, to come forth and be ready to step into the ring. The arena was jammed with young boys and older boys of every shape, weight and size.

I was hoping Mr. Anderson had entered me in the featherweight category. A punch from someone my own height and weight didn't frighten me. As it turned out, Mr. Anderson had filled out the application in the newspaper a few weeks earlier than when he first brought up the subject. I deeply regretted having boasted of my skills as a boxer when I was twelve and thirteen years old. I didn't take it seriously myself then and I hadn't expected Muriel's father to think much of it either when I'd related episodes of my childhood to him months earlier. The idea of me competing in the Golden Gloves had come to him in the form of some sort of revelation. Was it a secret wish of his to have a son?

I thought about all the possibilities and prospects as to why I was in the situation I was in this particular evening somewhere in the Bronx waiting to go into a boxing ring. Why was I volunteering to have my head knocked off me in the ring? I reflected that part of the reason I was sitting on a bench, waiting and waiting to enter a boxing ring for a three-round bout with someone I had never seen, met or talked to, was that I hadn't wanted to appear afraid or cowardly in Muriel's presence when her father proposed that I enter the contest.

It was a good thing Mrs. Axe was away in Ireland visiting Maggie. She would not have sanctioned this misadventure. Though she likely would not have believed that I would have allowed myself to fall into such a state of danger.

As the names of the competitors continued to be bellowed out over the public-address system it became crystal clear in my mind that the situation I was in had obviously something to do with my courting Mr. Anderson's daughter. It even occurred to me in my shivering state that my introducing Muriel to a Catholic church and showing her what Mass looked like was not a diplomatic thing to do to someone who was not inclined to be an observer still less a practitioner of another's religious faith.

As the voices, sounds and distinct aroma of where I was standing avalanched over me I began to think I was in some kind of dream that was morphing into a nightmare.

Mr. Anderson stood in front of me and offered supportive reassurance. He put his hands on my shoulders and told me everything would be easy going. He'd had a sneak preview of my opponent and I had nothing to worry about. He continued to tell me that from what he observed most of the contestants were the types who wanted to be professional boxers but he reassured me that my scheduled opponent was not of that ilk and calibre.

A boxer of any description was the last thing I wanted to be.

I was in too much of a self-induced coma to discern exactly what was happening to me. As I sat on the bench and waited to be thrown to the lions I regretted that I had let him decide I was a featherweight. Mr. Anderson was under the impression if I fought at that weight I wouldn't suffer much damage. My straight nose, however, might not have agreed with that assessment.

Rob Anderson tied the laces on the pair of boxing gloves that my hands were now shaking in. I was also wearing a new pair of boxing trunks as well as a pair of boxing boots that he had purchased in White Plains over the weekend. For safety and as the rules stipulated I was also wearing a metal cup to protect other parts of my anatomy. Everything happened so fast I seriously didn't know where I was or what I was doing. I was on the verge of crying and praying at the same time. I wanted God to forgive me for anything and everything I had done previously in my eighteen years of life. With all the noise and shouting going on around me I didn't think God would hear what I was trying to say. When word came in that I was the next entrant to enter the ring I prayed in as low a voice as I could mumble that my nose wouldn't be broken and if I was knocked unconscious and didn't wake up for someone to tell Mrs. Axe, Maggie and my mother what had happened to me. I also prayed that my opponent, someone of the same age and weight, would feel more scared than me and run away. Such hopes, wishes and prayers in this kind of arena were not likely to be answered and it didn't look as if a miracle would occur and suck me up to Heaven before the bell for the first round rang.

As I walked down the aisle towards the boxing ring all I could think of was that it was a good thing that Mrs. Axe and Maggie were away in Dublin. Otherwise both of them might well and with good reason have thrown me into the Hudson River from the top of the castle.

With a little push from Mr. Anderson I stepped into the ring and sat on the stool in the corner I was assigned. In the far corner I could see my opponent who was looking in much better shape than me and was definitely taller and more inclined to want to make a living from breaking noses.

For me, waiting for the bell for the first round might have been akin to what souls felt when they were wandering around Limbo with an eternity tag hanging from their necks. There seemed to be no beginning and no end and worse still, no explanation of my pained state of mind. The only half-pleasing thought I had was that I was glad Muriel had stayed home and wasn't here to witness my induction to martyrdom.

As I fell deeper into an abyss of nothing and nothingness I was awakened by the sound of the bell ringing to start the first round. It was a loud bell and my presence in the centre of the ring was helped by a slight push from Mr. Anderson who was in my corner.

The next thing I remember was another bell ringing forth at the end of the first round. I wasn't sure if the rounds lasted two or three minutes but each second felt like eternity. In the heat and hustle of being hit and fighting back at the same time, for three short rounds I found myself in a different universe. I had obviously been punched incessantly for a number of minutes but I actually hadn't felt one punch.

When the fight ended my opponent was awarded victory by a narrow decision by the judges and the referee. Mr. Anderson embraced me as if I was his long-lost and wished-for son. He showed the respect and appreciation for me that I had been hoping for. It was, after all, the main reason I had suffered a bruised lip and a bit of a headache.

* * *

Mrs. Axe had been gone for about two weeks and the length of her absence indicated to me that she had remained in Dublin because of health issues regarding Maggie. When I placed the breakfast tray in front of her the morning after she returned, and before I had a chance to ask how her trip went, she looked directly at me and said something I was not prepared for.

"She passed away peacefully. The nuns and the priest were with her. She had a funeral fit for an opera."

Without having ever seriously contemplated what the meaning of the word 'end' meant, the news of Maggie's demise was definitely the 'end' of an experience that existed in my mind since the day I stepped into her bedroom in the Shelbourne Hotel to serve her breakfast. After orchestrating my departure from Dublin she was also on hand to greet me when I first arrived in New York. When she had put her hand on my head that first day in the castle foyer almost two years earlier, I felt then and even more as I got to know her, that we had something in common. I came to the conclusion that she was deep down a shy person and in many ways like myself afraid to show emotion and tenderness. Maggie was great at reaching out but had trouble reaching in. Reaching in is, I suppose, more difficult because of the darkness of one's past and the memories that live in it. After hearing that she had passed away I felt I had lost an anchor and a guiding compass that had been an ever-present part of my life. I had known for months that she was in and out of the hospital in

Dublin and was battling in her diva-like manner to stay alert and alive. As the news of her death swamped my mind I momentarily felt lost and adrift.

Before I could rationalise and digest the implications of Maggie not being in my life, Mrs. Axe broke into my struggling and confused thoughts.

"She is in her final resting place in Glasnevin Cemetery."

The punches I had endured during my few minutes in the boxing ring while Mrs. Axe was away were nothing compared to what hit me directly in the head this morning. Even though I hadn't seen or even heard from Maggie in many months she was a constant presence in my life in Tarrytown. I had always secretly hoped for the day when she'd return and talk to me about her past and how I was preparing for my future. The anticipated joy and pleasure of talking about the future with Maggie had ceased to be and could no longer be even a wish. Although she had long since departed the castle I sensed her presence was always there. It certainly was in my sometimes insecure and wandering mind. Maggie wouldn't chastise my behaviour or correct my grammar any more. Her dissertations on opera and Ireland would now only be an echo of remembrance. Her near-obsession with her birthplace, County Mayo, would in and of itself be an opera of her legacy. During her absence from my life in Tarrytown she was a spectre and an angel that was constantly singing an aria of redemption in my ear while I went half-floundering about my life in Axe Castle. Maggie had brought me there, placed me there, and a part of me always sensed her instructive presence was always there. Her litany of social warnings permeated my brain on a daily basis and motivated me more than I knew or could measure. Almost every word and action out of me, in her presence or not, had to be vetted against her values and instruction. It is also possible that in the passing of time since she left New York I had acquired new friends and new values that might not have pleased her. My diminished devotion to Mass would not have satisfied her. Time spent away from the castle with Muriel and the hours on weekends I spent with Frank Dillon and his inebriated friends at the local pub would not have impressed her either. Maggie had an aversion to delusional people and for the most part considered them cowardly and even lazy. Sometimes the presence of Maggie in my mind was so dominant that I felt she had never left New York and returned to Dublin. This was particularly true when I was alone and rambling about the castle on deserted weekends and holidays.

My residence near the top of the castle was far away from everything and everyone. My nearest neighbours, since Maggie left, were the birds that flew by the window every so often. When I was in my room wondering what I was going to be doing that day, I would sometimes call out to the birds and ask them where they were going or what they would be doing for the rest of the day. Quite often the only sign of life was the feathered kind that waltzed about in the air outside. Since Maggie's departure, if the Axes were away in separate and different directions and not in residence, I found myself wandering about the place like an orphan cloud that couldn't make up its mind whether to cry or not.

Many times in my empty wanderings in and around the castle I wished I had been able to talk to Maggie about my confused reality. I would have told her about the awkwardness of living with two people who hardly lived with each other. I would have asked for advice on what to say and what to do when Mr. and Mrs. Axe asked me to accompany them on their separate activities at the same time. Would I walk with him

91

or drive with her? When they argued who would I sympathise with – even when I had no idea what they were arguing about? Would I invite myself to the dinner table when they appeared to be happy and content with each other? Should I have agreed to serve Mrs. Axe her morning breakfast before I went to school just like I had for Maggie? Would it have been improper and inconsiderate to complain about the encroaching isolation on weekends and holidays?

Would I have introduced Maggie to my dearest Muriel? Would I have told her how happy I was to be Muriel's boyfriend and half-considered a member of her family? Would I have told her about my brief boxing career? I had wished countless times for the opportunity to explain myself and my life since our initial encounter in the Shelbourne Hotel and now I knew that would never be. Maggie had been suffering from cancer but for her own reasons she had never, neither in Dublin nor New York, mentioned it to me. And now she never would.

* * *

Mrs. Axe was noticeably hurt by Maggie's passing. Periodically she'd interrupt the silence in the room by humming a piece from an opera Maggie had appeared in. She'd hum for a few seconds then she'd articulate the lyrics of the aria. It was as if she was communicating in her own way with Maggie. It was this mutual affinity for the arts that had brought Maggie Sheridan into her life. Maggie had given up or had lost her operatic career years earlier and was afloat in life, travelling between Rome and Dublin. After meeting the Axes one evening at a dinner and opera party in Rome, she and Ruth Axe bonded. Up until then Maggie had lived frugally off her recording royalties. The friendship of Maggie and

Ruth, with Emerson slightly to the side, formed an entity that suited all three individuals. Maggie's presence kept the Axes alive and sparkling after their work hours. And the Axes became Maggie's dependable patrons. They took care of all her living expenses and almost nothing was denied her when it came to paying for any of her material needs. This included her bi-annual trips to Ireland and sometimes to Italy.

* * *

Even though I was trying to catch up and accumulate enough credits for graduation I wasn't able to study and concentrate on school work in the castle no matter how I tried. Because of my age – I was two years older than the average student in my class – I was beginning to feel like the class idiot. I hadn't had the luxury of being a freshman in high school and the consequence of not having accumulated enough academic credits put pressure on me to take several summer courses in my junior year. The prognosis in my present senior year was neither encouraging nor positive. Carrying the burden of extra courses than was normal impacted on my ability to excel in any one course that I was taking. Algebra and geometry were as elusive as second-year Latin and more than a few times I just gave up. The slowdown and an unimpressive report card from school did little to enhance my presence in the castle.

Mrs. Axe called the school once or twice to find out if I was really attending classes. When she discovered that I had not missed a day of school, she appeared even more disappointed but didn't seem to know how to rectify the problem. There were times when she asked me about my comfort factor at school and suggested I make an extra effort to tell the school teacher that I was not used to being in a classroom where I wasn't afraid of being physically punished. Mrs. Axe was of the mind that I was so used to withdrawing from authority that I closed my mind to what I was being taught at school in Tarrytown. When she made an effort to explain the dilemma to me I got even more perplexed and confused. Having any problem of mine explained to me was an experience that was more foreign to me than the actual problem itself. But whether I knew or could acknowledge my drawbacks, inefficiencies and failures, I was still missing out on what I should be learning, and if I was to graduate with Muriel and the rest of my senior classmates I would have to study more and comprehend faster.

Apart from his occasional casual tutoring in history, art and opera, Mr. Axe took almost no interest in my everyday existence: particularly if it involved anything social or personal. He had no interest in my accomplishments on the soccer field nor did he ever inquire about my friendship with Muriel. He might, I often thought, in the oddest way be interested in hearing Frank Dillon reciting Shakespeare but Frank Dillon could only recite passages from Hamlet when he was drunk. I didn't tell him I had learned and memorised most of the famous monologues off by heart. My relationship with Mr. Axe seemed solely based on and dependent on his whims. Whenever he felt like talking to anyone or expressing himself on something that was taking place on the world stage he'd call me and we'd walk around the estate.

His persistent fixation on Churchill interested me the most. He claimed to have knowledge that Churchill faked his capture in South Africa during the Boer war and that he wrote dispatches to the London *Daily Mail* exaggerating his exploits and his internment when he was a correspondent there for the paper. He also went out of his way to tell me that one of Churchill's most famous sayings: "*I have nothing to give but blood, toil, tears and sweat*," was a quote from "The Age of Bronze", a poem by Lord Byron. As far as Mr. Axe could determine, Churchill didn't credit the poet with authorship of the famous line.

It might well have been Mr. Axe's Scottish ancestry that motivated him to cast aspersions on Churchill. In warm weather he periodically wore a Scottish kilt. The sight of him walking up and down his driveway often brought a smile to my face and to that of his wife. When we'd finish our walks and talks he'd inform me that his conversations were the method and syllabus of instruction practised at Oxford and Harvard. He also reminded me – even though I had already heard it from a drunk on a Dublin bus one night – that listening was generally the best way to learn anything. I don't recollect ever having the confidence or the impulse to question him and he would not question me to see if I had learned anything at all from him. To say he exhibited an air of presumption would be an understatement but with my present struggle in high school this arrangement suited me fine. I looked forward to walking with him often because I knew I would neither fail nor succeed with regard to whatever subject he waxed on about during the course of the daily walk. There were many days in school that I wished the teachers would ask questions on the subjects Mr. Axe frequently discussed with me. Only rarely was I obliged to raise my hand to answer a question that underlined the benefits of the attention I paid to Mr. Axe.

* * *

The exuberance and excitement of the pending graduation from high school permeated just about every moment and activity of the senior class. The looming commencement date was so looked forward to that the transformation of the high school seniors' attitudes towards each other was palpable. In fact it would not be too far a stretch to say it took on a religious zeal. The concoction of youth, freedom and ambition generated an energy in the school corridors that wasn't too far from being combustible. More than any other day in the life of a high-school senior, graduation heralded a liberation of both mind and body. But I was neither confident nor secure in the fact that I would be graduating with the rest of my classmates and the feeling I carried with me as my class got closer to graduation day was more sorrowful than celebratory.

My struggle to pack four years of high school into two was beginning to show strains in my syllabus. I had not accumulated the required number of official scholastic credits and I was also falling behind in the subjects I did have. Two months before the appointed date of graduation I was informed by my high-school guidance counsellor that I needed another two credits to graduate and the only way I could get them was to go to summer school. I would have to complete two courses during the summer months to receive my diploma.

This meant that I wouldn't graduate on the same day as my classmates and more importantly I wouldn't share the stage with Muriel. It also meant that at the upcoming senior prom I'd likely be the only senior who wouldn't be looking forward to the traditional graduation ceremony. Another depressing factor was that the presence of family and friends at graduation underlined the transition and I knew I'd have no family members in attendance even if I did graduate on the anointed day.

The first person I told about my disappointment was Muriel. She commiserated with me and invited me back to her house where she related my disappointment to her parents. Muriel's father was as comforting as he could be and did his best to ameliorate my painful and sinking state of mind by telling me that I would only be missing a ceremony and that I would still receive my diploma when I finished summer school. Since I had first known him, apart from a few rare instances Muriel's father had never really asked or inquired about my life and circumstances at the castle. Today, when he accepted that I was in an emotional quagmire, he questioned me on my present plight of living with the Axes and asked again about my past. I had assumed he had queried Muriel in detail about the young man she was dating but as it turned out Muriel hadn't added anything much to the bits I had told him myself. For the past twelve months I had been under the assumption Mr. Anderson knew as much about me as I did about myself.

Over a barbeque in the back yard I related as much as I could remember about my life in Dublin to Muriel's parents. When I got stuck for words or when I was feeling self-conscious Muriel filled in for me. She told her parents all about how, when I worked in the Shelbourne Hotel in Dublin, I met a great opera diva who orchestrated my journey to New York. Mr. and Mrs. Anderson seemed impressed by the circumstances that had me standing in front of them in their back yard. What they thought or imagined about me dating their beautiful daughter they kept to themselves.

They did express a curiosity about my relationship with the Axes. When I tried to explain it to them I only underlined the fact that I really didn't have a full comprehension of the situation myself. I told them as much as I could and as much as I knew about Mr. and Mrs. Axe and how I often felt like I was living in a kind of limbo, floating between Mrs. Axe and Mr. Axe. Muriel's father expressed concern that neither of the Axes had ever asked to meet his daughter. I attempted to defend them on that point by telling him that they were rarely ever home at the same time and when they were it was late at night. Deep down I accepted the fact that Mr. and Mrs. Axe did not seem interested in meeting anyone I had got to know since my arrival.

During dinner Mr. Anderson congratulated me on having endured the struggle that had got me as close to graduating as I was. Muriel also made a special effort to lift my spirits by reminding me about the senior prom. Prom Night was coming up and that would be such an occasion of youthful pageantry that I wouldn't have the time or the inclination to worry about graduating on schedule from Sleepy Hollow High. By custom the senior prom was a celebration and a dance into adulthood. The adulthood part of the ritual was something that I paid little heed to. The compass of my present emotional odyssey was pointed away from the actual reality of being a grown-up. Such a concept didn't reflect beautiful skies and gentle sunsets. My present seemed to overlap on itself each time I considered my state of affairs. Having brought Maggie Sheridan her breakfast every morning while she lived in the castle and presently delivering Mrs. Axe her breakfast before I took off for school every morning also contributed to a dilution of my present identity. In school, seniors displayed indications of who, what and where they wanted to go in life when they took on some of the responsibility for their own lives after high school. An inner cloud or darkness of some kind blocked my impulses and thoughts with regard to reaching out and owning a part of tomorrow.

I wanted to cry, protest and present my past as an excuse for my lack of intellectual acumen but the splinters of my yesterdays were still stuck in my ass and every so often when I tried to sit down on my early upbringing a volt of pain ran up my spine and I ran as far away from it in my mind as I possibly could.

* * *

Two weeks after Muriel and her parents commiserated with my plight the senior class was abuzz with a crescendo of excitement regarding plans for the senior prom. The social celebration was a ritual my classmates were obsessed with. As was evident to everyone who knew her, Muriel had a flair for the artistic and she was elected by her classmates to choose the theme for the dance. The theme she submitted to the class officers was an Oriental one and it was accepted enthusiastically. It was promised that on the night of the dance the gym would be adorned with a motif of Japanese lotus blossoms and all things Oriental.

* * *

While serving Mrs. Axe her breakfast a week or so later I told her about the possibility of me not graduating with the senior class and she responded by telling me yet again that I was spending too much time on weekends with individuals at the local bar and not focusing on my homework. She was on the verge of demanding that I not frequent the bar at all. I had not in the past mentioned Frank Dillon to her but I guessed she had heard about him from Mr. Axe. I had eventually told him about Frank's flair for quoting Shakespeare. When I jokingly told Mrs. Axe that at least I learned a bit of Shakespeare from Frank she didn't find it funny. She also remarked that when I spent time in the research office at the castle, where I was supposed to be learning "the business", I was often late and showed little interest in what her executives were showing me. A proclivity for sitting behind a desk watching and listening to businessmen talk about the stock market to each other was not an exciting way for me to spend my spare time. Although I was persistently encouraged to go to the office by Mrs. Axe on school holidays and even on Saturdays, I did my best to avoid it. Looking over charts, spread-sheets and graphs and other financial indicators was like a reincarnation of doing Catholic Church penance for sins I didn't commit. Mrs. Axe wasn't impressed when I made the comparison and reminded me that I needed to pay attention to my future. By that I assumed she meant that I should concentrate on having a profession, or learning something useful that would serve me when I got older. When I reminded her of my ambitions to be somehow involved or connected with the theatre or the arts in general, she fell back into talking about her own time when she wanted to be a violinist. Her attitude always changed when she talked about her own past, particularly if it had anything to do with her youthful ambitions to play the violin. She said she still kept the violin she'd had since college but hadn't opened the case in years and wasn't likely to do so. Unlike Mr. Axe, however, she didn't usually elaborate on the subject of music. For Mrs. Axe the subject was a reminder of something she had apparently abandoned at an earlier age.

After a long pause she reverted to the subject of attending college, implying that I had avoided that reality altogether. Not knowing if and when I'd graduate from high school was akin to having a migraine headache that wouldn't go away. Consequently I developed an insecurity about college that kept me from bringing up the subject at all. When Muriel and other classmates queried me on the matter I unhesitatingly changed the subject and told them I'd probably be returning to Ireland. Muriel, of course, didn't believe this and I reassured her in private that it wasn't true and was only a ploy on my part to cover up my insecurity.

When I defensively told Mrs. Axe that I would have liked to exchange thoughts and ideas on whatever my academic future held with her, she confessed that, apart from not having any experience with a younger person's life and world, her busy schedule and life didn't permit it. She volunteered however that the activity of me serving her breakfast gave her an opportunity to talk to me and be knowledgeable about my social life and school activities.

With this encouragement and with my last encounter with Mr. Anderson still in mind, I found a modicum of courage to tell her all about Muriel and her family. She listened but didn't respond in a manner that I would have liked or wished for. I was always hoping for approval from Mrs. Axe and partly because of that need I had minimised the existence of Muriel in my social life. It hadn't taken long for me to fall into the same psychological pattern of avoidance that I attributed to the Axes, Mrs. Axe in particular. Whether it was courage or foolhardiness, I pursued the subject of Muriel and how important she was to me in my life. Mrs. Axe, to my surprise, didn't seem to acknowledge my half-protesting attitude while at the same time she didn't hesitate to remind me of her promise to my mother and Maggie concerning my welfare in general.

Before she had finished her breakfast most of what she didn't know about me and what I didn't know about her became clearer. Mrs. Axe found herself in a situation she had no experience of and wasn't well versed in: what were fundamentally emotional equations as opposed to financial ones. I, on the other hand, had no inkling on how to relate to the person who was directly responsible for me being in her home and her world, without a compass that pointed to an understanding of the present much less a clear picture of the future.

When I added the fact that I would be taking Muriel to the prom Mrs. Axe implied that I had been socialising too much with Muriel as well and not paying enough attention to my teachers in school. She even admitted that, unbeknownst to me, she had made several private calls to the school and spoken with some of my teachers there. The report from the teachers, according to Mrs. Axe, was that I had a "sharp intelligence" but it was essentially "dream-like" in nature. Hearing this assessment of myself brought a smile to my face because I not only understood it, I agreed with it. Mrs. Axe however didn't find it funny or amusing. She informed me that I needed to plant my feet on terra firma and pay attention to my school work. I defended myself and told her that part of the reason my focus and concentration was blurred was the fact that I had to get up too early every morning and serve her breakfast. Mrs. Axe retaliated by saying I didn't have to do it and that I was complaining about that chore much too late. She said I should have told her that I was in need of sleep and that I didn't like serving her breakfast. I replied that I didn't mind serving her breakfast but on some mornings, if I was out late or tired from playing a soccer match for the high school, I wouldn't be as alert when I traipsed off to school that particular morning. There was the odd morning when I was late in getting Mrs. Axe her breakfast and consequently also late for school and at school it was difficult to explain to my classmates that I had a chore to do every morning before I arrived in class. When I presented this information to Mrs. Axe she ignored it. For every excuse that I could come up with Mrs. Axe retaliated. She chastised me on the fact that I was delinquent in corresponding with my family in Dublin. I defended my inactive connection with my parents back in Ireland by reminding her that it was only my mother and sister Rita who took it upon themselves to see me off the day I left two years earlier and that no one back in Dublin ever wrote to me or inquired about my life since I departed. Father Clifford's name came up again and Mrs. Axe reminded me that I had on several occasions refused his invitation to visit him in New Jersey at the religious campus or institution he lived on. That hit home because the truth was I was frightened of going to New Jersey to visit the priest and maybe being pressurised into confessing to him about everything I'd done since I arrived in America. I didn't want to tell him about my relationship with Muriel in the confession box. The memories of confessing all my thoughts, words and deeds in a confession box when I lived in Dublin were still prevalent and active in my brain, even though they didn't haunt me like they had done two years earlier.

Certain aspects of my life had changed for the better since I'd come to Tarrytown and the thought of returning to some of the practices of my religion was overwhelmingly unpleasant. The ritual of confessing and admitting to sins was beginning to reveal itself as a betrayal of my inner self. I had long given up on receiving Communion and at this point my attendance at Mass was only once in a blue moon. However, Mrs. Axe didn't seem concerned about my lackadaisical attitude towards my church attendance, mainly because I had never seen her attend any church at any time. She and Mr. Axe expressed no particular liking for any brand of religion and never in my presence, before this morning, had brought up the subject.

When the conversation regarding Father Clifford passed Mrs. Axe reminded me that I was failing to take advantage of walking about the estate with Mr. Axe when he was exercising. She was insinuating that I was avoiding Mr. Axe and his penchant for talking about serious subjects. I reminded her that I was always available and happy to walk with him and it was he who always initiated wanting my company. The occasional walk about the estate with Mr. Axe not only exercised my body but my mind as well and I very much enjoyed it. I reminded her that I had learned more from Mr. Axe in a month than I had learned in high school in two years. This particular piece of information seemed to irritate her and for the first time since I was in her presence she was loudly argumentative with me. She reminded me that I was in reality close to disappointing her and by extension Maggie Sheridan. As she continued to berate me for what she characterised as my unproductive use of time I found myself wanting to crawl into a hole. There was no place to hide, however, so I picked up her breakfast tray and walked towards the door. As I was halfway out Mrs. Axe called after me and told me she was going out of state for a week and that obviously meant I could and should get a bit more rest every morning.

* * *

The night of the prom arrived. I donned a white jacket and black pants and almost sailed out of my room at the castle. When I got down the marble steps I bumped into Mr. Axe who was coming in from his daily walk. He seemed surprised to see me all dressed up. Before I opened the front door or could close it behind me he told me he had spoken to Mrs. Axe, who happened to be somewhere in Connecticut, and that she passed along her best wishes for me to have a great night at the prom. I was happy to hear that she hadn't forgotten about me and appreciated the fact that she had said something nice. Three days had passed since she berated me for being lax in just about everything I did and I got the feeling she was apologising to me – even if it was only indirectly. Mr. Axe added that if the weather was good, and since I wouldn't be bringing Mrs. Axe her breakfast, he'd be interested in having me walk with him the following morning. I was tempted to tell him I would be out late and would probably be too tired in the morning to walk, but I didn't. For reasons I didn't question in myself I had fallen into the habit of not saying no to anything I was asked by either Mr. or Mrs. Axe. Maybe it was because I was still sensitive to Maggie's memory and I didn't want to betray her almost daily instructions when she was alive on how I should behave. At the same time I began to realise how emotionally and materially dependent I had become on both Mr. and Mrs. Axe. Mr. Axe's companionship, particularly when I took walks with him as well as when I attended the opera and theatre, kept my mind alive and even hungry.

As the time passed for me while living in the castle I felt increasingly that my life was akin to a pendulum in a clock. One day I'd feel like I was a member of the family. The next day I'd come to believe that there was no family to be a member of. In the need and perhaps search to find a centre for my existence I had, intentionally or not, replaced both my mother Molly and Maggie in my life with Mrs. Axe and most of my emotions were influenced by what she observed and even thought about me. Her concerns regarding my welfare made me want to please her and live up to what I imagined her standards to be. The problem I had with that illusive perception was that I was never sure what she truly wanted of me. On drives or on weekends at the castle when she had a few glasses of wine under her belt she'd talk about me working my way up in the company and learning everything there was to learn about her business. She talked about how I would make a good lawyer and that I had some natural instincts that would auger well for me being a successful executive in her company. Almost always her conversations with me were peppered with anecdotes about Maggie. She would, even though it was infrequent, ask me about my parents and how they managed to get along with having so many children. When I related that I had never heard either of my parents speak an affectionate word towards each other Mrs. Axe would end the conversation. There were also times when she'd be impatient, cool and indifferent: when she displayed these characteristics in my presence I retreated from her emotionally and became intellectually confused. Although it was less frequent and even impersonal at times my relationship with Mr. Axe was more succinct and definitive. When such thoughts about my see-saw life at the castle permeated my mind I usually retreated to either Muriel's home, which because of school could only be on weekends, or to the dingy bar in town where Frank Dillon held court and waxed on about his theatrical fantasies. For longer than I wished, my mind and sense of self bobbed between more realities than I could comprehend and feel comfortable with.

The advent of the school prom had beckoned to me like some sort of coming-of-age ritual, except in this case I felt it was my mind and not my body that had evolved and a sense of confidence followed. The formal new suit and the collective association of camaraderie that I looked forward to floated through my head. It was akin to being washed ashore on a new island that had me excited by the possibility that I would be the first to explore it and discover the world around me and even facets of myself that I wasn't fully sure I understood.

As I approached my newly washed and polished 49 Ford, Pat and Jim pulled into the parking lot in their old antique green-and-white Pontiac. The car looked as old as the castle itself. Jim had told me that they'd had the car since it was new and he was attached to it as if it was a member of his family. He talked and even bragged about how many times it had broken down and how he learned to be a mechanic by his attempts and efforts to fix the thing. He blabbered on about how the old car had on several occasions acted as a home and a shelter when he and Pat went travelling about the country years earlier. He glanced at his wife for confirmation about their relationship with the old Pontiac but Pat ignored his silent invitation for affirmation with a smile and a shake of her head. When I asked Jim what year the car came off the assembly line he had trouble remembering.

The McCluskeys had been away on a week's vacation that coincided with Mrs. Axe's departure. They had driven to the State of Maine where they originally came from and where they still had relatives. Both of them bragged about being of New England Yankee stock. That meant almost nothing to me at that point. I was under the assumption that everybody in America was a Yank, as we called them back home. Pat was anxious to set me straight on the term 'Yankee', explaining that it properly referred to the descendants of colonial English settlers in New England. But Jim differed from her when he confessed to having some Irish blood in him. Pat retreated slightly also when she admitted a forebear of hers on her mother's side was a Cajun Indian with roots in New Orleans.

When they saw me in my prom attire they gave out a happy and excited yell. Seeing me dressed in my white formal jacket and black slacks was a pleasant shock to them. Jim said I looked more like a 'Yank' than anyone he had seen in a long time. Pat reminded me of the first day I arrived when my attire was not so fancy – in her words I was "lost like an unremembered dream".

As I moved away from the couple and attempted to get into my car Pat asked me if Mrs. Axe had returned and I told her she was due back in two days. She asked me how I managed to know that. I related that she had phoned Mr. Axe and she had apparently told him to inform me of her imminent arrival. I did mention also that Mr. Axe was up in his suite listening to an opera. Pat then complained about having to listen to opera while she did her domestic chores. I responded by admitting that I was always happy when Mr. Axe had an opera playing on his record player. That revelation brought the merriment of the three us standing in the parking lot to an end.

I got into the car and, without looking back at Pat and Jim, turned the key in the ignition and drove off the estate. I promised myself that I would not dwell on the erratic and domestic complexities of my home life at the castle.

As I drove down the long twisting driveway I turned the car radio on full volume. Guy Mitchell was just coming to the end of his hit tune "I Never Felt More Like Singing the Blues". This special evening of attending the high school prom with Muriel made me feel like I had grown a pair of wings befitting a swan. The joy, excitement and anticipation of walking into the high school gym this evening dressed in my formal attire went a long way to erasing almost all of my perceived and imagined insecurities. The image of the old worn-out suitcase with the second-hand shirt and socks that Pat had reminded me of brought a smile to my face – but I wasn't really sure as to why.

As I sped along the highway the image of Muriel waiting for me made me feel and believe that I was becoming or had become a different person to the one who had emigrated from Ireland a few years earlier. As this slow and creeping metamorphosis crawled over me I got a fleeting sense that I was beginning to lose or had finally escaped from some inner reality that had for most of my life kept me from truly knowing and accepting that my life was my own. For a few brief moments I dwelled on the thought that the reason for this might be that I wasn't as concerned or worried about committing 'sin' as I used to be. The concept and shape of 'sin' in my mind had gone from a dark presence that was omnipresent in my past to a pale vapour-like outline that was slowly floating away from me, like a burnt-out fire that was breathing its last warm breath under a persistent rainstorm. As I welcomed these thoughts I began to accept that liking myself was not a *sin* now nor was ever going to be one. The paradox of observing my own confusion and understanding it was as liberating as it was pleasurable.

Earlier, as I prepared for the evening – and with very little experience of self-perfuming – I had sprayed on so much underarm deodorant while I got dressed that the car began to stink like a hairdressing salon and I wondered if Pat and Jim had noticed the aromatic change in the air as they stood next to me. For a second or two I felt I should have asked them or even apologised, but I quickly dismissed the thought from my mind as I sped along the road towards Muriel's house.

The anticipation of dancing with Muriel at the prom erased just about every memory of ever feeling responsible to anyone for anything at any time in my past. In my head, as I hurried to pick up Muriel, I could hear the voice of Marty Robbins singing "A White Sports Coat and a Pink Carnation" as well as Johnny Mathias serenading me with "Chances Are Because I Wear a Silly Grin".

When I neared Muriel's house I began to feel much happier and more secure than I had in a very long time. The fumes of my underarm deodorant had receded and the fresh air of summer caressed and maybe even congratulated my dear little car for getting me safely to my destination. When I pulled up alongside Muriel's house she was already waiting on the veranda with her parents. Both her mother and father were holding wineglasses in their hands and appeared to be as excited as Muriel who stood next to them. My date was wearing a beautiful white dress and the shoes on her feet appeared to be silver. She looked so sparkling she could easily have been a modern Cinderella. To make up for my tardiness I waved to her and she immediately ran to the car and got in beside me. With a wave of my hand I bid hello and goodbye to Muriel's parents and sped away down the street.

* * *

After dancing our feet off and imbibing a bit more than usual, Muriel and I decided to leave the prom before the last dance. Neither one of us wanted to be around the rest of our classmates who were themselves splitting off into couples. It was a night of celebration and discovery. The air was filled with the energy of lust, commitment and impatience. Couples left the dance floor more joined at the lips than hands. Outside the school the June air was warm and the nearly full moon was witnessing and maybe even laughing at the youthful stampede from the annual ritual of the high school prom. Muriel and I, after bidding adieu to some of our friends and fellow revellers, got into my convertible and drove off.

The students who had left the prom earlier had got a head-start and had driven immediately to the secluded spots around the outskirts of town and the nearby lake as well as other less-travelled hideouts. The local police, on prom night, purposely took the night off from patrolling the 'make-out' hideouts. Not having a romantic place to park the car available I drove all around and about the township of North Tarrytown and the fabled locations of Rip Van Winkle and the Headless Horseman. At one point, under the vast and late summer sky, I drove my old Ford up to the front gate of the Rockefeller Estate but quickly made a U-turn to avoid a confrontation with the security guard at the gate.

Slightly after midnight and anxious in the extreme to hold and embrace Muriel, I parked the car in front of Marymount College. Marymount, a Catholic girls' college, was situated on the highest point in Tarrytown. From the front lawn of the school one could see both up and down the Hudson River. There were statues and crosses and symbols of Christianity all over the front of the building. It was as if the shadow of my childhood in Ireland had followed and ambushed me on the highest hill in Tarrytown. The magnificent glow and aura of the moonlight sky had a surreal effect on the huge cross on top of the college building. The restive light bounced off the cross and with so many memories of the image of Jesus dancing on the rim of my mind from my childhood I had an urge to stop and salute it and obliterate all that I was looking forward to in my present situation with Muriel by my side. The Christian symbols stood out like a proclamation that suggested some kind of a Biblical gesture of triumph. The stone statues of the saints looked as if they were sentries and guards of the college, appearing animated and lifelike. In their immobilised state they could have been witnesses to all that went on below and before them. Standing in the night they glimmered with impatience and seemed to be hoping that the sun wouldn't rise.

I wanted to censure every impulse that was dashing through my body and I almost betrayed the beauty and newness of the moment by focusing on the religious symbols that at this late hour made me think I was committing sin. When the late-night moon passed behind a cloud, a warm comfortable darkness engulfed the hilltop. My mind returned to where I was and who I was with and I blamed the images I had been seeing on the fact I'd had too much beer to drink earlier at the prom. Also I was stampeded by uncontrollable physical urges as the aroma of Muriel's presence intoxicated my brain.

Then Muriel fell into my arms. The impulse was fast, furious and immensely exciting. All manner of fear, trepidation, apprehension and accountability fled as both Muriel and I consumed each other as if we were crashing and colliding stars in search of a physical galaxy that fuelled and explained the concept of time itself. We embraced and conjoined in a newness that obliterated individuality, creating a oneness that heretofore was forbidden in the memory of every cell in my body. The indefinable language of not wanting or wishing to express oneself in words complemented the stillness and the darkness that surrounded the old car we were in. It was a baptism of the flesh that obliterated sight and sound and all thoughts that struggled to define my ability to understand my own mind. In the birth of the moment the physical connection to Muriel promised an infinity of joy. The consummation of passion and desire was an exuberance that blanked out any sense of wishing for a tomorrow that would remind Muriel and me of who we were before this night in the back seat of my car in front of the religious icons that adorned the college on the hill this summer night of the high school prom.

* * *

A week later I was officially informed that I would not be eligible to graduate and be part of the graduation ceremony that was to take place in two weeks' time. This was most painful and humiliating. My indifference to algebra and biology had finally taken its toll.

Muriel and her parents did their best to ameliorate my disappointment and sadness. Her father even took me and his family out to dinner twice that week to reassure me that he was in my corner.

During the drive from Tarrytown to White Plains Mr. Anderson expounded on the union movement in America and a few times he mentioned several Irish names. He probably did this to make me feel that I was in some way connected to causes he believed in. I had told him when we first met that I was once in the Irish Hotel Workers Union. That fact might easily have been my most appealing feature as far as he was concerned. A serious union with his daughter Muriel in the future would likely be less endearing.

For a special treat Mr. Anderson would drive to White Plains for what he and Mrs. Anderson considered extraordinary homemade ice cream. It was during one of the forays in pursuit of ice cream par excellence that Muriel informed me that she had been accepted to Williams College in Vermont, and was very much looking forward to going there. This meant that she'd be going away not only from her family but from me as well. Williams College was a liberal arts institution that pioneered a more open approach to education. It seemed to me at the time to be a choice made by Muriel's father. Mr. Anderson's philosophy about life in general was very much in line with the curriculum at Williams. Study at Williams, in contrast to other academic institutions, was considered to be geared towards subjective expression as opposed to objective analysis of the world outside one's own perception of self. This concept of academic development at Williams was not popular with many members of my senior class who were also heading for college at the end of summer.

Mr. and Mrs. Axe had on many occasions talked about me going to college but Mrs. Axe in particular was of the mind that I should have patience and see how I navigated my way through high school. A part of me felt that she needed to be doubly reassured of my ability and commitment to books rather than the flights of fantasy that I often portrayed when I talked to her and Mr. Axe about the future. My childhood years of having been exposed to the world of celluloid continued to be in conflict with Mrs. Axe's idea of a more grounded reality. She reminded me on occasion that she was carrying out Maggie Sheridan's wishes and instructions. At times I felt she had Maggie's interest in mind more than mine, even though Maggie had been deceased for way over a year. Maggie's memory in some ways continued to be a reality that inadvertently diluted my relationship with Mrs. Axe. The question and problem of graduating from high school was the first time a serious issue had surfaced that required a solution that didn't involve Maggie's wish or opinion.

Knowing I wasn't likely to graduate without going to summer school to make up two courses I was in need of had been akin to having the Sword of Damocles hanging over me for the final six months of my senior year and at least one of the bulbs that kept the light on in my brain had gone out. But I had kept this from Mrs. Axe. These days she was away on business trips more than ever before. She came back after being away for over a week after I had been given the bad news of not graduating. I informed her while retrieving her breakfast tray one morning that she shouldn't look forward to seeing me on the high-school stage receiving a diploma. She had been away at a health spa and was looking more refreshed than I had ever seen her. She appeared to have recovered the sense of joy and lightness she had when she was in Maggie's company. When I finished relating my sad tale to her she got upset and called the high school principal. Despite her pleas and protestations she was not able to convince the school faculty that I deserved to be granted a diploma on the official day of graduation.

That same evening, as I sat on the balcony overlooking Tarrytown with the Axes, Mr. Axe did his best to comfort me by talking and reiterating to me about how the early Greek and Roman civilisations sowed the seeds of democracy for the present Western World. And how early China was so civilised it had neither laws nor police. Early Chinese culture and respect for the elderly seemed to be the summit of Mr. Axe's civilised perception and he didn't hesitate in his instruction on that matter when he talked to me on many of our walks around his estate. To encourage me he mentioned that if in the future I showed signs of pursuing an academic career he'd do his best to get me into his alma mater Harvard.

Mrs. Axe went out of her way to remind me not to be in a hurry. She wasn't able to resist reminding me about my life in Ireland two years earlier. She also couldn't resist mentioning that I might have paid too much attention to my social life rather than my studies at school. My accomplishments on the soccer field didn't impress her much either. I took her comments on my social life to mean that I was spending too much time with Muriel and her family. The only thing she left out was my excursions to the local pub and my time spent with Frank Dillon and his inebriated buddies.

After a toned-down diatribe from Mrs. Axe I decided to refrain from defending and explaining myself. My immature mind resisted dwelling on the past, be it recent or ancient. This was one night, however, when I had more interest in not having accumulated a school credit in Intermediate Algebra than in how democracy took hold thousands of years earlier – or how, before I met Margaret Sheridan and Mrs. Axe, I was hardly able to spell my own name.

* * *

Later that evening I decided I couldn't deal with the insecurities I was feeling so I jumped into my car and drove to the local watering hole where Frank Dillon and his crew were holding court. When I entered the place I was greeted like a long-lost friend. Frank seemed more than happy to see me. He was bragging about his plan to go to New York and try out for several plays he had seen mentioned in *Show Business*, an entertainment tabloid. Some itinerant patron at the bar apparently had left the newspaper on the counter and the barman, knowing Frank's obsession for Shakespeare and the theatre, had kept it for him. The paper advertised for actors and actresses to audition for upcoming theatrical productions both in New York and in nearby summer-stock theatres – theatres that presented stage productions only in the summer, as Frank explained. With excitement equal to having won the lottery, Frank practically ate the newsprint off the paper. He read out every audition notice that he imagined himself to be right for. And as he leaped from audition notice to audition notice he quoted his favourite bits of Shakespeare: *"Is this a dagger which I see before me, the handle toward my hand?"* from Macbeth. And the obvious overused soliloquy from Hamlet: *"To be or not to be, that is the question."*

The Hamlet quote put me in touch with my own dilemma. To graduate or not to graduate? Or put another way, to please Mrs. Axe or not to please Mrs. Axe. Unable to solve the riddle of myself, I decided I would join Frank Dillon and the gang at the bar and drink another beer and another.

With the passing of two hours or so I found myself leaning over the bar more inebriated than I had ever been in my entire life. Frank Dillon and his friends were singing at the other end of the room but I was so drunk I couldn't focus or concentrate on the lyrics of the songs they were singing. Some of them appeared to be a blend of "Danny Boy" and "Galway Bay", presumably being sung in my honour, but I wasn't sure. While the spontaneous vocalising continued I made my way to the exit.

Outside on the street and hardly able to stand up I fell on the hood of my car, but before my nose and face made an imprint a pair of hands turned me over and picked me up. Sergeant John Gilroy of the Tarrytown police department had me half hanging over his shoulder as he transported me to his patrol car that was parked right behind my old Ford. Before I could crystallise a word of inquiry or worry about where I was or where I was being taken, John Gilroy had me stretched out in the back of the patrol car. Later, whether it was seconds or minutes or an eternity, Sergeant Gilroy was entering the gates of Axe Castle and driving up the long twisted driveway.

I had been very much aware of Sergeant Gilroy's presence since my arrival in Tarrytown. When I first got my driver's licence I had driven over a front lawn in a pristine neighbourhood of Tarrytown and he was called to the scene. At the time he hadn't been promoted to sergeant and was very lenient towards me when I told him I had recently arrived from Ireland. He told me he was second-generation Irish and even though I had squashed somebody's flowers and was inches from breaking their front garden wall he was most sympathetic.

Back then Maggie was still residing in the castle and John Gilroy got me back on the road and directed me home while he cruised behind me. He took it upon himself to ring at the front door of the castle. Pat answered but immediately turned the situation over to Maggie who was walking in the foyer nearby. Mr. Gilroy inquired about my presence and informed Maggie of my driving mishap. What transpired during the course of their meeting was that John Gilroy became very respectful of Maggie and she didn't hold back in praising him, his Irish mother and father and all his Irish relatives. She even invited him to get in touch with her if he ever got the opportunity of visiting Ireland. Unbeknownst to me, later John Gilroy and several members of his family did make the journey to Ireland. Before they departed Tarrytown he contacted Maggie by mail and informed her of his impending Irish visit. Maggie, because of her failing health, had only recently returned to Ireland but I am told she made it possible by way of her friendship with President Éamon de

Valera for Sergeant John Gilroy of the Tarrytown police department to visit the residence of the President of Ireland in the Phoenix Park with several other American notables, and have a ten-minute audience with the president. The invitation and the event impressed the policeman so much that afterwards whenever I bumped into him on Main Street in Tarrytown he gave me a salute.

For the second time in my life Sergeant Gilroy was delivering me to the castle. This time, however, it was Mrs. Axe who came to the door when he rang the doorbell and she wasn't at all surprised when I stepped across the threshold hardly able to stand up. In fact she laughed a bit and thanked John Gilroy for his charitable impulse and for the supervision of my welfare on this particular night.

Seconds later and almost tripping over myself, I began the effort to make my way up the marble staircase to my room. As I proceeded with the task of putting one foot ahead of the other, Mrs. Axe approached me and put her arm around my waist. She apparently sensed I was in danger of falling backwards. I tried to pretend that I was safe, sound and stable but she knew better and held me even more firmly. As we trudged and traipsed up the winding staircase Mrs. Axe told me it was no coincidence that John Gilroy had come to my aid outside the pub. She said she had called him earlier after surmising that I was going to the pub to meet up with Frank Dillon and his cohorts.

What I hadn't known was that Mrs. Axe had had Sergeant Gilroy's phone number ever since the day Maggie greeted him after I had driven my car into the neighbour's garden. More than likely, with both Maggie's and Mrs. Axe's approval, Sergeant Gilroy had been keeping an eye on me without my knowledge.

As we slowly made our way towards my room Mrs. Axe was giggling away as if she was enjoying my folly. She appeared to have had a few drinks herself. Wine specially imported from France by Mr. Axe was her preference in alcohol.

When we entered my quarters I flopped on the bed face down but I could still hear Mrs. Axe's voice saying she was going down to the kitchen to make me a cup of strong black coffee. In the limbo of silence that followed, I rolled over and faced the high ceiling above me. While I stared into the void and without looking at my feet I managed, while lying prostrate, to kick off my shoes and simultaneously stretch my arms and my body out in the shape of a cross. Why I automatically choose this configuration likely had something to do with my upbringing and dark days in Dublin. Everything there was symbolised by pain and suffering. The very meaning of life itself was represented by the man on the cross with nails hammered into his feet and hands to keep him from falling off it. In my tired, sad and semi-incoherent state I felt sorry for myself and I thought it appropriate to conjure up the image of the Crucifixion. Our toilet out in the back yard in Dublin had a cross with Jesus hanging on it, put there by my mother.

As I stared at the ceiling it morphed into a floating mirror above me and I became dizzier and dizzier. After a minute or two I began to see blurred images of myself wandering around the streets of Dublin asking anyone who would stop and listen for directions to the Shelbourne Hotel. I also heard the voice of my mother telling me to get up and go to Mass. Also Maggie Sheridan's voice kept reminding me to conduct myself properly whenever I was in the company of Mr. and Mrs. Axe. An avalanche of thoughts and faces I had known in my childhood surged into my mind like rainwater gushing into a street sewer after a torrential storm. I wasn't sober or awake enough to hold or focus on any one of them and in the tunnels of my ears the echoes of the gang at the bar singing Irish songs, apparently in my honour, were still ringing.

As my grip on consciousness got weaker I vaguely heard my bedroom door open and I grasped the thought that it was Mrs. Axe returning with a cup of black coffee.

I heard her say, "Are you still among the living?"

I couldn't muster up the energy to respond but I managed to move my left hand to indicate that I was still somewhat coherent but I immediately realised Mrs. Axe might have interpreted the gesture as a signal for her to sit on the bed next to me – which she did unhesitatingly. I could feel her presence and weight as she sat close to the edge of the bed. I almost stopped breathing when I tried to apologise for my present condition. Before I could find a word or the strength to say anything to her, Mrs. Axe spoke to me calmly and reassuringly. "I brought you coffee. It'll wake you so you can retire properly."

The extra beers at the pub had diminished my capacity so much I thought I myself was uttering the words coming out of Mrs. Axe's mouth. An eerie kind of silence followed that gave way to the aroma of the coffee that she had placed on the side table near me. I didn't know if Mrs. Axe wanted me to continue to engage with her or if I should thank her and say goodnight. Bereft of energy and clarity, my eyes involuntarily closed and my ability to hold on to a single and simple thought deserted me. I felt myself floating about in a hollow void with a feeling of warmth and heat creeping upon me as if I was being returned to a previous but forgotten state of innocence, excitement and pleasure.

In the darkened state of my closed eyes I could smell the

perfume that was Mrs. Axe's signature. I could tell she was very close to me but I didn't want to open my eyes and look up at her. The scented perfume was as intoxicating as the beer I had consumed earlier. I wasn't sure why it was affecting me so profoundly but it was. My physical state abruptly appeared to be lighter than the emptiness of my mind, while at the same time all of my energy had retreated and assembled in my genitals. My nervous system felt like it had been struck by lightning and every bone holding up my flesh began to shake until my entire body was no longer in my control. I wanted to blame the presence of the alcohol in my system for what I was experiencing but the feeling was too overwhelmingly powerful and pleasurable for any kind of independent judgement that entertained the concept of compromise.

I felt my belt buckle being unfastened without my touching it. My trousers was slowly unzipped and a sensation, gentle in touch, was caressing me so much that I could feel myself rising and rising with all nineteen years of my life wanting to burst out of my skin in a celebration of sexual abandonment. After I erupted I opened my eyes and saw Mrs. Axe with her head bent downwards caressing and embracing my penis with her tongue and mouth. I wanted the image and the feeling to last forever and for a moment I thought it actually did. The only interference in the stillness of the room was the aroma of coffee. Its fragrance permeated the air like religious incense at a church benediction. I wanted to talk but couldn't. I was less able to conjure up words than ever before in my entire existence.

Mrs. Axe, seemingly floating in her own aura, slowly regained her posture, licked her fingers and quietly exited my room without saying a word or making eye contact with me.

* * *

As it had been previously set to do, my alarm clock began to ring at seven in the morning. It was the hour to get ready and arrange breakfast for Mrs. Axe. This morning the image and presence of her in my room last night was so present it kept me from jumping out of the bed as I routinely did. With my head still buzzing I couldn't muster the strength or even the will to move my body out of the bed. I was so unable to move I began even to think I was lying in my own grave after I passed out and away during the night, and thoughts that had occurred to me during the course of the night were still spinning about in my mind like flies hovering over a heap of fresh dung.

With my head pulsating like a frog in heat I began a self-interrogation. "Did it happen? Did it happen?" For a moment I was hoping it hadn't and that I had experienced some odd hallucination. "Maybe it was the drink that played games with my mind," I said with an assurance that might have indicated I knew what I was talking about. Frank Dillon had told me more than once that he suffered from delirium tremens, a condition that transported him to a different reality after he had imbibed too much, particularly if he mixed beer and whiskey, which he did on a regular basis. I convinced myself that I too had slipped into a similar mental dimension with regard to my encounter with Mrs. Axe. "Maybe she wasn't in my room." I paused to think about what I was saying to myself. "I wasn't touched or caressed by her last night and what happened didn't happen. She didn't help me up the stairs and assist me in falling down on my bed." I kept insisting to myself that the images and memories of the previous night were products of fantasy and wishful thinking.

The alarm clock rang again as if I needed to be reminded of my morning routine. I was already late and that added even more anxiety to my state of mind. To face what was ahead of me was hard to imagine if what I couldn't get out of my mind was actually true. It would be awkward and difficult to face Mrs. Axe if last night had actually happened. As I slowly began to roll myself out of my bed I began to believe that it was all a dream and I was delusional. Unattainable wishes are sometimes imagined and wished for. The excessive drinking binge was more than likely the reason I was wrestling with what I was accepting as a distorted reality.

Half convinced that I was being delusional I fell out of bed with a modicum of renewed energy and enthusiasm. As I did so I bumped into the side table and knocked over the cup of coffee that on was on it. The coffee began to seep onto the carpet. I rushed to the bathroom, grabbed a towel and immediately threw it over the spilled coffee. While I soaked up the coffee the unambiguous reality of the previous night became crystal clear. It had indeed happened. I knew I didn't go to the kitchen and make myself a cup of coffee. I never brought coffee up to my room. Mrs. Axe was here! The scent of her perfume was still lingering in the air.

As I got dressed and readied myself to prepare and serve her breakfast I kept asking myself, "What can I say? What could I say?" And "What will she say?"

* * *

When I got to the kitchen Mrs. Axe was already there and so was Pat. Both women were sitting at the kitchen table and by the looks of the dirty plates and coffee cups in front of them it was obvious that they had eaten breakfast already.

Ever since Mrs. Axe had come back from the week she spent at a health spa a month or so ago she had been looking slimmer and more youthful, though still slightly rotund and

Botticelli-like. As I looked at her sitting at the kitchen table I accepted the fact that she didn't, at least at this point in time, exude many maternal concerns towards me. The impression I had of her when we met in Dublin had been gradually changing: from a friend old enough to be my mother, to a woman whose influence had gone from physical, intellectual and material protection, to what was beginning to be an emotional obsessions for me. I began to realise I was losing my ability to resist thinking about her in this way.

While I shyly and silently observed her with my new-found image of her in mind, she and Pat in unison bid me good morning. I did my best to avoid eye contact with Mrs. Axe and was glad that Pat was present.

"Pat and Jim are going away for the weekend and we're sorting things out," Mrs. Axe said without a hint or a suggestion of any kind that might have reflected on the event in my room hours earlier.

"I'm up early, Gabriel, to get an early start. Jim is outside polishing up that old car of his," Pat volunteered with her usual warm smile in full swing.

"Where are you going and when are you going?" I asked as indifferently as I could to display an attitude that showed I was not at all focused on the event in my bedroom earlier.

"We're off to Maine for a few days, Mr. Walsh," Pat replied, using my surname for the first time since I met her – maybe taking her cue from Mrs. Axe who used it occasionally in a playful way.

I sensed Pat was in a good mood so I got myself a cup and poured coffee into it from the pot that was between her and Mrs. Axe.

"I took it upon myself to make the coffee this morning, Gabriel," said Mrs. Axe. "Pat needed to see me because she was anxious for cash as the bank won't be open when she leaves this early."

I then sat down on a chair that was near the cooking range. Before I could hide in the coffee cup Pat started talking to me again.

"I'm sorry to hear that you won't be graduating with the class, Gabriel. Mrs. Axe told me about the whole situation and I'm terribly sorry. I don't think it's fair."

Mrs. Axe then cut in. "Oh, he'll be fine. He'll make up the two credits in summer school and get his diploma. The only thing he'll miss is the ceremony."

I wanted to respond but I was still feeling somewhat ill at ease sitting with Mrs. Axe so close by.

Pat blurted out, "But that's the fun part! Isn't it, Gabriel? I'm sure you'll miss that – with all your friends and everything parading up there on the stage. I remember when my daughter graduated. She was as happy as a pig in you know what . . ."

Mrs. Axe laughed at Pat's animal reference.

By the intensity of her laugh I got the feeling, if not the signal from her, for me to relax and not to be so caught up in what had transpired between us during the night.

I then looked past the two ladies and noticed my car was back in front of the castle door. I was about to ask how it got there when Pat said, "Oh, the policeman brought your car up here this morning, Gabriel! He woke me up."

"Sergeant Gilroy?" I asked quickly.

Pat continued as if she was holding court. "He's the one. I don't think that man ever sleeps. What he was doin' with your car in the first place I don't know. He didn't tell me and I didn't ask him either."

I looked at Mrs. Axe and was afraid for a moment that

she'd inform Pat of how my car got into the possession of Sergeant Gilroy but before she could say a word, Jim came into the kitchen.

The first thing he did was tip his hat to Mrs. Axe. "Mornin', ma'am," he said with a gentility that was becoming.

Mrs. Axe reciprocated.

"Ready when you are, Missus," he said to his wife with a movement of his head that indicated the direction of the door.

Pat took the cue, got up from her chair, shook hands with Mrs. Axe and then turned to me and planted a kiss on my forehead. "I'll be back Monday, Gabriel." Somehow she couldn't resist adding, "When you have time, keep this kitchen sparkling!"

There was still in existence a part of my early Dublin upbringing that was attached to being a servant and helping a servant. "You'll be able to eat off the floor, Pat, when you return," I said with a touch of defensive humour.

"Bye to you all!" Jim said as they departed.

After a moment or two of a palpable silence I moved from my chair and sat on the one Pat had vacated, which was on the opposite side of the table from Mrs. Axe. To avoid looking directly at the lady of the manor, I turned from her and focused my attention on Pat and Jim getting into their car. I kept my eyes on them until Jim drove the car out of sight. Before I could even think of uttering a word Mrs. Axe asked, "When is the graduation ceremony, Gabriel?" She spoke to me as if we hadn't talked to each other in a long time. "Tomorrow night," I replied.

"Don't feel left out. It will pass. You'll make up for it."

I was happy she was talking to me and the fact that she was sympathising with me about not graduating was comforting.

"This weekend Mr. Axe and I will be away. We're going to Boston for his class reunion at Harvard. I think he is one of ten left from that class. Don't ask me what year he graduated. I won't tell you if you do." She shook her head sideways a few times and smiled. The physicality of moving her head left to right and then right to left made her appear childlike. It was as if she had just received a gift or a pleasant surprise. It was something she always did when she was in good humour. She then placed her elbow on the table and rested her chin in the palm of her right hand. This gesture seemed to re-enforce her confidence. She faced me with a look that was more questioning than words and continued to talk. "Anyway, after the colossal event of Emerson's reunion we're spending three or four days on Cape Cod. We used to have a summer house there and he wants to revisit it. It's like Harvard reminds Emerson of his salad days when he was there." She paused. "So, Gabriel, I'd like you to relax and forget about anything and everything and that includes my breakfast for a while. Concentrate on the mornings you'll be in summer school chasing those two darn credits. Do think about your future as well when you are ploughing through algebra and second-year Latin. You're a long way from looking forward to a reunion but the future shows up faster than you know it. I suggest you spend more time in the office here. There's a lot to be learned and in the end it can afford a good future for you." She stopped talking for a moment as if to think over what she had just said to me.

She had said so much I wasn't sure what she really meant or if she even had a genuine concern for me or my future. I even wondered if she was purposely dismissing what went on in my room during the night.

"Any plans for the weekend?" she asked me very perfunctorily.

When I mentioned that I was to attend a party at Muriel's house after the graduation ceremony Mrs. Axe reached across the table, took hold of my hand, and squeezed it a little.

She got up from the table and spoke down to me. "I'll see you in a few days – five at the most." She then exited the kitchen.

As if to express an indifference similar to what I was feeling from her, I picked up my coffee cup and swallowed the remnants of what was left in it, trying to accept that Mrs. Axe was not as concerned as I was about the nocturnal encounter in my bedroom, where I began the evening imaging a crucifixion that turned into an emotional and physical baptism for me.

*　*　*

I came to the graduation ceremony late and, as pre-arranged, I stayed outside the auditorium until the ritual was over. When the doors to the auditorium opened I joined Muriel and her parents and congratulated them. After chatting for a few minutes about the last few years, perhaps in deference to their daughter, Mr. and Mrs. Anderson bid us good night.

Almost immediately after that Muriel and I drove away from the school to attend a party given by one of the graduates. Upon entering the home of our classmate I found myself sailing through a sea of friends expressing their regrets about my being left out of the happiest day in high school. Many of the young people I'd spent two years with in class and on the soccer field encouraged me to put my sadness behind me and join in the shouts and cheers that were overwhelming any and all sense of civility. So many sad expressions were bestowed on me I was tempted to rush down to the pub and meet up with Frank Dillon and drown my feelings with the contents of every bottle that looked down on me from the top shelf. In the pub I could escape into a world of fantasy and be shielded from the painful reality of a night I wasn't really a part of.

While we danced, drank and reminisced about our past, Muriel kept telling me and others about how she looked forward to attending Williams College. The same was true of just about every other graduate at the party, each of them boasting about the university he or she was going to attend in the fall. The consequence of hearing and listening to my schoolmates talk about leaving town and attending college in other parts of the state and country only made me feel more disconsolate. Muriel picked up on my dejected mood and made every effort to revitalise me by hugging and kissing me and telling anyone who would listen that I would be getting my high school diploma within six weeks after I attended summer school in Ossining, a township about ten miles north of Tarrytown. I reminded those who were listening that I'd be applying to a college of my choice where I wouldn't have to focus on Intermediate Algebra. That wishful thinking got a small applause. I had trouble accepting anything positive about the evening. It was as if someone had hit me with a baseball bat months earlier and I was only now feeling the impact and pain.

On top of wallowing in self-pity, my mind simply couldn't come to terms with the fact that in a very short period of time Muriel would be leaving town and going away from me. Her anticipated new life in college was a reality that didn't include me and the more I thought about it on this vulnerable night, the more forlorn I became. I was also tempted to tell her about my encounter with Mrs. Axe but I was too insecure and uncertain about how she'd react.

I had once, when the Axes were away, taken Muriel on a tour around the grounds but she didn't take to the place or consider it very welcoming. In many ways the imposing sight of the castle was simply forbidding to anyone who lived in a normal or regular house. Almost everyone I talked to, particularly my schoolmates, knew about the castle but very little about the people who lived in it. When I told friends that I lived in it I was always asked if it was haunted. When in conversation with schoolmates in the local luncheonette, Muriel would sometimes humorously quip that I was related to the ghosts that walked the stairways at night. In turn I would add that there was only one ghost but under the threat and penalty of being turned into the son of the Headless Horseman or Rip van Winkle's sister I was sworn to secrecy never to reveal its name. Muriel often encouraged me to take notes when I walked about the place on weekends and bring them to our English literature class. In that particular class I was introduced, mainly through Muriel, to William Blake, an eighteenth-century English poet who said, "*It is important to see life through the eye rather than just with it.*" I took the position in the class discussion that perhaps the poet meant that to see life with the eye is a limited experience that separates us from a lot more than our own perceptions of self – living, so to speak, as if we are only our own shadow rather than the figure that casts it. Muriel countered with something to the effect that, according to her interpretation of Mr. Blake's poetry, humankind is forever trapped between enlightenment and ignorance. She insisted on quoting Blake to me quite often. "*A robin redbreast in a cage puts all Heaven in a rage*" and "*Truth told with bad intent beats all the lies I can invent.*" A few times I accused Muriel of equating me with the robin redbreast in Blake's poem. She denied it but it was clear

131

to me that she considered the castle a cage that I was in. And as far as I could comprehend I was never objective enough to distance myself from the environment of my jigsaw-puzzle-like relationship with the Axes. This was particularly true when it came to explaining what Mrs. Axe meant to me and what I meant to her.

Muriel was such an anchor for me in school and in the community I felt I'd simply float and fade away if she turned away from me. Listening and hearing her share her future college plans with others who would also be leaving Tarrytown added to my disappointment and drove me into a deeper sense of insecurity. When I thought about her going away to college a feeling of abandonment engulfed me and I felt like a fish out of water. When it became clear to Muriel at the graduation party that I was sinking into a state of melancholia she asked me to take her home, which I did.

Outside her front door we sat and talked very quietly to each other so as not to attract the attention of her parents who were very likely awake and waiting for us to call it a night. Muriel was in good humour and still concerned about my mood. In as sweet a voice as I'd ever heard she began to reminisce about our relationship.

"Remember the first time?" she asked me.

"The first time what?"

"The first time we did it!"

"Yes, I remember. I remember it every day." I looked up at the summer sky as if to be sure it was bearing witness to what I was saying.

Muriel then broke into my pensive hesitation. "The first time for you was the first time for me: a wonderful experience to share at the same time. A cosmic-like thing, wasn't it?"

"That's a fact," I answered, feeling a bit self-conscious.

Muriel laughed and questioned me again, more to tease me than anything else. "It is true, isn't it?" she continued as if she had nothing else to talk about.

"It's the truest thing I know about my whole life."

A moment of complete silence followed. I waited for Muriel to say something that would change the subject but she didn't. Finally I concluded that she was waiting and perhaps even anxious for me to comment on the night we both shed our virginity.

"At the time I hardly knew how to do it or what I was doing," I said, looking at her directly and hoping she'd compliment me in some way for being honest.

She giggled again. "I couldn't tell if you hadn't been at it since the day you were born," she said with a bit of a laugh.

I replied, "I think I've been thinking about it since the day I was born but on the day I was born in Ireland I was told not to be thinking about it. With that kind of thinking it's a bit of a miracle that anyone is born at all in Ireland if you ask me."

"You came all the way from Ireland and we did it up there on the hill in front of Marymount College." She was now in a happy and even cheerful mood and doing her best to cheer me up. She continued to interrogate me. "Why did we end up there, do you remember? Was it because it was a Catholic school?"

I couldn't wait to answer her question. "There was no place else to park. Every make-out place was taken by everybody we know."

"Do you know who got pregnant that night?" she asked me.

"Not you!" I quickly blurted out.

"No! Not me! Fool!"

"Who?"

"You don't know?"

"No. Tell me."

"Joan Paltorsky – that's why she wasn't at graduation. That's why she quit school not long after the prom."

"I don't know Joan Paltorsky that well but I remember a lot of boys in school used to make gestures with their hands about how big her breasts were when she walked up and down the corridor."

"She was a cheerleader," Muriel said.

"Yes, the guys went to see her at the football games."

"Did you?"

"Once."

"And?"

"She did have a big pair."

After another moment of silence Muriel moved closer to me. "Can I tell you something?"

"Tell me anything you want."

"This is about me. No, it's really about us."

At that point I got acutely nervous. I worried that Muriel was going to tell me she was now in the same way as Joan Paltorsky. A few times in the past she reminded me that her 'monthly' was late but it always eventually came and banished the shock and fear of early parenthood for both of us.

"Go ahead! What?" I said.

"We first did it on the prom night, remember?"

"You asked me that already."

"I didn't."

"I thought you did."

"I didn't."

I was now unable to hold on to any remnant of patience or humour. "Tell me what you want to tell me. I'm afraid to hear but tell me! Tell me! Go ahead and tell me!" All of a sudden the pain and rejection of not graduating seemed minor compared to what I was thinking I was going to hear.

"The dress I wore to the prom, remember?"

Was Muriel going to tell me that the dress didn't fit her now and wouldn't for a few months?

"Remember the dress, Gabriel?"

"I remember that it was a beautiful dress. Wasn't it white?"

"Yes, it was."

"You looked beautiful in it. You still look beautiful. You are beautiful!"

"Yes, but I'm not wearing that dress now."

"Where is it? What happened to it?"

"That's what I want to tell you about."

I braced myself for the news – à la Joan Paltorsky – that Muriel was going to clinically deliver to me.

She then leaned back on the reclining summer chair that her mother and father usually sat in. "I wanted to tell you about my prom dress because, after I got home that night after we did it, I was so happy and excited that when I took it off I didn't hang it up. I just jumped out of it and left it on the floor of my bedroom."

"So your dress got messed up."

"Well, sort of."

"Sort of?"

"The next morning when my mother came into my room to wake me up she almost tripped over the dress."

"Is that all?" I asked with a great sigh of relief.

"Is that all? Sort of! Except when she picked the dress up it was covered in blood. My white dress was soaking in blood. My blood! When my mom saw that she knew what we did that night."

"She knows?"

"She knows. I don't know if she told my dad. I never asked her."

I had no response. I felt sad, sorry, confused and admittedly relieved. I then reached over and kissed Muriel and she was very responsive but she got up from the reclining chair, opened her front door and entered her house. I sat alone for another minute or two then walked to my car and drove back to the castle.

*   *   *

I began my summer school course in Ossining New York, a township north of Tarrytown. Classes started at nine in the morning and ended at noon. Mrs. Axe requested I not serve her breakfast while I attended to acquiring my high school diploma. This gave me a bit more time to concentrate on the homework I was assigned. Every morning I sped off the estate in my car after having a quick breakfast with Pat and most of the afternoons I spent with Muriel. One or two evenings a week I'd join her and her parents for dinner. When her parents were out of the house or away for a protracted period of time I'd spend hours on the sofa with her. How she managed to avoid getting pregnant had mostly to do with my use of contraceptives. When such an item wasn't readily available we took our chances and – for both our sakes at the time – got lucky.

As the weeks passed Muriel visited Williams College more and more. She had acquired accommodation on campus and spent a lot of time decorating it and making it her new home. The inevitable day also came when she packed the last of her personal belongings and left home for Williams.

For me, Tarrytown then became a ghost town. With Muriel

in Vermont I felt and looked like a dead spider caught in a web that wouldn't stop spinning.

While she was away I would join Mr. and Mrs. Axe and reported to them weekly on my scholastic progress. It so happened that I was doing well in algebra and Latin and my spirits were lifted considerably. Mrs. Axe went out of her way to say – more to reassure me than anything else – that because of my association with Mr. Axe I was a bit more classically educated than almost any other student who had graduated. And she went on to say Mr. Axe, being a Harvard graduate, was likely to pull strings and have me admitted to his alma mater if within the next year or so I could show and display an ability to grasp a few more sophisticated and complex academic subjects. What the subjects were she didn't say. As encouraging as this sounded and as positive a spin as Mrs. Axe was putting on it, I couldn't shed the feeling that I had failed at high school.

* * *

On the odd weekend the Axes and I would go and see a play on Broadway. Of the plays – and there were quite a few – that Mr. Axe and I had seen, our favourite was the musical *My Fair Lady*. Mrs. Axe was less committal about favouring one play over another. She seemed to like them all.

When my last day at summer school came about, after I had passed my two courses, I was listed and registered to receive my diploma from Sleepy Hollow High School, which I officially received close to the end of summer. That same week, while I was still in a celebratory mood, I decided that I would go unannounced to visit Muriel in Williams. I had been there twice before and knew my way to Vermont. More than a month had passed since I had seen her. I drove along the Taconic Parkway feeling like a new man. The acquisition of the high school diploma was out of the way and, with the exception of serving Mrs. Axe her breakfast on weekday mornings and putting in a few hours in the office at the castle, I was free to go where I pleased. After informing Mrs. Axe that I was planning on visiting Muriel in Vermont, I chose the weekend for my journey. I also bought a small pocketbook edition of William Blake's poems as a token reminder of our days in class. My car had recently been tuned up and it performed like new. With four wheels under me and William Blake's poetry in my back pocket, I was in great form as I drove to Williams.

It was late afternoon when I pulled into the parking lot at Williams. As I headed towards Muriel's residence I noticed girls and boys dancing on the huge lawn in front of the Commons. Many of them looked like they were active participants at a carnival. There was a palpable sense of looseness and freedom in the air. The place was abuzz with students coming and going in every direction. There was a banner between two trees extending a welcome to 'freshmen'. Some of the young men from Williams had grown their hair as long as the female companions they walked about the campus with. A few even seemed to have fallen out of the nearby trees. Their attire was anything but uniform-like. Everybody seemed to be doing their own thing. Whether it was a good or a bad thing, respect for authority didn't appear to be in vogue at Williams. Musicians seemed to be everywhere, playing instruments that might easily have been as old as mankind itself. There was the odd character who still had the courage to wear a crew-cut and a three-piece suit with a shirt and tie to match but that sighting was rare. The voices, the singing and the songs were also of the kind that advocated social change. Woodie Guthrie – "*This land is your land, this land is my land, from California to the New York Island . . . this land is made for you and me . . .*" – might well have been the patron saint of the college. Freedom of individual expression, it seemed, was overtaking or at least challenging the collective and corporate bunker mentality of national isolationism. The button-down shirt generation had hatched an offspring that resisted buttons both literally and metaphorically. The curriculum may have had its roots in the 'McCarthy era' – the plague of Senator Joe McCarthy, a senator from Minnesota, a man who smelled a Communist under every bed in America. Recently he had been exposed for the ideologue he really was. His campaign against communist and godless Russia was a plague on the American landscape that had only just lifted. The college, it seemed to me, was a repository for a new kind of politic that in itself was in danger of falling over the same cliff it had chased its advisories over. As I crossed over one pathway after another on my way to Muriel's dorm the atmosphere of no perimeters permeated the very air I walked in. A traffic light of any description or function, metaphorically or otherwise, would easily have been the most superfluous sign and symbol of life there. Apparently this was part of the attraction and philosophy of the school. Students who applied for admission were very much inclined to be anti-establishment and that meant rebelling against just about everything that the culture of the three-piece suit and the crew cut offered at the time. Their parents were more than likely of the generation and the engine that saw extreme capitalism as a threat and a scourge to self-expression. I sensed this kind of politic with Muriel's father. It was almost a sure thing that he encouraged his beautiful daughter Muriel to enrol there. What he probably didn't plan on was that

Muriel was way ahead of him when it came to being liberal, charitable and caring. Proof of that was when she invited me to dance with her at my first school dance. One of the most appreciated characteristics of Muriel was her artistic inclination. She exuded a spontaneity that challenged convention and saw almost everything in life through the eyes of art. It was one of the reasons she was able to cope with my existence of floating directionlessness. I might well have been to Muriel a splattering of paint in search of a canvas. She touched a part of my being that helped open my mind to see beyond the obvious. She was accepting and even forgiving when I frustratingly struggled with being loyal to the Axes and to her needs. Compassion and creation were her twin engines. I was also aware that she had defied her parents' wishes by continuing our relationship. The love note she sent to me when I first attended high school was an impulse that foreshadowed an artistic sensibility.

I had digested a full serving of the college imperative by the time I arrived at Muriel's dorm. After knocking at her door two or three times it opened and I received what I considered to be one of the great shocks of my life. A young man, about my own age, opened the door and invited me in. He looked like any one of the many carnival-like figures I had seen dancing on the commons. He bid me enter with a spreading of his two hands. Had I not known for sure I was in Muriel's dorm I could easily have been entering a temple of some sort. I stepped into the room and immediately recognised the familiar photographic display of Muriel's family as well as several art posters she'd had since I had known her. She liked the paintings of Van Gough and Picasso and had copies of them hanging on opposite walls.

Before I had time to introduce myself to the stranger he

had with amazing indifference – at least from my perspective – sat down on the sofa and lit up a cigarette. The second thing I noticed about him was that he wasn't wearing any shoes or socks. He did seem to be very much at home and he greeted me as if I was his brother. My shyness, which I considered to be an Irish disease, soon overwhelmed me and I felt as the seconds passed that I was going to melt and evaporate off the face of the earth. To stop myself from fading and vanishing into the wallpaper I managed to sit on one of the two armchairs Muriel had in her room. As I was about to address the barefooted stranger, Muriel emerged from I could only surmise to be the bathroom. She was wearing her nightgown and made no effort to apologise for it. My plan to embrace her with the element of surprise had vanished with my confidence. I sensed I had walked into a situation that was not sympathetic to my feelings. My mind was ringing the alarm bells of 'ambush'. My new-found confidence since I finished summer school instantly evaporated and I wanted to run for cover. Before I could organise a thought on how to retreat, Muriel approached me and kissed me on both cheeks. This kind of formal greeting I didn't want. It told me in no uncertain terms that Muriel's lips were off limits and, for a moment at least, my mind detached itself from whatever rationale it was heretofore attached to. And for the briefest of time I felt bereft of the ability to act responsibly. In a moment of what I imagined to be total paralysis I stood pained and even frightened.

I then heard the man, Mr. No Socks, calling to Muriel. "Who's the dude?"

Muriel turned to him and introduced him as her new house guest. Surprisingly she even began to tell him about our relationship in high school and Tarrytown. She told him we even acted in a high school play together and jokingly added that we were destined to become lights on Broadway. When she got into telling him about my journey from Ireland to the castle in Tarrytown I asked her to stop. Her barefooted house guest wasn't showing any interest in my past and it was clear that he was becoming uncomfortable listening to Muriel wax on about me. Sensing my catatonic state, Muriel asked her house guest if she could have a bit of privacy with me. Her guest jumped over the sofa and made a hasty exit.

The prolonged silence that followed told its own story. Both of us knew that the situation explained itself. I had never felt so helpless and thought for a moment that if I told Muriel about my encounter with Mrs. Axe she might see me differently. Would a confession from me change or alter the situation I found myself in? Would it mean anything to Muriel if I admitted to her what had happened the night the police sergeant took me home and placed me in the company of Mrs. Axe who was herself intoxicated that night? A gush of guilt came over me and I began to blame myself for what was happening now between Muriel and me. I had in my own way, sober or not, strayed from our private and youthful sense of idealism.

Before I could come to terms with my inner confusion Muriel took a deep breath, thanked me for making the journey, and uttered the words "I'm in *love!*"

I naïvely responded, "With him?"

She replied instantly and calmly. "Yes. David is an artist. His work is really innovative. A bit like . . ." She stopped for a moment.

I wondered if she was going to compare him with Picasso or Monet or Cézanne but she didn't.

"Jackson Pollock is the closest I can describe . . . him as

being like . . ." She hesitated again as if to retract her comparison. Finally with a sense of impatience, she added, "He lives off campus. Well, he used to in any case. I met him at one of his exhibits in town."

I felt I had been hit by a bolt of lightning. A starving artist was fodder for Muriel's charitable and creative instincts and I knew that her proclivity for ambiguity was non-existent and when she went in any direction she didn't look back to see if she'd made the wrong turn.

I dropped back onto the sofa and practically cried my eyes out. After a bout of weeping I got up and began to punch the walls to rid myself of the anger and pain I was experiencing. As I pounded on the wall Mr. No Socks returned to investigate. I looked at him for a moment and had all kinds of pugilistic thoughts but I was able to dismiss them by forcing myself to believe that Muriel had just gone off on a new artistic adventure and a part of me loved her even more for being direct, honest and even brave. As I fumbled with thoughts as to why she had changed course in so short a time, Muriel approached me, held my hand and said something to the effect that she was "obeying her heart and was sorry if she hurt me".

While she was explaining the genesis of her emotional U-turn I retrieved the book of poetry from my back pocket and placed it on the coffee table. Muriel impulsively picked it up and randomly leafed through the pages. I hoped she'd come across a poem, perhaps even one of her favourites, and recite it but she didn't. While she stared at page after page I took her withdrawal and silence to be her way of saying goodbye. This brought on another wave of insecurity and anxiety that almost obliterated me completely. When I tried to identify in my mind where the unbearable pain was coming from I couldn't. It had converged on me like a massive rainstorm with each raindrop a spike piercing my heart. The anguish that flooded my mind had in many respects rendered me helpless but somehow I mustered the will to leave the room as quietly as I could. I knew Muriel wanted it that way.

In less than a minute I was back on the highway, heading back to Tarrytown and the castle.

* * *

When I began again the morning duty of bringing Mrs. Axe her breakfast she seemed genuinely concerned about my break-up with Muriel. I hadn't told her till she inquired about my visit to Vermont. Communicating aspects of my personal life to her always helped me regain a bit of self-confidence.

Mrs. Axe began to encourage me again to write home but I told her that most of my family had relocated to England. And my mother and father had separated and separately moved in with different siblings in England. I had only found out about it via a neighbour who lived on the same street in Dublin. With the exception of my sister Rita, as far as I was concerned, all my brothers and sisters behaved as if they were in a prison camp and separately and secretly making plans to escape from it.

After the debacle with Muriel, my morning talks with Mrs. Axe became a more and more important event for me. I looked forward to getting her breakfast. I was even impatient to see her and observe how she readied herself for the breakfast tray when I placed it in front of her every morning. She always had a smile on her face and would invite me to sit next to her for a minute or two while she looked over the contents of the tray.

Every morning while I sat in front of her I hoped she

would mention and remind me of the night she leaned over me while I lay half drunk in my bed. She didn't. She acted as if it had never occurred and I was simply too afraid to even remotely touch upon it. Mrs. Axe seemed not to want to revisit the night she brought coffee to my bedroom but every day it silently played a role when the conversation turned to my personal and social life. Our bedside conversations were sometimes interrupted by early-morning phone calls coming from who knows where.

In a very short period of time and after spending so many mornings sitting by her bed, I found myself wanting to be in her presence more and more. So much so she was not only omnipresent in my everyday reality, she was also beginning to inhabit my dreams.

* * *

The external membrane of my existence was smooth and polished and impervious to the claws of poverty but inwardly and perhaps too secretly I was often feeling close to turmoil. One reason for this was that almost all my high school classmates had gone off to college and left Tarrytown. I did meet up with some of them occasionally when they came home for a visit but the contact was minimal. My visits to the pub and the ritual of drinking two beers with Frank Dillon usually ended with me swearing never to drink again. It didn't take long for me to realise and accept that two beers for me was one too many. The coincidental ritual of occasions when I'd have two beers always seemed to be punctuated by the appearance of Sergeant Gilroy. It only occurred to me later that the bartender and the policeman were in cahoots. What I should have known and paid attention to but didn't, was that Mrs. Axe had a pact with

Sergeant Gilroy to keep me under surveillance whenever I entered the bar. The bartender's phone call to Sergeant Gilroy, made in the back room, completed this caring and innocent conspiracy.

*　*　*

To keep my mind occupied Mrs. Axe suggested I spend more time during the day at the office, where she had arranged for me to have a desk next to a few senior executives. She still clung to the belief that if I was close to one or two of the vice presidents I was likely to pick up on some of the details of what went on in the running of the company. She also arranged for me to be paid a weekly salary of sixty dollars from the company payroll – a raise of twenty on my former salary – which was essentially used for pocket money. If I needed extra money she told me to just ask her. With almost no expenses, other than filling my car up with petrol, I rarely had a situation where I needed more cash.

For two weeks, after serving her breakfast, I went to the office and did my best to be an intern in the world of finance. A read of the *Wall Street Journal* wasn't mandatory but it was required when it came to the coffee break. The paper didn't appeal to me but at the morning coffee break I did listen to those who read it. The financial news of the day was debated back and forth for about fifteen minutes in the staff lounge and there was very little agreement on what upstart company or product was worth investing in. After the morning coffee interval I delivered financial statistics and morning newspapers from one desk to another. In the afternoons I collected office mail and dropped it off at the Tarrytown post office. When the mail wasn't available to be posted I operated a machine that addressed envelopes.

On the rare evening when I stayed home or when Mr. and Mrs. Axe sat down to eat at the same time, I ate with them. Sometimes this took place in the kitchen when Pat had the night off and Mrs. Axe went about cooking dinner herself.

* * *

At least once a week and usually just before noon, I now drove Mrs. Axe into Manhattan where she conducted business from an office at 730 Fifth Avenue. I got a visceral pleasure from driving her big new Cadillac. The car was almost as big as my bedroom in the castle. Mrs. Axe used her time in the car to read reports, sift through papers and write notes and reminders to her staff both in Tarrytown and New York City. On the drive into Manhattan most of the chat was brief and perfunctory. We hardly talked or said much to each other. In the city I would drop her off outside the office entrance on 56th Street and park the car in a designated garage a few blocks away. After parking the car I had the option of going to the office and chatting with the staff there, as well as doing whatever chore Mrs. Axe had prearranged to keep me occupied. When I wasn't expected at the office I wandered about Midtown. The odd time I would take in a movie or if it was a Wednesday I'd go to a theatre matinee. If there was an important exhibit at any of the major museums in Manhattan Mrs. Axe usually supplied me with a ticket. A few times when her workday ended early I'd accompany her to the Museum of Modern Art, which was only a few blocks away from her office. Jokingly, while viewing an exhibit she'd remark that her physical stature would be ideal for an artist who shunned lines in favour of circles. Body-wise and perhaps from an artist's point of view, Mrs. Axe's shape and body was more bouncy than bendable.

At approximately six and sometimes seven in the evening I'd pick up Mrs. Axe and drive back to Tarrytown. Infrequently her calendar required her to stay in the city longer than the already usual late evening hour. Sometimes she'd meet with business executives for dinner at the Metropolitan Club on Fifth Avenue. Such events required that I be available to pick her up at the club after the meetings and drive her home. Whether it was because of fatigue, or over-imbibing at the club or just a sense of letting go of her professional responsibilities Mrs. Axe, after sitting in next to me, would change from the tireless driven businesswoman to being more like a girl going on her first date. On the journey back home our conversations were varied but for the most part they had to do with what was happening in the arts. We talked and sometimes argued about plays, painting, music and opera. She was pleased and impressed that I had been paying attention to what Mr. Axe had been dishing out to me in our walking chats.

I routinely checked the clock on the car dashboard when I pulled into the driveway. One evening, after a long day in the city, the clock indicated the time was some minutes past ten. When I was halfway up the long twisting driveway Mrs. Axe asked me to stop the car which I did. She then asked me to turn off the headlights which I also did. She then reached towards me and turned off the ignition. For a second or two we both sat in total darkness, parked halfway up the driveway. In the darkness and isolation I could hear myself and Mrs. Axe breathing. Then, and as it had happened before, Mrs. Axe moved her body to give herself room, bent downwards to my lap and ceremoniously unzipped my trousers. Once again she held me gently in her hands and with the warmest of breath caressing my genitals she placed her mouth over me. My excitement was instant and in an even briefer period of time I was sexually exploding. I kept my eyes open and stared into the abyss of darkness and wondered again if either one of us could be a witness to what was happening. As on the previous occasion, because of the position we were both in, I couldn't see or look directly into Mrs. Axe's eyes. As I disintegrated with erotic pleasure and excitement Mrs. Axe sat back up in the car and, without looking at me asked, almost in a whisper, if I'd mind walking to the castle on my own. She said she would drive the car the rest of the way and park it outside the front door. Normally and routinely I used the back entrance because it was a more convenient pathway to my place of residence. After absorbing the implication of Mrs. Axe's request, I stepped out of the car and began walking up the long driveway in the dark towards the castle. In the darkness the castle's silhouette stood majestically and seductively under the late night sky. As I approached the back entrance and turned the heavy black doorknob I heard Mr. Axe calling and complaining to Mrs. Axe about her tardiness. As quietly as I could I made my way up the marble steps, entered my room and wanting to stay in the darkness I fell onto my bed without turning on the lights.

* * *

Mrs. Axe informed me that Father Leo Clifford was back in New Jersey and, according to her, he was in need of a respite and had called and asked if he could visit. She gladly invited him and a few business associates to dinner later that week. She informed me that Father Clifford had become a very popular pastor in the community of Paterson. So much so he was assigned the parish as his permanent parish. The day before the small dinner party she asked me if I would take her car and drive to Paterson New Jersey and bring Father

Leo to the castle. I happily accepted the assignment. It had been some time since I had seen Father Leo and I looked forward to being in his company again. Unlike many of the priests I had met when I was growing up in Dublin, Father Leo didn't overtly act as if he had God on his side. He was confident enough to rely on his own humanity and that distinguished him from many of his fellow travellers. Remembering our previous wrangling about my religious observances, I was confident I could now handle the whole subject better should he choose to probe about it again.

* * *

That afternoon I got behind the wheel of the Cadillac, headed south, made my way across the George Washington Bridge and headed further south to Paterson, New Jersey.

As prearranged, Father Clifford was standing, small black bag in hand, outside the entrance of the priory that was adjacent to a church. I pulled up alongside of him and he jumped in a spritely fashion into the car and sat next to me. He proceeded to bless himself as I started the car up again but I reassured him I was a safe driver. He laughed and said it was his final prayer of the day. By the time I exited the George Washington Bridge and got on the Saw Mill River Parkway heading north towards Tarrytown, my favourite priest had relayed about as much news from Ireland as I could possibly handle. He seemed disappointed that my enthusiasm for the "land of my birth" as he put it, had waned considerably. It wasn't that I had lost interest in Dublin or anything associated with Ireland. It had more to do with the fact that in Tarrytown I wasn't living in an Irish enclave and, apart from the Irish parading up Fifth Avenue on Saint Patrick's Day, I had few opportunities to celebrate Irish culture. Without being asked, I told my priestly friend that my family back in Dublin were now mostly in England. And my mother and father had finally separated and were living in different accommodations. When I was asked if the break-up of my parents bothered me I admitted it didn't. I had never really accepted that they were ever together in a living way.

Seemingly disappointed with my innocent and unintentional disconnect when I talked about my immediate family, Father Leo predictably turned the conversation to religion. He might well have assumed that a dilution of national chauvinism on my part was concurrent with a disinterest in the religion I was born into. He reminded me as usual of Margaret Burke Sheridan and how she would react if she knew that I was negligent in my sacred duties. He also reminded me that Margaret Sheridan (he didn't refer to her as *Maggie* as most people who knew her did) was responsible for me being in America in the first place and it was through her good graces that Mrs. Axe was persuaded to bring me to New York at such an early age. When I didn't disagree with him on that subject he smiled and I told him about my high school graduation and my break-up with my high school sweetheart. He congratulated me on the graduation and suggested I say a few prayers for Maggie the next time I found myself in a church. He also said she was in his prayers every day of his life and when he was in Dublin he made the pilgrimage to her gravesite. He informed me that Mrs. Axe had paid for a gravestone over Maggie's burial place with the inscription: "*The praises of the Lord I will sing forever.*" I told him I looked forward to the day when I could stop by her grave in Dublin and relate to her how my life had turned out since she arranged for me to go to New York.

"It's good you believe she could hear you, Gabriel. I think

that's a positive on your part." When he asked if I was still devout I admitted I was not as observant as I was when I was a child. I also said that I wasn't as aware of committing sin as I was in Dublin.

"Sins or no sins, Gabriel, I strongly recommend you say a few prayers – not only for yourself but for everybody else as well. I am of course suggesting you remember your unfortunate mother as well. From what Margaret told me, I sense your mother was close to being a saint. How she managed at all I don't know."

I promised I'd make an effort to say a prayer for Maggie Sheridan and my mother Molly the next time I was in church. My clerical friend quickly reminded me that I need not be in a church to say a prayer. With that I had no argument.

As we got closer to Tarrytown Father Leo asked me the question I hoped he wouldn't. "What about Confession, Gabriel? Have you resumed that? I trust and hope you have! The last time we talked you told me you were drifting away from it."

I didn't want to answer the question and tried to avoid it by telling him about Sergeant Gilroy. "On the occasional Sunday I've gone to Mass with a policeman who lives nearby. He's Irish and he goes to Mass every day."

"Who?" Father Leo asked, sounding relaxed and satisfied that I was talking about a policeman. He also seemed to be happy with the fact that I was driving him to the castle for dinner. "You know a policeman? Is that what you just told me?"

"Yes. A sergeant. Sergeant Gilroy."

"Always good to know a policeman – can help if you get into trouble."

"This policeman was told to keep an eye on me."

"Who told him that?"

"Mrs. Axe told him."

"Mrs. Axe?" Father Leo responded incredulously as if not believing his ears.

"Yes, Mrs. Axe told him!" I replied.

Father Leo seemed to take that as a criticism of me. "Well, you were not so committed to Sunday Mass the last time we chatted. Were you? Am I right about that?"

I didn't answer that question either. "It's good you're going once in a while in any case, but you didn't answer my earlier question, Gabriel."

"What was the question, Father?" I asked, pretending I didn't know.

"Have you gone to Confession lately? I am of course referring to the sacred ritual of saving your soul and acquiring a second chance to truly repent for your sins and make a pledge not to repeat them, real or imagined."

I hesitated again in answering about the question of Confession.

When I went to Confession in Dublin from the age of seven I used to make up imaginary sins so that the priest didn't feel he was wasting his time listening to me. I was afraid to tell the priest that I hadn't done anything wrong or had 'bad' thoughts or anything like that, so I would make up silly stories about how I kicked a dog or strangled a cat or threw a neighbour's unwanted kittens into the canal. I was always looking for something to confess to the priest that I didn't do. On a few occasions I even thought that if I told him I took my clothes off during Mass or if I committed murder he'd be impressed with me. The bigger the sin and crime I confessed to the more it seemed to justify going to Confession. Whenever I heard about a really bad and serious crime happening in Dublin I thought about the person who committed the crime rushing to Confession and confessing. I often found myself wanting to commit a sin so that I could confess it and please the priest. Not having sins was a bit like not having money. Without 'sins' there was little to say to the priest to get his attention. Without money there was little to eat at home. When I made my Confirmation at the age of ten, according to the local priest in Dublin at the time, I became a more important and independent Catholic because aged ten I was obliged to take full responsibility for being a Catholic. At ten and with Confirmation bestowed on me I was a real official soldier in God's army. That's what the priest said anyway. It was as if I had got promoted. Then one week I went to Confession and told the priest that I hadn't committed any sins or done anything bad or wrong since I was in the confession box the previous week. The priest got annoyed at me and told me I must have had at least a few bad thoughts. I told him I hadn't and he got upset. He accused me of lying and told me to say the Rosary six times for penance.

The subject of Confession and me confessing, particularly to Father Leo, was more than impossible. I would definitely not be able to tell him, or anyone else for that matter, about the dark night on the driveway and the drunken night of the cup of coffee with Mrs. Axe.

My silence and obvious retreat from the subject didn't please Father Leo. I could tell by the way he turned his face from me and looked out at the scenery as I drove along the highway. Each time I drove by a landmark or something that I thought Father Leo might be interested in I pointed it out, but he didn't react or acknowledge me or the place I was pointing out to him.

After what seemed like a sentence in Limbo I told him the story about how Maggie put Sergeant Gilroy in touch with the President of Ireland when the policeman and his family visited Dublin. Father Leo avoided commenting on the policeman's trip, perhaps because he was well aware of it at the time. With a tinge of annoyance he raised his voice and said to me: "If you want me to hear your confession when you get home tonight I will."

"I can't think of anything to confess, Father," I replied.

A silence followed.

"Did you hear me, Gabriel?"

"I did."

"Well?" he asked in a challenging tone.

I retreated by leaning my head forward to distract him by showing I was concentrating on my driving.

As we approached the gates of the estate and to ease him away from wanting to hear my confession, I told my religious passenger that I would think about having my confession heard the next morning before he went back to his parish in New Jersey. I added that I was too tired just then to remember the sins I had committed since I confessed last. I wasn't sure he was fully satisfied with my response because he fell very silent. When he scratched his bottom lip with his upper teeth several times I sensed my apparent indifference to the sacrament hadn't gone down well with him.

"Well, there's always tomorrow," he said and a smile came back to his face.

I knew, however, in my head and in my heart, that I would not follow up on it.

* * *

I placed glasses on trays and carried bottles of wine and

liquor out to the main buffet table at the party Mrs. Axe gave for Father Clifford. There was a scattering of different types of people at the function. Some were executives in the company. Other individuals were invited perhaps more because of their notoriety than their acumen in finance and business. At the party I did my best to avoid Father Clifford by running in and out of the kitchen and bringing in food platters. I knew if I approached him he'd bring up the subject of Confession and how Maggie Sheridan would turn in her grave if she knew I was not attending Mass or receiving the sacraments.

As I was heading towards the service door that led to the kitchen Father Leo called me from across the room. "Whenever it dawns on you, Gabriel!" he called with a smile on his face.

I wasn't sure if he was just joking or if he was being serious about hearing me confess my sins to him. He did appear to be enjoying himself and it was apparent by the way he made his way around the room that other guests appreciated his company. Father Leo had a great sense of humour and applied it to his ministry. He was also quite a handsome man and he stood out even more by wearing the black suit and white collar.

Anyway he stopped me in my tracks and I felt obliged to walk up to him.

As I stood in front of him he calmly made an effort to reassure me. "Relax, Gabriel. I realise that this is not the time or the place to confess and atone for one's sins."

Just then Mr. Axe approached holding two glasses half filled with wine.

"Look what I've got here!" he proclaimed as if he had won two trophies. "Nobody here tonight could tell me what wine came from where. Can you tell by looking at the two, Father?"

Stepping back to get a better view of the two glasses, Father Leo said, "I think one of the two is . . ." He hesitated then shook his head. "I honestly can't tell, Emerson."

I wasn't sure if Father Leo was drinking alcohol or not. He had a glass with something in it but I wasn't sure if it was wine or ginger ale or some other concoction. He hadn't come to the wine bar when I was serving the wine. He might have, however, when I was back in the kitchen. In any event I didn't want to question him on his alcohol consumption even if he was drinking it. I feared he might take my questioning him as a criticism.

Mr. Axe then turned to me and asked me, "How about you, Gabriel?"

I drew a bit closer to both glasses. "They are the same, sir," I said.

"How do you know that?" Mr. Axe inquired of me.

"I poured the same wine into both glasses when you went down to the wine cellar to replenish the supply at the bar."

Both Father Leo and Mr. Axe laughed just as Mrs. Axe, wearing a broad smile, entered the circle of three. "What's so funny?" she wanted to know.

"Gabriel here has poured the same wine into most of the glasses – that's what's going on," Mr. Axe said.

"I only did it when Mr. Axe went down to the wine cellar for a different label," I said apologetically and defensively.

"You kept the party going, that's all," Mrs. Axe said.

"Wonderful, wonderful party, Ruth," Father Leo said.

"Thank you," she responded.

Hearing Father Leo refer to Mrs. Axe as 'Ruth' I thought to myself that Ruth was a nice name. What would Mrs. Axe say if I called her Ruth? As I entertained the thought Mrs. Axe turned her attention back to Father Leo.

"I'm glad you're having a good time."

"I am indeed and my forever thanks to you!"

"You're most welcome."

Mr. Axe turned away. "I'll be right back," he said as he made a beeline for the wine bar. Mrs. Axe looked at me for a moment and then at the priest.

Father Leo then asked Mrs. Axe, "What do you think of our young man now? What would Maggie say?"

Mrs. Axe put her glass down on a tray that was already stationed on a cabinet that was almost touching her right elbow and looked at me.

"I get very positive reports from the office. He's learning day by day."

Father Leo then interjected, "I can attest to the fact that he is a very good driver. He got me here safe and sound."

For a few minutes I stood between Father Leo and Mrs. Axe while they discussed my life at the castle. Mrs. Axe would mention my high school situation and Father Leo would comment on my weakening religious observance. Mrs. Axe would speculate on my future as an executive and Father Leo would raise his glass to that prospect.

As I stood mute and immobilised Pat came by and handed me a large tray filled with empty glasses and asked me to take them into the kitchen which I happily did. It was a welcome rescue. When I got into the kitchen I helped Pat arrange and rearrange food platters. I then tackled a mountain of dirty plates and prepared them for the dishwasher. After that I sat down at the kitchen table and decided that I didn't want to return to the party. The thought of meeting up with Father Leo the next morning wasn't at all comfortable. There was a strong possibility that I would be asked to drive him back to New Jersey and it was likely he would, with the zeal of a missionary, pursue his vocation and do his best to keep me from falling into the hands of the Devil. I was also concerned that he might, intentionally or not, influence Mrs. Axe in a way that could change or end what I believed to be an evolving friendship. To help alleviate the thoughts that were making me feel insecure by the second I decided to get in my car and drive to Tarrytown and visit the crowd at the bar.

* * *

Frank Dillon was sitting in his usual spot when I entered the pub. When he saw me he jumped off his seat and greeted me as if I was a long-lost cousin. Or, at the very least, someone he was definitely looking forward to seeing. He gave me a hug that nearly choked me.

"Where the hell have you been? I wait here for you and you never show up."

I was a bit taken aback by his exuberance. I attributed his air of confidence to the fact that he might have had more than enough to drink.

"I've been working at the office in the castle and doing other things up there," I said.

"Well, let me tell you what I've been doing, Mr. Irish." He used the word *Irish* as a term of endearment. It definitely meant he was on a roll of some sort. "The newspaper I was showing you – remember it?" He waited for me to respond.

I couldn't remember.

He continued. "The *Show Business* newspaper! Someone left it here once. I got one when I went into the city last week and I checked out places where they were looking for actors."

For a second or two I thought he was going to tell me he was soon to be starring on Broadway.

A friend of Frank's called out: "Yeah, he definitely went into the city. I didn't think he'd come back though!"

Frank told me he had gone to an office in Manhattan that had an ad in the newspaper. A woman at a front desk told him to come back on Tuesday if he wanted to audition for one of their productions. After a few more drinks Frank informed me that the office he went to was a summer-stock-producing one. Most of the summer-stock productions attracted stars, he said. Sometimes even the ones who originated the roles on Broadway went on to work in the out-of-town productions. The place Frank kept referring to was Buck's County Playhouse in New Hope, Pennsylvania. It was the premier stock theatre on the east coast. I asked him when he calmed down if he had gone to Pennsylvania.

"Hell, no! That's where the theatre is. I went to their office in the city because that's where actors live."

I couldn't resist teasing him. "*You* don't!" I said.

"No, but I will if I get a job."

His enthusiasm was contagious and I began to feel a bit more confident about myself after avoiding Father Leo and the possibility of Confession. Frank went on and on and bragged that he was finally going to be on stage. The pub, it seemed, wasn't a big enough theatre for him and the five or six half-inebriated patrons leaning on the bar wasn't an appreciative audience. Judging from the hug and welcome from Frank, he wasn't going back to the city alone. Before the pub closed he convinced me to go into the city with him on Tuesday to try to convince someone else that he had the talent to be an actor. I happily agreed and had another beer before both of us were told to go home because the bar had closed.

* * *

The next morning when I brought Mrs. Axe her breakfast she asked me where I had vanished to the night before. I wanted to tell her that I was simply afraid of being around Father Leo too long in case he asked again if I wanted my confession heard. I was terrified the Reverend might bring up the subject, even in jest, in front of her. The consequence of such an event would likely have serious implications for my relationship with her. Although the odds on me confessing anything to Father Leo was zero, I was still filled with trepidation.

I told Mrs. Axe of my trek to the pub and meeting up with Frank Dillon. She wasn't too pleased and abruptly dismissed me from her room.

"Ah, I can't talk to you!" she said and as I walked towards the door she called after me, "Wasting too much time! That's what you're doing. Goodness gracious, I don't know what you get out of going down to that den."

I didn't stop to respond.

"You should focus your attention on work at the office. Do you hear me?"

I didn't answer and kept walking.

A few minutes later I was in my room lying on my bed, looking up at the ceiling and thinking about my silent confrontation with Mrs. Axe. I questioned as to whether I should have defended myself and talked back to her but the feelings I had for her inhibited me and I was afraid that she might suggest that I leave the castle once and for all.

In an hour or so I would be called on to drive Father Leo back to New Jersey. To escape my thoughts about him and the incident with Mrs. Axe, I turned on the radio next to my bed and William B Williams on *WNEW* was playing Frank Sinatra songs. Most of Sinatra's songs, certainly the ones I identified with, had to do with wishful thinking and aching hearts.

While Frank's voice singing *"What's new? How is the world treating you?"* caressed my pained and confused feelings, a knock came to my door.

For a second or two I wasn't sure I heard it. When the knocking persisted and got a bit louder, however, I turned the radio off. I assumed it was either Pat or Jim coming to tell me the Cadillac was washed and filled with petrol and ready to take Father Leo back to his parish.

Then the door slowly opened and Mrs. Axe entered. She was wearing a silk Oriental bathrobe over the usual long white cotton nightgown she had on every morning I saw her in bed when I brought her breakfast. The bathrobe was either Chinese or Japanese. I couldn't tell the difference.

"I was walking about and I heard your radio playing," she said.

I didn't know how to respond to her comment so I kept quiet.

With the heel of her right foot she closed the door behind her, walked to the small chair near my bed and sat down.

"Pat came up – I gave her the tray to take back to the kitchen and . . ." She hesitated.

I guessed she had called Pat to come and retrieve her breakfast tray because she didn't want to put me through the humiliation of having to explain why I went to the bar in Tarrytown. Her whole demeanour was quite apologetic and it definitely made me relax again in her presence. I remained silent and made sure I didn't talk back when she started to speak while I lay stretched out on my bed.

"I'm sorry about what I said. You've a right to go where you want be with whomever you choose. I was just . . ." She stopped talking but continued again almost immediately. "Well, I got annoyed and maybe I shouldn't have, Mr. Walsh . . ." She hesitated again and smiled at me.

Calling me Mr. Walsh was her way of breaking the ice. Whenever she referred to me as Mr. Walsh I knew she was being affectionate and humorous. The tag of Mr. Walsh fore-shadowed a different mood and a warmer kind of connection. Mrs. Axe knew from past encounters that I'd at least grin when she called me that. And I did. The air and light in my bedroom changed as if the sun had burst through the windows and all memories of the past had been hurled out towards the Hudson River in the distance.

As I lay motionless, even corpse-like, Mrs. Axe mentioned that she and Mr. Axe intended to go to their house on Long Island that Saturday afternoon and I was welcome to come along if I wished to. The weather forecast for the weekend was for a particularly hot one. The house on Long Island was a beautiful one and its location on an almost isolated beech made it even more alluring. Mrs. Axe waxed on about how she had neglected the house but was determined to pay more attention to it. She was not hesitant or ambiguous about how she felt like vacating the grey castle for the sunny shore of Long Island.

"I should spend more time out there and I definitely know it's good for me. Why I don't take advantage of it is another story. It's part of my own indecisive mind. Mr. Walsh, don't tell anyone that I think I'm indecisive. Some people think I'm the opposite." She paused again.

I wasn't sure if she was waiting and wanted me to comment on her self-evaluation. I didn't. I didn't know what to say. Even if I had a response I would certainly have kept it to myself. A few seconds of a very heavy silence passed.

Mrs. Axe continued. "I know Emerson doesn't take kindly

to long drives and he is less predisposed to walking along a sandy beach regardless of where it is or even if he owns it. So come along. You can help me with the drive as well."

I was simply incapable of saying no to her no matter what her request was and I accepted the invitation. Then, to my joy and surprise and maybe to humour me even further, she added that she would be dropping off Father Clifford in New Jersey on the way to Long Island. It would be a slight detour but in the big Cadillac it would be a comfortable drive. This was a great relief to me. I knew Father Leo would not go near the subject of Confession or religion with Mr. Axe sitting next to him in the back seat. All the apprehension I had been feeling earlier melted away from me and I felt I had a new lease of life – not only about myself but about Mrs. Axe.

The air was clear again and I was about to jump out of the bed and tell her why I had left the party when she told me to relax. Again I was reminded that when Mrs. Axe had something on her mind she didn't want to be talked back to. On the other hand, over the last few years I had learned that when the conversation was personal she was calmer, warmer and more affectionate, and that was how she was now. Her conversations with me, as opposed to Mr. Axe's, had more of an emotional content.

When Mrs. Axe and I first met in Dublin I wasn't sure she really noticed me. Maggie was such an imposing and demanding presence back then that almost anyone in her presence would have to take a back seat and be almost invisible. This part of Maggie's diva personality seemed to make Mrs. Axe more alive. It was as though Maggie was constantly performing and Mrs. Axe was always applauding. When the two of them were in each other's company they were definitely a happy duet. Maggie had reached out to Mrs. Axe and asked her to take me out of Dublin and ensconce me in her home. At the time Mrs. Axe had no awareness of me or my family history. She had then met my mother and learned as much as she could from her but that was about it. Maggie's influence on Mrs. Axe was substantial and it was a testament of Mrs. Axe's affection for Maggie that she consented to be my legal guardian and have me reside in her home in America. Mr. Axe had only heard about my existence by telephone. While at the Shelbourne Mrs. Axe had called her husband and informed him of her plans to bring me to New York. He acquiesced, not only because he generally left everything outside of corporate financial decisions to her but also because of his respect and friendship for Maggie. For Emerson Axe, Maggie was a living breathing diva who constantly humoured him with her tales of a life in opera. His affinity for opera was at the very least slightly fanatical. Mr. Axe wallowed in the tales Maggie told him about her life in Rome and her career at La Scala. The fact that her earliest benefactor Marconi, the inventor of the radio, played a part in her life impressed Mr. Axe greatly. Many times I listened to Maggie's duets with the great opera singer Gigli when Mr. Axe played them. The presence of Maggie in the castle gave the place an air of festivity. Mrs. Axe enjoyed letting Maggie have centre stage. On that stage I felt at times that I was a minor character in Maggie's real life opera. I took this to be the case particularly after she died.

I was still lying almost motionless when Mrs. Axe leaned towards me. I turned my head in her direction and with a combination of shock and excitement I felt her lips kissing me on the forehead. For the second or two while her lips rested on my forehead I could see her bare breasts. They were actually falling out from her bathrobe and towards my chin. On more than a few occasions when I brought breakfast to her, a part of her body would be exposed. Sometimes it would be her leg that was uncovered by the bedding. Other times it would be her naked shoulder after her bathrobe slid off during the course of her sitting up and readying herself for the breakfast tray. There were times, when I entered her room just as she was returning to her bed after being in the bathroom, that her nightgown would be half hanging from her body and there were times when I was retrieving the breakfast tray she'd inadvertently have her breasts half exposed. When she wore a dress or a blouse during the course of the day I would create in my mind the half-naked image of her total body and focus on her breasts as I wished to see them every morning. Now this morning, after chastising me about my behaviour the previous evening, I could smell her breasts, see them and touch them. As I had imagined they were large, round and exuding palpable warmth and I had the feeling that they had finally found me and that I had found myself as well. There was a sense of completeness in the room as if it too had come in the window with the sun. Instinctively I reached downwards to the breast that was closest to my mouth and I kissed and suckled the nipple for a while, then released it. Without looking at me Mrs. Axe reached for her other breast and placed it in my mouth. The smell of her skin and the heat from her flesh electrified every cell in my body. My appetite to consume her grew rapidly while she unbuttoned my pants and placed her hand under my testicles. While she held me in her hand I exploded over and over. Thoughts, perceptions and anything to do with understanding anything heretofore rational became obsolete. Life for me in this moment had no past and the consuming present obliterated any need for me to contemplate a future.

* * *

The next morning I helped Pat load the big Cadillac with food left over from the party and, with Father Leo and Mr. Axe sitting in the back seat, I drove out of the estate. The morning sunshine and the anticipation of going away seemed to suit everybody. The weather was beautiful as I pulled away from the castle and headed for the George Washington Bridge and Paterson, New Jersey. Mrs. Axe sat in the passenger seat next to me but for most of the time she had her head turned towards her husband and Father Leo in the rear seat. Father Leo periodically talked about Maggie Sheridan and mentioned more than once that her gravesite in Dublin was a well-attended fixture and because so many famous people were buried in the graveyard it had become an important tourist attraction. Glasnevin, Ireland's national cemetery, was a repository of Ireland's past and visitors and visitations to it often surpassed the crowds that attended national sporting events or religious shrines that promised eternal life. In an earlier time it was a source of income for grave-robbers who supplied Irish hospitals with corpses for medical students to dissect.

Glasnevin Cemetery had visited me twice: first with my brother Nicholas and again with Maggie Sheridan. Both people were in many ways my protectors and heroes. In my eyes when I was a five-year-old my brother Nicholas was my knight in shining armour. Long ago he was buried in Glasnevin Cemetery. This day, hearing that Maggie, my protector, was buried in the same place brought back memories to me. Glasnevin is the main and official burial place for ordinary and extraordinary Irish citizens, particularly the citizens of Dublin. If it was to be seen in an objective peaceful reflected and downward slumber, the cemetery would be a fossilised mirror of Ireland's history and culture. In a dark and unseen sort of way the burial ground is Ireland at peace with itself. Most of Ireland's political heroes, famous and not so famous, are buried there. If the inscriptions, dedications and prayers on the many oversized tombstones memorializing the famous dead were to be pooled it would guarantee that Heaven would be a hell of a place.

The image of my twelve-year-old brother Nicholas and the memory of his coffin being lowered into a hole in the ground there is as vivid an image as any that was ever branded in my brain. At the age of five and on the day of his burial, I sat crying at his gravesite while he was lowered into his final resting place. It was my first experience and awareness that the finality of one's relationship with life and time is close to overwhelming.

I also thought back to the day when I introduced my mother to Maggie and Mrs. Axe. In a conspiracy of love and caring, all three women had reached out to me and for the first time in my existence I felt wanted and important. The sense of self that I now lived with would not have come about had Maggie not initiated the replanting of my mind and body in a soil that was conducive to enhancing the evolution of my existence.

The Axes had funded a large gravestone for Maggie in Glasnevin and both of them seemed pleased to hear that all was in order at her final resting place.

Before I got to the Jersey side of the Hudson River, Father Leo, after hearing more than he probably wanted to about the history of World War I and Winston Churchill's exploits during the Boer War from Mr. Axe, directed his attention to me by asking if I was interested in joining the priesthood. If I was he would recommend the Dominicans, the order he had committed his life to. Before I had a chance to even respond one way or another Father Leo broke into a sermon. It probably was because he was trained to preach whenever he saw the opportunity. In this case it appeared that I was the person he was preaching to. It might also have been that he wanted Mr. and Mrs. Axe to hear him expound on his background as well.

"Members of the order carry the letters OP on our lapels after their names, standing for the Order of Preachers. But, Gabriel, you've already guessed that my trade is that of a preacher."

Mr. Axe laughed but it didn't interrupt.

Father Leo continued. "To meet the needs of his life and times, Saint Dominic – 1170 to 1221 – initiated a new type of society in the Catholic Church, one with all the dedication and education of the older monastic orders but which would be organised with greater flexibility to deal with the problems of the growing populations of European cities."

Now Mr. Axe couldn't resist joining in. "And in England and certain other countries the Dominicans are referred to as Black Friars because of the black cloak they wear over their white robes – as opposed to the Carmelites who wear white over black and are called White Friars. Or the Grey Friars – Franciscans who wear grey. Augustinian Friars wear a similar habit but that's another story."

"And, Gabriel, if you should want to know, the name *Dominicans* gave rise to the pun that they were '*Domini canes*' or 'the dogs of the Lord'."

Father Leo laughed this time as if he was congratulating himself and patted Mr. Axe on the shoulder as if to compliment him on his earlier reference to the order. The priest then reached over to me and touched my shoulder as if to remind me of his original intention but, before I had a chance to tell him I wasn't cut out for the priesthood, Mrs. Axe interrupted him and added that I was more inclined to be a businessman and bolstered her opinion by adding that her associates at the office where I sometimes worked had verified that. It was an unexpected compliment that I appreciated and I admitted that I did like the people in the office and overall enjoyed my part-time work there.

Then Mr. Axe joined in on the conversation and suggested that I'd be more drawn to the theatre or some such show-business activity. I beeped the car horn when I heard his comment but immediately Mrs. Axe told me to pay attention to my driving. After that, the conversation in the car regarding me and my future came to an abrupt halt and for about the next ten miles or so as I drove towards Paterson a silence followed.

To change the atmosphere in the car I reached to the car radio but Mrs. Axe touched my hand and told me not to turn it on. By the time I pulled up outside Father Leo's parish house in New Jersey I noticed in the mirror that Mr. Axe had fallen asleep in the back seat and Father Leo looked sadder than I had ever seen him. I wondered at that moment if he had second thoughts about his vocation. He had been the life of the party the night before at the castle – not only did he enjoy himself but he was very popular with the other guests. His happy state last night was probably the best thing that had happened to him in a long time and I sensed he was looking forward to visiting the castle again. In fact he mentioned that he was looking forward to it. I was also happy that he didn't bring up the subject of Confession. He did however tell me to make sure I prayed for Maggie and to promise that I would one day visit her grave. I acknowledged his requests by promising I would. How that would come about in the near future I had no idea, nor had I any plans to fulfil it. Lately my mind was focused on places like Manhattan and Los Angeles rather than Dublin.

As carefully and as quietly as I could I brought the car to a halt, stepped out onto the sidewalk in front of the religious establishment and retrieved Father Leo's travel bag from the trunk. As I did this Mrs. Axe, still sitting in the car, reached out to him and shook his hand. Both of them then looked at Mr. Axe asleep in the back seat and smiled.

Seconds later I was behind the wheel again and making my way towards the house on Long Island. The drive to the beach house took about two hours. At times, and maybe even out of boredom with the long drive, the chat in the car turned to my parents. Mrs. Axe asked once more if I had any contact with them and I said no. The alienation of my family was consistent. Mr. Axe, having woken up refreshed, attributed the alienation of my family to the economy in Ireland and suggested it had to do with the struggle to survive and that the reason the Walshes didn't openly embrace each other was anthropological in nature. He referred to Darwin several times. The debate about my family in the car as I drove had its comical moments. When my mother's penchant for suffering came up as a serious reason for the family alienation we all agreed that she would be canonised before Christmas. The reason for my father's silent indifference, at least according to Mr. Axe, was his experience on the battle front during World War I. Mr. Axe himself had been a 'doughboy' (that is, an American infantryman) in France during World War I. His thoughts on the issue were that my father, being an unwanted son at home and an Irishman in an English war, had a lot to do with all the Walshes being alienated from each other. My father, Paddy Walsh, according to Mr.

Axe, fathered a family just like him. Having an overzealous mother, who through her religious instruction was committed to suffering, sealed the deal.

Periodically, as we got closer to the beach house, Mr. Axe, from the back seat would interject and offer a philosophical reason for not being tied to one's family, particularly if the bonds and anchor were never really secure or solid.

* * *

The Axes' house on the North Shore of Long Island was quite a big one but small compared to the castle in Tarrytown. It was a pink two-storey residence perched on the beach and had three bedrooms and a small wooden front gate. After the car stopped, Mr. Axe got out and opened the gate. The hinges on the gate let out a squeak that sounded like someone was choking a duck. Mrs. Axe drove onto the property and stopped in the circular driveway directly in front of the house. Mr. Axe approached, complaining about the recent storms that had covered the place in litter. He immediately began to gather bits and pieces of seaweed and other discarded items. I got out of the car and helped him tidy up. Mrs. Axe then asked me to assist with unloading the food and the travel bags she had brought along with her. In seconds she had opened the door and the three of us entered the house. The place looked unused. "What happened to that woman you hired to keep this place clean and tidy?" Mr. Axe asked as he looked about.

"A few months ago I dropped in and discovered she was living here and I let her go."

Mr. Axe took two bottles of wine from one of his bags and walked into the kitchen where he placed them in the refrigerator. The living room was very large and had tables and bureaus with many photographs of the Axes when they were younger. Mrs. Axe almost instinctively began to wipe the dust off some of them. The photos she picked up depicted a couple who seemed to enjoy the activities they shared together. There were photos of them on fishing trips with each showing off their catch. There were photographs of their travels in every capital in Europe placed on the mantelpiece over the fireplace. The two of them with Maggie somewhere in Italy were prominently placed on a nearby side table close to the window that gave a view of the beach. I guessed the photos were probably taken at La Scala in Milan some time after Maggie's retirement from the operatic stage. By the look on Maggie's face the essence of the photo seemed sentimental. She had detached herself from her operatic career in Italy because she couldn't see past the veil of loneliness that seemingly was always in front of her eyes. In general, the photographic display in the rarely inhabited house reflected Mr. and Mrs. Axe as a happy couple in a happy time. One old, grey and faded one was of a very young girl sitting on a chair playing a violin. The young girl's face in the photograph was almost identical to the present Mrs. Axe.

The entire house was a bit like a neglected and unattended museum to the Axes' past. Mrs. Axe did say she had driven out to the place sometime during the fall and winter on her own but hadn't done so for many months. It looked as if she hadn't paid the place a visit since she fired the 'cleaning' woman. The houses itself looked lonely, forsaken and unappreciated. If Mr. Axe had to be here alone and with no one to talk to he'd likely put a match to the place. Emerson wouldn't dream of spending time here on his own. I got the feeling as I listened to him on the drive that he was not a happy traveller when it came to travelling to the house. Whether it represented a time in his life he didn't want to revisit or just that it was so isolated I wasn't sure. The Lord of the Castle was a scholar at heart and was most comfortable among his books and records or when people were listening to him expound on subjects that were intellectual in nature. Emerson Axe liked being alone provided there was someone nearby to praise his insight into relevant matters of the day.

After digesting my whereabouts I was directed up a flight of wooden stairs by Mrs. Axe, to one of the bedrooms. As I proceeded up the stairs Mrs. Axe called to me and let me know that the room had a view of the ocean. Then almost immediately Mr. and Mrs. Axe followed behind me. When the three of us arrived on the upstairs landing, just like their accommodations in the castle, the Axes entered separate bedrooms.

* * *

When I had unpacked the few items I had in my small travelling bag I sat down by the window and took in the beautiful view. The sun was setting slowly, the weather was beautiful and, as I looked in the distance to the water's edge I began to think about how I happened to be in this house this night at this time in my life. I opened the window and could hear the sound of the waves lapping against the shore, and the gawking cries of seagulls skimming the water in search of fish created a cacophony of images as well as a serious dose of confusion in my mind. Mesmerised by the sight of the ocean in front of me I thought of Ireland and that somewhere beyond the horizon my childhood and my family lived. I wondered if my parents, Paddy and Molly, were thinking about me. I still hadn't heard from my mother or anybody else in the family. I had never in my time in Ireland ever heard or experienced a sister or brother of mine writing to each other. No one in my family wrote anything to anyone at any time and even though I was so far away I was essentially no different. It wasn't that we were all shy and embarrassed about our handwriting or our inability to spell correctly. It was more likely that members of my immediate family had trouble expressing affection towards each other. Support and affection for one another wasn't practised in my home. For all practical purposes my parents and my family were gone from my life. I didn't write to my father and he didn't write to me. While at home I didn't feel wanted and now that I was far away and gone for such a long time I didn't feel missed.

Maggie was the reason I was staring out at the ocean from a bedroom in a beautiful house on the beach. Maggie took it upon herself to make sure I toed the line and kept myself out of everyone's way. For the first few months she was the bridge that connected me with the Axes. Since her departure the Axes and I lived like three kinds of goldfish swimming about in a large bowl.

When I thought about Mrs. Axe I didn't seek an answer as to why she occupied so much of my time and thoughts. I accepted that I was happily tormented. I thought back to the beginning of the journey I had never imagined could exist. In Dublin, when I first met her at the hotel, I didn't question myself about her becoming my legal guardian and agreeing to bring me to New York. This night, however, far away from the castle, I began to fear that her affection for me might evaporate and vanish. It was as though I had captured a butterfly in my hands and didn't want to open them for fear that the butterfly might fly away from me. The bizarre memory of serving Maggie breakfast on the hotel floor of the

Shelbourne in Dublin came into my head. That bizarre encounter had brought Mrs. Axe into my life and as I closed the bedroom window I was able to laugh and accept that Maggie Sheridan was in the cemetery in Dublin and maybe singing to her angels from the grave.

I then took a quick shower and, feeling refreshed and renewed, I went downstairs to join Mr. and Mrs. Axe.

* * *

For dinner that night Mrs. Axe unpacked the basket of food she had brought with her from the castle in Tarrytown. Mr. Axe put out a few bottles of wine which he unhesitatingly and expertly uncorked as we sat at the dinner table. When he poured some into my goblet, Mrs. Axe warned him not to fill my glass. I had in a small way gotten used to drinking fine wines at the castle and it wouldn't be an overstatement to imply that Mr. Axe enjoyed pouring his specially imported beverage to anyone in his company who appreciated, as he did, the fruit of the vine. This was very much in keeping with the evenings when Mrs. Axe was away in the city and Mr. Axe would call me into the dining room and have a small unscheduled wine-tasting event. He talked and bragged about wine as if he was talking about his ancestors in Scotland. Half of what he said to me about wine and its pedigree went in one ear and out the other. I could hardly remember drinking it much less remembering the French signature labels and the names of the areas in France it came from.

After Mr. and Mrs. Axe had emptied the second bottle of wine they began to argue with each other about business transactions that had taken place earlier in the week. Mr. Axe reminded his wife that while she was away in Dublin certain individuals in the firm had messed up financial contracts and suggested she dismiss the people involved. What they were arguing and talking about was as foreign to me as the names on the bottles of wine. The in-house debate and discussion went on throughout the consuming of the food from last night's party.

When it came to the welcome dessert, in this case sherry trifle, I gobbled it up fast, excused myself from the table and walked out on to the beach.

* * *

The beach was deserted and for a minute or two I was confused about what direction to walk in. Each direction seemed to lead to a curve in the earth. As I stood almost awash in indecision, the sea water splashed over my shoes. I then decided that it would be better and more practicable for walking on the beach if I took them off. As I bent over to separate my shoes from my feet an elderly couple entwined in each other's arms and a scraggy-looking dog walked pass me. The dog stopped and seemed to do a double take when it saw me. By then I was holding one of my shoes in my hand and for a moment I thought the dog wanted me to throw the shoe into the ocean so that it could retrieve it – but the animal didn't show that kind of energy or enthusiasm and seemed more curious about my presence than anything else. As I stood motionless and stared back at the dog staring at me, the man, way up the beach by now, took his arm away from the woman he was walking with and whistled. The whistle rang through the night air and interrupted the momentary communication I had with the four-legged animal. The dog ran and quickly caught up with the whistler. Something about the dog seemed friendly and I decided that it had to be going somewhere so I turned and followed it. After a few minutes I lost sight of the dog and its people but at the same time I also realised that I had forgotten about Mr. and Mrs. Axe back at the house behind me, arguing about business deals and maybe other issues they wouldn't admit to.

With my mind a bit clearer and not so laden down with what Mr. and Mrs. Axe were up to, I turned back and walked in the opposite direction. The beach and the night were becoming more and more familiar to me and the further I walked along it the closer my past seemed to follow me. The more my feet pressed into the shifting sand under me the lonelier I felt and the sadder I became. It was as if my entire past was a canvas on the water in front of me and I was being instructed by the observant moon in the sky above to form it, paint it and sign it. The first colour that clouded my eyes was religion. It had one dark dense colour and that was black. It seemed infinite and endless like the ocean in front of me. The thought of floating, swimming or sinking in it took my breath away and I felt helpless. All the rituals of observances came back to me like the sloshing ocean water that caressed and followed my feet as I walked along the ocean front. As the night aged, the canvas of my past became clearer and I felt less frightened and more in control of it. In a broad and general sense I began to understand the seemingly ever present fear a bit more than I ever had in the past. Fear was a belief and a perception that had many shapes and dimensions. A bit like a ball of malleable putty that dared and challenged the hand that held it to shape and change it. The first change in my religious observance was when I stopped going to Confession. Although I had slowly been retreating from it in Ireland I was now in an environment that didn't remind me so much of doing penance for anything I thought, said or did. Going to Confession and Communion faded away from me much quicker than I would have imagined two years earlier.

With thoughts that were becoming as heavy as my head felt, I walked back to the house. When I approached it, a small light was on in the living room and another was on upstairs in Mrs. Axe's room. Mr. Axe's room was dark and I presumed he had retired for the night. With my head still filled with bags and buckets of self-pity and regret, I entered the house and walked directly to the kitchen where I discovered a bottle of wine left on the kitchen table. Had Mr. Axe been up and awake I would have thanked him. I uncorked the bottle and retreated to the sun deck and stretched out on one of the two chaises-longues where, with as much gusto as I could muster I began the ritual of drowning my thoughts and feelings. In almost no time at all I had consumed half a bottle of wine and rapidly reached the point where I couldn't tell if time was going forward or backward. Way out in front of me the reflection of the shimmering moon on the water seemed to dance, spin and bounce in harmony with every thought that was spinning around in my head. If it hadn't been for the sound of the waves hitting the shore I could well have been, thanks to the amount of wine I had just consumed, a random star flying about in the summer sky above me.

While I gargled on the wine and mumbled incoherently about my life the screen door opened and Mrs. Axe stepped onto the deck. When she approached she didn't look at me or acknowledge my presence but sat and leaned back on the other reclining chair that was next to me. If she hadn't seen me I knew she had definitely heard me and because of that I didn't acknowledge her arrival. I was a bit surprised that she was still up and awake. I took note of the fact that she was wearing a thick warm-looking bathrobe and appeared refreshed as if she had just emerged from a hot bathtub or had taken a swim in the ocean. I wasn't sure she had noticed the now half-empty wine bottle that was situated on the small utility wooden table next to me, so I moved it out of her line of sight.

Mrs. Axe stared straight ahead. "You don't have to hide it, Gabriel," she said.

I felt embarrassed and trapped at the same time. I couldn't think of anything to say in my own defense so I remained silent. I was a bit unsure if my semi-inebriated state and the presence of the wine bottle had anything to do with her nocturnal attitude.

After what seemed like an eternity but in reality was less than half a minute, Mrs. Axe broke the silence again. "Finish it off if you want. Emerson won't remember he left it in the kitchen."

While I pondered her surprising instruction Mrs. Axe got up from her chair and walked back into the house. Before I could figure out why she was leaving or where she was going, she returned almost immediately with a wineglass.

"I don't like to see good wine wasted," she said as she reached down and picked up the wine bottle.

With my mind still in a tailspin I watched her pour some of the wine into her glass and begin to swallow it as if it was a lemonade or orange juice. She seemed to be in a celebratory mood and whether it was caused by the beautiful night air, the sound of the ocean pounding the shore or the fact that she might have won the argument with her husband I wasn't sure. In any event she appeared to be, to say the least, calm and content.

She stretched out and began to talk again as if our conversation hadn't been interrupted. "You know, you shouldn't pay any attention to what you hear going on between me and Emerson. We talk and argue but it's not as serious as you might imagine. A good percentage of it has to do with business and, although you may not know it, our arguments are really discussions. It's the way we function. And by the way, we didn't plan on arguing in front of you." She stopped talking.

For a few moments I thought she was waiting for me to comment on what I had just heard. Although I digested the tone and content of her words, my instinct was very much like I had when I was first in her company: and that was to listen and hear but not to counter-argue or even debate the issue at hand. At the same time I realised that many things between us had changed since my arrival and I considered expressing myself, perhaps for selfish reasons. Nevertheless I didn't know what to say in return. I wasn't really confident she wanted me to respond or make any kind of comment. This evening was in many ways a reflection of what our relationship really was. There wasn't a thought in my head that would have made sense even if I had replied. The back of my head felt as if it was peeling down my neck and falling away from the rest of my body. A silence fell over the deck and only the shaking reflection of the moon on the water, tied to the harmony of the ocean lapping against the shore, kept me from retreating further into myself.

As I made every effort to appear sober Mrs. Axe broke into my drenched thoughts.

"You should know, Gabriel, and I don't doubt that you do . . ." She hesitated as she usually did when she had some important announcement to make.

The tone of her voice and the patience she took with her words convinced me that she wasn't asking for a response from me. I watched her stare out into the distance and wondered what she was going to say to me. With her eyes fixated on the sea she began to talk again.

"When we get back to Tarrytown I suggest that you take time off from bringing me my breakfast. Pat will take care of it – at least for the next month or so. She's planning on retiring and I'm not sure what to do about replacing her."

Hearing this almost sobered me up. I wasn't sure what she really meant by it and was a bit afraid of what else she might say. My nerves tingled with the feeling of rejection and I felt somewhat abandoned and practically helpless. The experience of bringing breakfast to her every morning was in some ways a private and magical ritual. I inhabited a little universe in my mind that made me feel special and wanted. Nobody in Mrs. Axe's circle – including her husband – shared this moment every morning. I felt and believed that Mrs. Axe had venerated me above all others in her domain. Her business associates whom she presided over at board meetings were excluded from an intimacy that only my eyes saw before she tackled the day. The chore, which was by now for me a privilege, afforded both of us private time and a chance to know each other better. It was an assignment that I looked forward to every morning, even when I was attending high school. It was the only time when Mrs. Axe didn't behave like the business executive she had to be during the rest of the day.

As I was absorbing the shock of Pat's potential departure and the discontinuance of me serving Mrs. Axe breakfast, she spoke again.

"I know you know that I love my husband. I do love

Emerson." She then reached out for her glass, slowly drank what was left of the wine, bid me goodnight and walked back into the house. After a moment she returned to the screen door and called out to me. "I'll leave the light on upstairs!"

Why she said this or what she meant by it I couldn't determine. Before I had a chance to respond she moved away from the door and headed towards her bedroom. I persuaded myself that Mrs. Axe was beginning to feel bad about what had transpired between us. Still, her silence made me feel she had gone from feeling sorry for me to reminding me that what had happened had been more of a mistake than a statement of love and caring. I had not been able to put the events between us into any kind of meaning that answered my emotional turmoil. Since the first event I found myself falling deeper and deeper into a dependency that I couldn't define or articulate to myself and even more importantly to her. When I wanted to express my feelings with words to Mrs. Axe I was not able to think of any. Paradoxically, the idea of defining my emotions only served to prevent me from doing so. Yet in an awkward way the emotional incapacity seemed to be safe and comfortable. I was actually comforted by the fact that I really didn't know or understand the consequences of what my relationship with Mrs. Axe had become and that provided me with an excuse to believe that it would and should continue. The unknown and the confusion kept my desire alive.

After about ten minutes or so I managed to lift myself up from the deck chair and retreat into the house.

* * *

The drive back to Tarrytown was a long and mostly silent one.

With the exception of the odd comment from Mrs. Axe about the possibility of me attending college in the future and my working more often at the office, very little was said. I was hoping Mr. Axe would join in but he was nursing a hangover and his response and reaction to the little that was said was tepid to say the least. Mrs. Axe sat in the back seat and appeared to be half asleep while I drove. Once or twice I asked if I could turn on the car radio and was told I could do so if I kept the volume down. For my own sake I searched the radio dial but I wasn't able to find a song or a sound that would have suited the atmosphere in the car. After few snippets of a classical sound and wanting to make an impression, I mentioned the name of the composer, thinking it would impress Mrs. Axe, but she seemed purposely withdrawn and even indifferent to my efforts to make contact. I then turned the car radio off altogether. Periodically when I viewed Mrs. Axe in the rear-view mirror her eyes were closed and she looked as if she was dreaming of being someplace else.

Her words on the deck the previous night were still in my ears and as I drove along the highway and over several bridges I kept asking myself why she needed to inform me about her affection for Mr. Axe. The more I questioned her motivation the more insecure I became. My relationship with her had by now taken so many twists and turns I couldn't tell where I stood with her. One thing however was inescapable: I had become dependent on her emotionally and the thought that she was or might be disappointed in me plagued me like an unending toothache.

Over and over I could hear her words: "I know you know that I love my husband. I do love Emerson." The statements of affection for Emerson rang in my mind like an unanswered telephone that wouldn't stop ringing. I even imagined Mr. Axe, asleep in the back seat could hear the words that were pounding in my brain. In fact there were moments as I drove towards Tarrytown that I wished he did.

* * *

When I pulled up in front of the castle Mrs. Axe stepped out of the car and held the door for Emerson. By now he was halfway back to his normal self and walked briskly into the castle and, as he did so, he mumbled, "Would you sell that damn house?"

Pat appeared at the front door and helped me with a few bags that contained empty wine bottles and several dishes that Mrs. Axe wanted brought back to the castle kitchen. With a bounce in her step Mrs. Axe walked ahead of me as we crossed the foyer. She appeared to be attempting to catch up with Emerson but he had already gone to his apartment. As I headed in the direction of the kitchen Mrs. Axe called out, "I'm going upstairs to rest a bit!" Whether she was saying it directly to me or Pat I wasn't sure and I didn't turn around to verify it.

When we got to the kitchen Pat put the dishes away and I placed the empty wine bottles in an open cardboard box that I knew Jim would eventually pick up for disposal. I sat down at the table next to the window, looked out at the car that I had just driven from Long Island and wondered if the last twenty-four hours were real or if I had dreamed or just imagined it. The reality of the beach house, the old photographs, the wine and the smell of the ocean air continued to linger with me as if I was still intoxicated.

My thoughts were broken into when Pat placed a cup of coffee in front of me.

"So how was the trip?" she asked and sat down opposite me.

I held the coffee cup in my hand and for a moment wished I was holding Aladdin's Magic Lamp and could just rub it and be granted any wish I wanted. What I would have wished for sitting at the kitchen table in front of Pat I wasn't sure. In a tiny foggy corner of my mind I imagined myself wishing that I knew more about myself, particularly when it came to having a sense of what Mrs. Axe really thought about me. Also I half wished that she might even ask me what I thought about her. Or even if I had given any thought to being with another girl my own age. In another secretive narrow and shaded alley of my mind I wished I could have a talk with Mr. Axe and tell him all about my life at the castle and the secrets I shared with Mrs. Axe. I didn't wish to see his face if I told him that secret. He might have had me thrown off the top turret like what happened to the king's soldiers when Robin Hood attacked the old English castle during the reign of King John in the Middle Ages. It was an easy task to thank Mr. Axe for spending so much time with me when it came to imparting the happy and intellectual realms and regions of his own brain. Talking and listening to him was without exception an experience that was almost equal to the emotional and personal magnetic pull I had from and for Mrs. Axe. The pendulum-like life I was living at the castle was in many ways akin to the swing I experienced when I moved from Dublin, Ireland to Tarrytown, New York. My physical and mental existence had somehow become a similar kind of duality.

The coffee cup I held in my hand of course had no magic powers and the wish for celestial magic would have to remain hidden and locked in my brain. With no pathway to fantasy I retreated to the cup of coffee more out of fear than for any need for the brew. My thoughts were now more stretched out than ever before and I couldn't coalesce any of them to make any reassuring sense. Pat's question floated about in my head and I didn't know where to begin with an answer.

Mixed in with the memories of the beach house were the thoughts of what I was going to do for the next few days and the realisation that I was to go to work in the office every morning and learn as much as I could about the business.

I responded to Pat by telling her that most of my time at the beach house had to do with Mr. Axe explaining how the world of Wall Street operated. I volunteered that the subject of finance was boring and dry as far as I was concerned and I didn't respond to the economic tutorials given by Mr. Axe in a positive way. I added that my indifferent attitude didn't go down well and that I spent most of my time walking on the beach alone. Pat reminded me that I should take advantage of the opportunity to learn the business and if I did I could look forward to being a senior member of the company someday and maybe even make it to the board of directors. Pat, it seemed, couldn't stop encouraging me to be more attentive to my time spent at the office and reminded me time and again that unlike almost all the other employees I only had to answer to Mrs. Axe and Mr. Axe. She smiled at me and told me that she and her husband were happy to have had the weekend off and volunteered that they had gone away for the night and it turned out to be like another honeymoon. When she finished talking, part of me wanted to tell her everything that had happened at the house on the beach but I was still so confused in my mind I didn't know what I would say even if I knew how.

Pat had been a close friend since the day I arrived at the castle and in many ways had acted like a surrogate mother to me. There were times over the two or more years since we met when I had a cold or was not feeling well, and Pat brought food to my room or cough medicines and most of the time she did my laundry when I remembered to bring it to her. In the past I spent as much time in the kitchen helping her as I did attending the functions Mr. and Mrs. Axe gave.

As we sat at the table the service bell rang on the wall. It indicated Mr. Axe was back in the dining room apparently in need of something. Usually after a wine binge Mr. Axe resorted to filling himself with vitamins and fresh orange juice. Sensing this to be the case, Pat immediately jumped up, opened the refrigerator door, grabbed the jug of fresh orange juice and answered the call.

When Pat departed the kitchen to attend to Mr. Axe I got up from my chair and made my way to my room.

* * *

For the next two weeks I sat at a desk in the large research office of the castle and talked and listened to the senior executives who had been with the Axe Corporation for most of their adult lives. Mrs. Axe had informed me, indeed instructed me, to be neat and clean. That meant I had to wear a shirt and tie and have polished shoes. I sat close to senior executives of the company who scrutinised data on companies that were indexed on the stock market. When they concluded their research they'd report back to Mr. Axe and exchange information and he in turn would advise clients on what to invest in and when. I floated from department to department, attempting to learn and pick up as much experience as I could. At lunchtime I'd join one or two executives and drive into Tarrytown for lunch. The longer I worked in the offices at the castle the less time I spent in the kitchen with Pat and even my infrequent walks with Mr. Axe had, with the odd exception which was usually on Fridays, ceased. Instead of driving with Mrs. Axe into Manhattan every work day like I used to, she'd called me on Saturdays and sometimes on the odd Sunday to spend an hour or two driving about the Westchester countryside with her.

* * *

Frank Dillon got the address of a television production company in New York City and he was told he could drop by the office in Midtown Manhattan and leave a recent photograph of himself and his acting résumé at the reception desk. It was early in the day and Frank hadn't yet crossed the zone and threshold of sobriety into the smooth-sailing seas of delirium when he told me about it. Frank was sober enough to convince me that this time he was serious about going to Manhattan to pursue his dream of becoming an actor. At first I was reluctant to believe him as he had reneged the last time but when he pleaded with me to drive him there I wasn't of the mind to refuse him. He, like me, probably dwelled too much on the alternate universe we witnessed on the big screen. Being a person who earned a living setting tiles in bathrooms and toilets probably had something to do with his theatrical aspirations. Whatever the psychology, Frank convinced me he was going through a life-changing experience and I could contribute to it by driving him into New York City. Proof of this was the fact that he was cold sober when he made the request. Frank's only acting experience, a far as I could tell, was his weekend performances at the bar.

Nevertheless the following Monday I took half a day off from sitting behind my desk at the office in the castle and found myself in New York City with Frank. On the morning of the expedition Frank took with him a photo of himself and an acting résumé that was handwritten and almost one-hundred-per-cent false. The photograph Frank planned on submitting was only slightly larger than a passport image and it was of Frank when he was much younger – certainly before the ravages of his drinking career was underway. When he showed me the address, which was on Madison Avenue, I assured him that I knew exactly where it was. Having driven back and forth to Manhattan with Mrs. Axe for the past three years I could have driven each way with my eyes shut. I knew New York City almost as well as I knew Tarrytown. I had spent numerous hours and days walking about the place when Mrs. Axe was attending to business in her office. The streets and avenues of Manhattan were as familiar to me as the lines on the palm of my hand. I also had a strong attachment to the city and its rainbow of cultures and attitudes. I didn't need much of a reason or a lot of encouragement from Frank to get me to drive into the city. My roadster had had its monthly tune-up and it purred like a contented cat when I turned on the ignition.

* * *

Ten minutes after parking my car in the garage on West 56th Street where I normally parked Mrs. Axe's Cadillac, Frank and I entered the lobby of a huge skyscraper on Madison Avenue. A man in uniform was directing a small group of men, similar in age to Frank, to the far side of the lobby where others who had a *"lean and hungry look"* on their faces had congregated. We were then told to wait at a particular elevator and to join another small crowd who also looked as if they hadn't slept in weeks. For a moment or two I got the feeling that the group of men Frank and I had joined at the entrance to the elevator was being quarantined. It didn't take long to hear from the assembled individuals that they were all in search of employment as actors: or, more to the point in this case, as extras. Because *The Scarlet Pimpernel* was set in 18th century France during the aftermath of the French Revolution, the crowds had to look as if they hadn't eaten since the Papacy moved back to Rome. Most likely the producers of the production believed that unemployed actors were the ideal segment of society to mirror such deprivation. Talent Associates, a company led by a Mr. David Susskind, was acting democratically by having an open call for actors in his production. I had seen an old film version of *The Scarlet Pimpernel*, that starred Leslie Howard, in Dublin when I was a child and had remembered a few famous lines from it:

> "*They seek him here, they seek him there,*
> *Those Frenchies seek him everywhere.*
> *Is he in heaven or is he in hell?*
> *That damned elusive Pimpernel!*"

After standing in line with a dozen others the elevator doors opened and the anxious group of men entered as though they were storming the Bastille. A man, acting more like a traffic cop than an elevator operator, asked everybody if they were going to Talent Associates. In unison all the voices called out *"Oui!"*

"Next stop the thirtieth floor!" the man yelled out. Eight seconds or so later the doors of the elevator opened and the passengers, like cattle running down a gangplank, disembarked. Frank and I, who were less versed in the experience of what is known in the business as a 'cattle call', stayed at the rear of the group and followed the herd into the waiting room of the production company. This day had not only become a day of initiation for Frank but in an unexpected way for me as well.

Once inside the waiting room and after finding a place to sit we settled in quietly among the herd and pretended, more by our silence than anything else, that we knew what we were doing. While we waited for someone to come out of the office and address the gathering I silently observed Frank staring into the distance and he looked a little out of place and maybe even intimidated. His abnormal silence made me wonder if he was craving a beer or some kind of elixir to ameliorate his present reality. I looked around the room and wondered if I had seen any of the faces on television or in the movies. Almost to a man they were talking about their last job and what plans they had for their careers. I overheard talk from a few guys sitting across from me about how they had returned from Los Angeles as they preferred New York to Hollywood. Most of the group talked about having part-time jobs and some even expressed regret about having chosen to pursue an acting career in the first place. After hearing so many tales of woe my image and idealisation of actors and show business in general suffered its first battering.

After sitting for about fifteen minutes an attractive young woman come out from the long corridor and greeted the congregation sitting in front of her. At first she asked those who were already members of the American Federation of Television and Radio Artists (AFTRA) to raise their hands. Everyone with the exception of Frank and me did so. The young woman began to distribute a sheet of paper and asked all present to write their name, address and phone number on it. She then asked those who were not members of the union to raise their hands. Frank and I immediately stuck our hands in the air. The sight of the two hands signalling that we were not members of the union brought a groan and a mumble from the others in the room. Whether the men were protesting or booing I wasn't sure.

Not being members of the union did have one consequence however. Both Frank and I were directed by the young executive to go down the corridor to another room to meet the casting director for the company. Frank immediately got up and vanished from my sight before I had chance to think about my own feelings and situation.

A few minutes passed then Frank appeared again. Behind him was a different woman, whom I took to be the casting director he was referred to. As Frank was about to fill me in on what had happened, the woman behind him signalled for me to follow her which I did. When I got to her office the woman introduced herself and told me she was delighted to see that so many people had shown up. The first question she asked me as I sat down in front of her was if I knew anything about the proposed and upcoming television production. I told her I was aware of an old movie version and I quoted the few lines to her: "*They seek him here, they seek him there . . .*" Without being asked I also mentioned that *The Scarlet Pimpernel* was written by Baroness "Emmuska" Orczy. This knowledge had come to me courtesy of Mr. Axe while he was waxing on one day about the French Revolution during one of our walks around the estate. The woman seemed pleased that I knew the author and asked me if I could speak French. When I told her I spoke a little she said I looked like I was French and that I might fit in as one of the ten or so musketeer-type characters who were in league with Sir Percy Blakeney who secretly was the Scarlet Pimpernel, the English aristocrat who leads a double life in the drama. Before the four-minute interview ended I had given the casting director my name, address and telephone number at the castle. Her projection of employment for me was that I might be used for two days if I was called but I had to reassure her I could make it into the city. She seemed amused that I lived outside of Manhattan and had never acted in anything other than in a play in high school. Before I stepped out of her office she asked me where I was from originally. When I told her I was from Dublin she smiled and told me that the female lead in the production was Maureen O'Hara. I jokingly asked if John Wayne would be playing the Scarlet Pimpernel and she humorously replied: "No, Michael Rennie is penned in for that role."

* * *

By the time I drove off the Saw Mill River Parkway exit to Tarrytown and returned Frank to the front door of his apartment he had convinced me that he wasn't likely to venture out into the unknown again. New York City was too busy a place for him. He complained about the crowds and all the characters he encountered in the waiting room as well. In his gut he believed he was a better actor than ninety per cent of those who crammed into the elevator that took us all to the thirtieth floor. As far as he was concerned none of them could recite Shakespeare and feel the part the way he could – samples of which he pumped into my ear on the drive back. He didn't feel good about his interview and objected to the fact that he wasn't given a chance to show off his acting talent. He complained that, adding insult to injury, the casting director informed him that if he was hired he'd only be a nameless face in one of the many crowd scenes. The trek into Manhattan and the reality of the herd in the casting office was not something that Frank could digest or even tolerate. It was all too hectic and competitive.

I informed him that I might get a bit part in the television show because the casting director said I looked French and if I did I would be dressed in the uniform of a French soldier. With only a slight exaggeration I mentioned that I spoke a few French words and that added to my chances of joining the actor's union and getting the job. My projection didn't go over well with Frank.

"You're Irish for Christ's sake! You're not fucking French! What's with that woman? She couldn't spot talent if it jumped out of her wastepaper basket!"

It was clear that Frank was more than a bit annoyed that I was even called into the casting office. I was there to accompany him and support his ambition and not my own. By the look on his face it was clear that he might have been happier had I stayed seated in the waiting room or not have accompanied him to the office altogether. When I drove away from Frank's front door I found myself hoping that I'd be called in the next few days.

* * *

Inside a massive costume truck that was parked on Second Avenue on New York's East Side I was measured for and fitted into a uniform of the French army of 1778 and told to report to a sound stage a block away. With a bunch of other young men of similar age I was paraded down the street and directed into a big warehouse type of place that had been converted into the city of Paris as it might have looked a few hundred years earlier. Having seen so many old black-and-white films that took place in Paris I was half expecting to see The Hunchback of Nothin' Doin', as it was referred to in Dublin in my past.

The night before, when I told Mrs. Axe I was offered a bit part in the television production of *The Scarlet Pimpernel* and explained to her how it had come about, she laughed and seemed genuinely pleased. Mr. Axe had a similar reaction. He told me he had read most everything written on the subject of the French Revolution and jokingly advised me on how to act as a Frenchman. When I told him I only had one line and that I was to play a French soldier he congratulated me and advised me not to lose my head.

Once inside the building, myself and the others who marched down the street with me were introduced to the actor Michael Rennie who was playing the part of the Scarlet Pimpernel.

Mr. Rennie was sitting on a large sofa having his face powdered and drinking a cup of coffee at the same time. There were many stage hands around him attending to his requests and he seemed to be talking to all of them at once. However, when he saw his small army of young French soldiers, of which I was one, he officially welcomed us both personally and professionally. With a big smile on his face he asked all eight or nine of us if we knew our lines. Although I didn't know it at the time he was apparently making fun of us.

A few feet behind him sat Maureen O'Hara, being attended to by a hair stylist and a few dressmakers who were stitching a frilly-looking item to the big gown she was wearing. I had seen her years earlier on the screen in Dublin. If nothing else happened to me this first day on the set, it was all worth it because I was in the same room as the Irish icon. I was tempted to approach her and tell her we had homeland geography in common but I sat on the impulse. Diminutive as it was, my past and my present had happily found common ground this day as I found myself floating on the outskirts of my own fantasy. I was dressed as someone else and in the environment and atmosphere of the massive sound stage I wanted to believe I had become someone else. I was transported to an earlier period in history dressed up as a French soldier and I was mesmerised by the sight of Maureen O'Hara sitting not too far away from me in person. The star of *The Quiet Man* and *The Hunchback of Notre Dame* was sitting in the same room as me and I definitely felt and believed that I had been transported from one planet to another.

Earlier, when I was being dressed in my military outfit, I had been given a page from the script and a line was circled in red that said: "*Je suis trés fatigué.*" Another heading said: "*Soldier Number One is tired and wipes his face with his uniform sleeve.*" What the other actors, who like me were now members of the League of the Pimpernel had to say I didn't know. My nerves were shaking so much the sabre that was hanging from my waist was rattling like a church bell. I began to worry and thought I was going to be judged by the way I spoke French: in this case only one line of the language. Panic swept through my bloodstream and instantly I couldn't even remember the line.

A minute or two later Mr. Mark Daniels, the director, approached and asked me if I was ready for a camera rehearsal. What he meant by that I had no idea but I said yes. Mr. Daniels led me and the other soldiers to a long wooden bench alongside a table. There was another bench on the opposite side of the table.

To my amazement the director asked me my name.

I replied: "Gabriel Walsh."

He looked at me and shook his head as if it had been

severed by the guillotine that was situated at the far end of the Paris setting. "No! Not your own real name. What number soldier are you?"

I quickly grasped the idea that he was referring to the name of the soldier I was assigned. "I'm a number, sir," I obediently answered.

"You're the first. You're Number One. I want you to sit here at the end of the bench. You've just come back from a battle and you're tired. When you see or sense that the camera is across from you, say your line. You got that?"

I nodded my head affirmatively, too terrified to utter the word *yes*.

The director then placed the other soldiers along the benches. Some sat next to me, others across from me. Mr. Daniels stepped away and a stage hand placed a tin mug in front of me. This terrified me even more. "Take a swig from this before you say your line," the stage hand said. When I looked in the mug there was nothing in it but before I could ask a member of the crew what I should do with the empty mug the lights dimmed and someone called out: "Rehearsal!"

At this point in time I was tired from worrying and when I noticed the big film camera passing in front of me I was able to mumble "*Je suis trés fatigué*" while I wiped my brow with my sleeve at the same time.

When the camera reached the end of the long wooden bench a call for "Lunch!" was bellowed out and the lights came back up in the cavernous space.

During the lunch break I made my way over to the table where the stars of the show were sitting and eating. A company photographer was snapping pictures of just about everything and everybody. I tapped him on the shoulder and asked him if he'd take a picture of me sitting with Maureen

O'Hara and he agreed – providing the star had no objection. Without hesitation I sat down next to Miss O'Hara and quickly told her I was also from Dublin. Before she had a chance to respond to me the photographer snapped a picture of me sitting with the star of the show.

After lunch I was back sitting on the long wooden bench and leaning on the table with the empty mug in front of me. As I stared into the empty mug I kept wondering why there wasn't any beer or even water in it. I turned to an assistant, an older man who appeared to be wrapped in wires from head to toe, asking if I could have a little water, even a drop of whiskey put in the mug and he told me no and to pretend I was sitting in an Irish pub at home after spending my last penny. An actor, sitting nearby dressed in rags and looking like he had spent too much time with Quasimodo from *The Hunchback of Notre Dame*, told me to piss in the mug and to stop complaining. I was about to tell him to go fuck himself when the lights dimmed and the camera started rolling.

When the director called "Action!" I was more confident than before. I took my time with swigging my 'drink', wiping my forehead and saying my one line. Whatever way I said it seemed to please the director. He thanked me and a few minutes after that I was told that my assignment was completed. An hour later I was out of costume and while driving back to Tarrytown I was feeling more and more like a new person.

* * *

I continued to spend most of my time working in the office at the castle but I found that I was always waiting for a phone call that would take me back to New York for work as an actor. Several weeks after my first adventure Ruth Conforti, the casting director for Talent Associates, left a message for me at the castle. When I returned the call I was informed that there was another bit part for me in another production: *The Light that Failed*, by Rudyard Kipling.

The instructions and logistics were the same: report to the same office at a given date and be fitted again for a new costume. The star of this production, when I reported for work, turned out to be a Mr. Richard Basehart. This job came easily and went uneventfully but when it was over I was invited by a fellow actor, after we both finished our three-line speaking assignment, to accompany him to an audition for a play that was to be produced in the Bucks County Playhouse in Pennsylvania. This was the theatre Frank had been interested in – the premier showplace for plays that had recently been produced on Broadway. I arrived with my fellow actor at the office of Mike Ellis, the producer and owner of the Bucks County Playhouse. As was the norm and what I had come to expect, auditioning for anything in New York City had become a case of 'hurry up and wait'. While waiting and listening, a common ritual in such situations, I learned that Mike Ellis was producing Jean Giraudoux's play *Tiger at the Gates*, a play dealing with the Trojan War in ancient Greece. Yet again, a subject Mr. Axe had often talked about. The overall theme and thesis of the play seemed to be that man's proclivity for wanting 'more' of everything ultimately leads to conflict. The consequence of such an impulse is that war among mankind cannot be avoided. The setting and time for the play takes place inside the walls of the city of Troy only hours before the start of the Trojan War. The central plot line is that of the disenchanted Trojan military commander Hector. He tries to avoid war with the Greeks. His wife Andromache is about to give birth, and this reinforces his desire for peace. With his worldly-wise mother Hecuba, Hector leads the anti-war faction in his homeland and attempts to convince Paris, his brother, to return the beautiful captive Helen to Greece from whence he had abducted her. The abduction of Helen is the spark that ignites the conflict. Giraudoux pens Helen as an object of desire, but also a metaphor for human greed and its darkened destiny.

After sitting for at least an hour in the reception room at the producer's office on West 56th Street I was called in by the producer's assistant and introduced to the director of the play, a man who looked as if he had seen every pained face of every actor in New York City and beyond. The director took a look at me and immediately asked me where I was from. Apparently he had sensed I was not as fully American as he had anticipated. When I told him I was from Dublin he appeared to be a bit put off. He could obviously detect my accent and after having such a tiring day auditioning hundreds of actors he might well have thought he was wasting valuable time. But, with a certain kind of respect that he naturally had for the profession of acting, he handed me a script and asked me to read from it. He told me to focus on the character Troilus. It was a small but important role and I sensed, because of all the other young actors in the waiting room, it was the last one to be cast.

Three weeks later I was in New Hope, Pennsylvania, rehearsing for a one-week run of the play. Sitting opposite me around a large round table was Robert Redford, the actor who was chosen to play Paris in the production – Paris of course being the man who stole Helen of Troy and as a consequence set off the war. The actor Hurd Hatfield, who had become famous for his film portrayal of Oscar Wilde's

Dorian Gray, was also in the cast and playing the lead role of Hector. The part of Troilus, which I was picked for, was the very last character to appear on stage and, although the lines were few, I did get to kiss Helen of Troy, played by Louise Fletcher, as the final curtain dropped.

Every night after the show the cast and crew assembled at the bar of The Inn which was the place where most of the actors and crew stayed. I had a small comfortable room that overlooked a river. For my first week there and while listening to the after-theatre banter I learned a lot about the life of an actor from the professionals such as Hurd Hatfield and Robert Redford.

Mrs. Axe came to New Hope to see the last performance and stayed at The Inn. After the show I introduced her to as many people as I could. The evening was a happy and exciting one both for her and for me. The day before, one newspaper had nice things to say about the production and one of them even mentioned my performance in a positive way. Mrs. Axe became more celebrative when she read the review and she ordered another bottle of wine. I invited my fellow actor Hurd Hatfield to our table and she ordered yet another expensive bottle of wine for him. In no time the table had as many bottles on it as it had people sitting around it: six in all. When the bottles were emptied by the thirsty crowd, time itself appeared tired as the night of wine consumption slowly took its toll.

The closing of the show brought on a deluge of sentiment. Actors and crew members exchanged addresses and phone numbers and memories. I became more and more intoxicated and so did everybody around me. And that included Mrs. Axe. The proprietor was obliged to remind everyone of the late hour and he made noises about closing. Mrs. Axe picked herself up from her chair and, after excusing herself from the gathering, made her way to her accommodation. Fifteen or so minutes later I bid goodnight and in most cases goodbye to my friends and actors and proceeded up the wooden stairs of the inn.

As I walked along the small and very narrow corridor upstairs I passed Mrs. Axe's room and noticed that her door was ajar and a shaft of light from inside her room touched the corridor carpet. I thought for a moment she might have unknowingly forgotten to close it behind her. She had consumed a lot of wine, more than I had ever witnessed her drink before, and I guessed that she might not be aware that her door was left open. I leaned towards the door and gently began to pull it towards me in order to close it but then I heard, or thought I heard her calling out "Is that you, Gabriel?" Hardly able to stand straight I felt I had electrocuted myself when I heard her voice. With the ability to think gone from me I pushed the door open and saw Mrs. Axe stretched out on the bed wearing her bathrobe.

Slowly but unhesitatingly I walked into the room and sat on a chair as close to her as I could.

Again without looking directly at me she began to talk. "I really enjoyed this evening so much. You were good. You were excellent."

I wanted to thank her but my brain was spinning about in my head so much I couldn't think of anything so I sat in silence, looking at her stretched out in front of me. For a few long extended moments I began to think back and tried to put my future and the rest of my life at the castle in perspective. In many ways it was a wonder I wondered about it without being able to define it clearly for myself. Having floated and drifted between so many possibilities and disappointments, I felt like I was missing a piece of a jigsaw puzzle that had fallen to the floor and got lost. Mrs. Axe's pendulous personality kept me in an emotional darkness that obstructed me from expressing myself when I was working in the office or spending time with Mr. Axe.

I wasn't sure what frightened me the most: wanting to leave her or thinking about her leaving me. For an inordinate amount of time I lived beneath two clouds that were constantly threatening to burst.

As I attempted to focus my unhinged mind in her direction she started to talk. She spoke softly and slowly and was in a more sentimental mood than I had ever seen her. She started to talk about how we first met at the Shelbourne Hotel and how Maggie was so determined to have the two of us meet.

What would Maggie think now? I asked myself. She would rise from her grave if she was to know that Mrs. Axe and I were in some abstract way stranded in a hotel room in Pennsylvania. Maggie would flee from Heaven itself if she was to see her best friend and the boy she brought to America so intoxicated and hardly able to put two words together.

Stretched out on her bed in the dimly lit bedroom Mrs. Axe reminded me of the morning I foolishly attempted to serve Maggie her breakfast under the bed. She then told me it was at that moment in time that Maggie took a liking to me. Maggie, it seemed, as Mrs. Axe related, couldn't believe anyone could be so naïve and responded to the combination of innocence and ignorance that I paraded in front of her that fateful morning. That particular moment in Dublin might even have reminded her of a scene in some Italian opera. To think anyone would want to have breakfast under the bed was not only odd but comical.

"That incident really got my attention when Maggie told me about it," said Mrs. Axe. "I did honestly laugh and I was really interested in meeting you."

She stopped again as if to be reassured that I had heard everything she just said. Relying on past experience I remained silent.

Mrs. Axe continued: "It was during that week I decided to go along with Maggie's request to bring you here. I hadn't even told Emerson. He wouldn't have minded one way or the other. Emerson is happy with just being Emerson. He likes what he likes and that's that."

She paused again.

I got a bit confused and didn't know if she wanted me to respond, react or say something. I was tempted to reply and make a contribution to the conversation but my head was in such a spin I felt obliged to put my hands to my ears to keep from hearing the noise that was blasting away inside.

I commented on the first day I arrived at the castle door and was greeted by Mr. Axe and how we all reacted towards each other.

Mrs. Axe engaged with me again. "You were so lost and tired that evening when you arrived with me and Maggie – you just didn't know where to start or what to say and probably what to even think. And who could blame you? I wanted to reassure you more than I actually did that first day but I didn't and I want to apologise for that."

As I looked at Mrs. Axe from the chair I was sitting on I noticed for the first time that she had closed her eyes. I began to think she had fallen asleep and was not even aware of my presence. I then felt as if I was hit by a blast of thunder while simultaneously a cloud of confused thoughts burst inside of me and I felt like I was embracing a religious salvation and the ultimate forgiveness for wanting and wishing the pleasurable images that were suddenly engulfing me. Without having any control whatsoever I was instantly adrift on a mental roller-coaster and believed I was a captive of a happy kind of insanity.

I leaned over towards Mrs. Axe and lay down on the bed beside her.

Lying sideways with her eyes still closed, Mrs. Axe whispered, "Close the door."

I stood up from the bed, walked to the door and with both of my hands I secured it with a stillness and a quietness I didn't think I was capable of. When I approached the bed and looked down at Mrs. Axe she rolled over on her back and stared up at me. Her bathrobe had opened and her nakedness captured every aspect of my sight. The shock and excitement made me faint for a moment and I fumbled with dislodging my shoes from my feet. The same ineptness was repeated as I shed my clothing. My very nakedness appeared to be infinite and transparent.

I lay down again next to her and I could feel the heat of her body and the sound of her breathing. She seemed to be floating all over me. The space and distance between us instantly vanished. In the directionless and timeless space that was between our bodies Mrs. Axe's hand firmly but gently guided me into her. I pushed and pulled about in every direction that my erotic pleasure was taking me. At the same time a litany of deformed dreams and cravings were let loose in my non-sober brain. As Mrs. Axe lay prostrate under me I could feel myself detached from everything and anything material. Some part of my being still tried to escape and deny the reality that was overpowering me but whatever it was it dissolved or was smothered by the hunger of my body. In the shadowed bedroom I had for the briefest period of time thought that if I closed my eyes I'd vanish, but with each touch of Mrs. Axe's mouth I drowned in a reality that I didn't want to end. In an unwanted and uninvited invasion of my past I sensed every urge of desire since I sensed my singular identity. Mixed with the eruption of touch and emotion I could even hear my mother and the priest screaming at me as if I had sped through a red traffic light on a crowded street corner. The imposition of that thought brought forth a surge of guilt that had me believe for the briefest moment that I had deserted my own sense of self. Panic and a weird kind of ethereal abstraction, brought on by the feeling and sight of Mrs. Axe under my body and entwined around it, unleashed a massive passionate hunger. I crashed into everything that I had ever seen, heard and known about myself and there wasn't anything about me that I could make sense out of or even wanted to. Still and as if in opposition, Rosaries, Benedictions and a host of religious rituals and sacraments peppered me with fear and warnings of sin as though I was caught in an unexpected rainstorm of falling souls screaming from Hell or Purgatory. In the reality of what I was accepting I was able to push them away and felt I was saving my own life. In the exhilarating tumble I forgot who I was and where I came from or how I managed to be experiencing feelings that actively obliterated my identity. My youthful energy was bursting out of every pore in my body and I felt I had been turned inside out. With little ability to understand the erotic feelings that were obsessing and smothering me I could sense my past and childhood departing from me.

* * *

When I returned to the castle three days later I sat in the dining room with Mr. and Mrs. Axe. Mrs. Axe had apparently informed Mr. Axe of my stage debut and he congratulated me profusely. This night Pat was off and Mrs. Axe had prepared a light meal. By the time I had finished eating the dessert of crêpes and ice cream, Mrs. Axe informed me that she and Mr. Axe would be going away the following Thursday on a vacation that was predicated more on business than on pleasure. They were to attend a convention of executives from different parts of the county in Montego Bay Jamaica. Mr. Axe said he wasn't in the least looking forward to it but it had to be done for business reasons. He also emphasised that he hated travel as much as Mrs. Axe liked it.

Half in jest I asked if I could come along and Mrs. Axe, in a similar tone but with less humour, said I could but in reality it would not be a good idea. Mr. Axe said I was better off staying home. Mrs. Axe added that my presence at such a gathering would simply be distracting. When I mentioned that I didn't have any acting assignments on my calendar Mr. Axe told me to read and study Oscar Wilde's *The Importance of Being Earnest*. He said it was one of his favourite plays and I should keep an eye out for it in the event that I might act in it someday.

Mrs. Axe encouraged me to be in attendance every morning at the office while she was gone and to continue to listen and learn from the executives she had assigned me to observe. I wanted to confess and tell her that my ability to concentrate and learn the business was seriously compromised by my lack of interest as well as my limited education in the field. The world of statistics, charts, assumptions and board meetings was foreign to me and contrapuntal to the utterances that percolated in the depths of my mind that were unreachable to everybody but my silent inner self. My brief but professional venture into the world of the theatre had taken hold of a big part of me and it was becoming more and more difficult, if not impossible, for me not to nourish it. I was at last feeling inextricably and involuntarily attached to seeing and solving my personal social problems by indulging in wanting and wishful thinking. This was underlined and reinforced whenever I thought back to my days of deprivation in Dublin and my wanderings into the dark room of the cinema where I consistently witnessed the fantasy of good conquering evil and the triumph of beauty and righteousness over outrage and deception. In my childhood the world of the cinema had inadvertently become a moral compass. The celluloid altar was its own kind of religion. Its pantheon of stars were consistently battling with morals and values that I not only understood and identified with, but looked forward to on a daily basis. The reality of living up to the sacraments and sacrifices of the religion I was born into and was enveloped in got diluted when the ceiling and wall lights in the cinema went down and the flickering images appeared on the big screen in front of me. The lessons and curriculum of film fiction suited me more easily than the imposed and enforced doctrines of the clergy who lived all around me in Dublin. To me the priests and Christian Brothers, with their propensity to administer corporal punishment, were like prison wardens of the mind. Added to that, the absence of love and affection between my parents and in my immediate family promoted a hunger for the simple unattainable pleasure of just being noticed and wanted.

* * *

After dinner I went to my room and fell down on the bed. I wanted to talk more to Mr. Axe and in the private regions of my mind I wanted to tell him about my ever-changing relationship with Mrs. Axe. I felt I was in a situation very similar to the one I was in with Father Leo. A confession to Father Leo would have done serious harm to his relationship with Mrs. Axe. A confession to Mr. Axe would have severely impacted on all three of us. We were essentially and definitely an odd and awkward threesome. For the majority of our time together the Axes and I seemed to be sliding down different rainbows and only occasionally making contact with each other. Within each relationship was satisfaction that supported an inner hunger. Private person as he was, Mr. Axe loved to talk and I loved to listen. From me he rarely demanded or insisted on anything. Our unplanned walks and conversations filled some void in him that he kept secret. Once, in humour, he told me that "One must make the effort to have serious conversation with oneself if one really wants to learn." Consciously or not I often found myself testing this social and personal theory. Mrs. Axe, a business executive up to her teeth on weekdays, was on weekends an angel with loose clothes and flowing hair. A part of her personality had a hunger for things spontaneous. She liked broken lines and unformed images. When she was of this state of mind and when I was in her company I felt imprisoned in her loose tresses and holding on for life.

The few weeks at the theatre in New Hope, Pennsylvania, and away from the castle was more than just an affirmation for my sense of self and, delusional or not, I felt I could unequivocally do something and be independent of exterior influences. It had been a long time since I first lay on my bed in the castle and hung my second-hand shirt out the window to dry. Since that day my unfolding world with the Axes and the castle had become an overpowering reality that I seemed to be forever wrestling with. Externally my life was in many ways a shining one. I had my own car and I could drive about whenever and wherever I wanted. I had more meals available to me every day than I could eat. I could come and go at the castle with ease and freedom. My clothes were mostly always new, courtesy of Mrs. Axe. When I asked for a glass of wine Mr. Axe had the best that money could buy. I had an allowance that provided me with enough money to buy items that got my attention, such as records and record players. I had come to know opera, history and world culture in a general way via the tutelage of Mr. Axe.

I tried to imagine how content or happy I would be sitting behind a desk for years to come dressed in a shirt and tie and talking about monetary matters from one end of the day to the other. My brain didn't respond favourably to the images I was conjuring up. At the same time I felt I had an obligation to follow the advice and instructions Mr. and Mrs. Axe imparted to me on a daily basis. Both of them had more often than not been kind and supportive. Mr. Axe opened up my mind and imbued me with the seed of intellectual curiosity. Every moment I spent in his company I learned something about the world – both past and present – that I was oblivious to before. When I first arrived the confusion of not knowing my place with the Axes grew by the day and I literally roamed about the castle like an orphaned ghost looking for someone or something real and stable. The consequence of being adrift obliged me to spend more time in town with some of my friends at the pub. I wasn't really sure how I arrived on the podium of self-awareness but I was convinced that experiencing a different routine had a lot to do with it. I was sure that I had arrived at an awareness that felt satisfying and fulfilling. Whether it was the experience of appearing on stage or seeing my name appear in a newspaper coupled with the night of intoxicated passion with Mrs. Axe I couldn't fully determine. Whatever the combination of time and events, I was convinced and secure in believing that my recent past was for me a new and definite baptism. The obligation of what I would do with my new perception of myself remained another matter.

I still lived and worked and earned money in the castle and Mrs. Axe was omnipresent in my mind and often in my body.

* * *

The Axes had returned from their Jamaican sojourn and I hadn't heard from or received a phone call from the casting director in New York. Living so far away from Manhattan also kept me out of the loop when it came to hearing about auditions.

I had learned some of the basic tools for maintaining a profile when seeking work in the world of show business. I was encouraged by Ruth Conforti at Talent Associates to get myself a proper and professional photograph of myself. This I accomplished the first week after I returned from the theatre in New Hope. New York City was a Mecca for photographers because of the large population of aspiring actors. Also via the good graces of Hurd Hatfield I had made contact with an acting agent in New York who advised me that I would be far better off if I pursued work as an actor in Los Angeles. During the rehearsal period of the play Robert Redford offered the same advice. He had already appeared on Broadway as well as in many television productions. Hurd Hatfield was in demand on both coasts. His classical training as an actor afforded him the luxury of working on the stage and the screen. Robert Redford had the same ability.

Still, even armed with new photos and an agent, I remained somewhat incapable of being able to make a decision with regard to pursuing an independent life. Leaving the castle was not an option I could fully commit to.

* * *

The excursions I took away from the castle on weekends were likely spiritually and creatively restorative for Mrs. Axe but for me they underlined her continued vacillation as far as my relationship with her was concerned. Weekdays, at least during some of them, I felt as if I was simply a file in a large file cabinet that was taken down, perused and quickly returned to my alphabetical position. By appointment I'd meet her in the kitchen after she concluded her domestic appraisal and personal chores with Pat. Her first priority had to do with making sure Mr. Axe had everything he wanted when he wanted it. When the chores of overseeing the domestic life of the castle was in order Mrs. Axe would greet me with a smile and apologise for taking me away from my schedule. I assured her when she did that I was anxious and even happy to accompany her. For the most part my schedule consisted of traipsing around the grounds or wandering about the interior of the castle.

* * *

Finishing work one evening I dropped by the kitchen to have dinner. This was as habitual with me as was going to bed at night. I had been a regular visitor to the kitchen since the day I arrived and I knew every square inch of the big room better than the odd mouse that came to hibernate behind the massive industrial stove during the winter. When I opened the door I encountered Pat. She wasn't wearing her usual white apron and she was sitting at the table writing on a notepad. Her mind appeared to be in another place until I bid her good evening.

She immediately got up and poured coffee for me and placed it on the opposite side of the table from her. Her mind still seemed to be elsewhere and she didn't say a word to me. Not wanting to interrupt her thoughts I quietly retreated to the coffee.

While I sat pensively drinking Pat stopped writing in her notepad and asked me: "You know Jim and I are leaving?"

The shock of what she said almost made me spill the coffee on the floor. The pain in my mind at the news immediately shuttled me back to the first minutes of the first day when I stepped out of the car and saw Pat and the castle for the first time. Back then, when I was in a daze from the ocean voyage, Pat took hold of me and the old suitcase I brought with me from Ireland. I remembered her smile when she first looked at me. It was warm, welcoming and very reassuring. Broader than any I had ever seen on a face in a long time. That day she humorously commented on my old and essentially empty suitcase. She often reminded me of that moment more than four years ago and that she wished she had a camera to record how lost I looked back then. Also she found the old tattered suitcase particularly touching and wondered if I grew shamrock in it. The news that she and Jim would be leaving the castle and retiring to the town they had originally come from in the State of Maine softly paralysed me.

Mrs. Axe had forewarned me the weekend I was at the beach house but maybe because I had imbibed too much wine that particular night I didn't dwell on it or even contemplate what it would mean to me. Mrs. Axe hadn't brought up the subject since and I hadn't thought about it either. At first I didn't know what to say or how to respond. Mrs. Axe's words from the night at the beach house echoed in my ears. But like then I simply didn't grasp the implications or even accept Pat and Jim's impending departure as a reality. Finally when my nerves stopped dancing all over my brain I replied, "When, Pat? Are you sure? When?"

I was hoping she'd say next month, or even in three months, but she didn't.

She calmly responded, "This coming Saturday – Monday at the latest. Jim's out readying the trailer to hitch onto the car. He wants to retire more than I do but I still think it's time for us. Five days is all that's left."

This day being Tuesday made Pat's departure the following Saturday or even the following Monday much too soon for me to accept with any rationality.

"Mrs. Axe told me she told you and for the last week I wondered why you didn't ask me or Jim," Pat said and put a sheet of paper into a stamped envelope.

In five days she and Jim would be packed and gone from the castle. This news was akin to throwing me out of my bedroom window.

I rushed to declare my innocence with regard to being aware of their departure. "Mrs. Axe mentioned it, Pat, but I didn't think it was definite or for sure. I heard nothing since and I thought you had changed your mind or something." My plea reminded me of times I protested my innocence to my mother in Dublin when she often and wrongfully accused me of stealing food that wasn't allotted to me from the kitchen. The sensation that flooded through my body was also akin to some of my early schooldays with the Christian Brother in Dublin who accused me and whipped me for not reading schoolbooks I didn't have because I couldn't afford them. The gusts of early injustices stormed through my veins once again and I was not able to escape the grey damp shadow of victimhood.

Pat smiled and was on the verge of laughing. "I did change my mind. I changed it twice since I told Mrs. Axe but I've a new granddaughter up there in Maine and I figure there's no time like the present."

They had been such a support to me. If I hadn't spent a lot of time in Pat and Jim's company after my break-up with my high-school sweetheart I might easily have become a regular in the pub with Frank Dillon. The couple commiserated with me the day I returned from Williams College and convinced me that I was only suffering from 'growing pains'. They shared memories of their daughter, who they said went off with a new boyfriend after she graduated from high school.

"My grandchildren are the main reason I'm giving up my work here," Pat repeated. After a painful moment of silence she continued. "Mrs. Axe is comfortable with our decision. She understands. She's been good to us. We appreciate it."

In those early days, only on weekends when I was out for a drive with Mrs. Axe or walking about the estate with Mr. Axe did I absent myself from Pat's domestic world. When she asked me to help her in the kitchen or even tidying up after a party I didn't hesitate. I was used to cooking, serving and cleaning. Pat was always happy, even appreciative that I served Mrs. Axe her breakfast every morning before I went to school. Preparing and serving breakfast was as automatic with me as tying my shoe laces. Such chores didn't require much planning or comparisons from my point of view and participating in physical labour was for the most part bereft of judgment and ambition.

It was left to her to accustom me to my new surroundings. She was my guide and at times my salvation when I wandered about the huge mansion half lost for days on end. Early in my residency Jim took it upon himself to drive me to every corner of the estate and show me where he kept the salt that kept the driveway free of ice and snow in the winter as well as the garage where he helped repair and ready the cars that the Axes used. And that included my roadster. Had Jim and Pat not been concerned about my welfare for my first couple of months at the castle I might not have adjusted as easily as I had. While Maggie Sheridan lived at the castle Pat filled me in on the custom and idiosyncrasies of getting along with the Axes.

Now after she delivered the sad news that she and her husband were leaving the domain it took all I could do to keep from crying in front of them.

The kitchen door suddenly opened and Jim entered.

"We're gone this Saturday," he said to Pat as he wiped his hands with the colourful kerchief he usually had tied around his neck. He then registered my presence by gently slapping me on the back. "Remember the first day, Gabriel?"

I wasn't sure what he meant and I responded, "What first day?"

Pat handed him a hot cup of coffee and he sat down on the chair opposite me.

"He's talkin' about the first day you arrived here," Pat said.

Jim looked out the window that gave a view to the front entrance as well as a good section of the estate. "You know every bloody blade of grass out there, young man, 'cause I showed you."

In the past I often sat next to Jim in the snow plough when he cleared the driveway of snow. In spring and summer I frequently volunteered to cut the grass with him as well. I enjoyed being on the tractors and listening to Jim complain

217

about everything with what he called his "Yankee sense of humour".

"Maybe the next time we show up around here, Irishman, you might be the Lord of the Manor – it's yours to dream for!"

Pat, who knew me better than her husband, volunteered, "I don't think he'd want that, Jim. Gabriel's not cut out for workin' behind a desk and wearing a pressed pair of pants every day."

Jim looked over at me and shook his head as if he was of two minds and didn't know what thought to decide on. "If he's the boss he can wear what he likes. Mrs. Axe is more than keen on grooming you, son, for a chair on the board. I know that because I've heard her say it more than once."

Pat then chimed in, "And I know I shouldn't say it, but the old man ain't goin' to last forever and somebody's got to step in."

Jim looked at the kerchief he was holding in his hands as if to inspect it for perspiration or anything else that might have landed on it since he came in from the garage.

"Who's goin' to be in this place twenty years from now: the ghost that prowls about the garden every night?" Pat clapped her hands again but even louder this time. "No! The ghost thing that walks up and down the big staircase every morning. I know that 'cause I bump into it every morning I bring Mrs. Axe her breakfast."

I joined in on the merriment. "That's Hamlet's father you bump into, Pat." I couldn't resist quoting from the play: "*My hour has almost come when I to sulphurous and tormenting flames must render up myself.*"

Jim laughed even louder than before. "The old boy, Mr. Axe, has you all learned up with that artsy crafty stuff."

For a second I was tempted to defend and even explain my appreciation of Mr. Axe and his scholarly demeanour but I resisted the temptation. Jim was not one to pay much attention to pronouncements from the gods of literature or to even know or understand Mr. Axe's obsession with Shakespeare and the English language.

Pat then walked to me and looked directly into my eyes. "I think you like the other world better, Gabriel, don't you?"

"What other world?" I asked.

"The world of runnin' about! Singin' and actin' and goin' where the devil takes you. Isn't that so, Gabriel? I think you have that in you and you like it better than sitting downstairs at the desk that has your name on it."

I wasn't inclined to influence Pat's thinking. I stood up and looked out the kitchen window again. "I like looking out there, Pat. I like seeing the seasons change and I know all of this and all of you have been almost like religious guardians to me." I stopped talking because my throat seemed to want to burst and my mouth went dry. I sat down and covered my face with my hands to hide the fact that I was trying to stop the tears from drowning me. I took my hands from my face and put on as brave a face as I could. Jim approached me and gently massaged the back of my neck.

"Make sure he's got our address in Maine, Pat," he said as he pointed his finger to the notepad in front of her.

She immediately retreated to the pad in front of her and scribbled, in almost illegible handwriting, their address in Maine. I questioningly looked at the piece of paper and was about to ask for clarification when Pat took it from my hand and rewrote what was on it. When she handed it back to me I smiled in approval. The handwriting and information was legible and clear.

I had put the page into my pocket when Jim called out, "Give him the phone number as well!"

I retrieved the piece of paper and handed it back to Pat. She in turn and very clearly wrote their phone number in Maine on the slip of paper.

"When I drive up to Maine you will be my first port of call," I said and I meant it at the time.

* * *

It didn't take long for Mrs. Axe to replace Pat and Jim. Within three days of their departure I was introduced to a couple from France who the night before had taken up residence in Pat and Jim's apartment above the kitchen. Mr. Axe had had a few men from the grounds staff clean and paint the accommodation. The transfer and transition of domestic power depressed me somewhat. For the past three years I had spent a good part of the cold winter sitting in Pat's living room watching television. As I observed the French couple standing in front of me and blabbering away in French, I accepted that past form of recreation had come to an end.

After the introductions Mrs. Axe asked me to help her show the couple about the residence. We started in the kitchen and took a tour of the main areas of the castle. As I made the rounds with them I kept thinking about Pat and Jim and how much I missed them. What made it even more awkward for me was the fact that the French couple didn't really speak English very well. I did my best to make the couple feel welcome and comfortable. As I contributed to the tour I tried to impress the new domestic staff with my limited knowledge of the antiques and some of the paintings hanging on the wall. By the look on their faces I wasn't confident however that they understood me. When I advised them against touching and changing the book order on one of Mr.

Axe's bookshelves they seemed to think that I was offering them the books to read. I got the same reaction when I tried to explain Mr. Axe's obsession with his collection of musical recordings. Mrs. Axe on the other hand spoke French and had to keep translating for me and the couple as we moved from room to room. When they spoke I hadn't a clue as to what they were saying. At one point I told them that I was in a television production of *The Scarlet Pimpernel* and that I wore the uniform of a French soldier. The mention of 'French soldier' caused a little concern with the woman and she turned to Mrs. Axe for an explanation. Speaking in French Mrs. Axe explained in detail what I intended to be humorous. By the look of both faces I was glad I hadn't mentioned the word *guillotine*. The dame of the couple then turned and spoke to her husband in what I considered to be a harsh tone of voice. He immediately raised his voice at her and they both were quiet for at least a minute, but just as fast as they went silent they turned to each other and began to argue – at least that was how it appeared to me. The gist of the conversation, according to Mrs. Axe as she simultaneously translated for me, was that Adele, the Frenchwoman, was anxious to get to work in the kitchen and to show off her culinary skills. Her husband, Jacque, looked more like a domestic butler than an outdoorsman. He was constantly complimenting the décor of the castle interior. This made me think he could not replace Jim, particularly when it came to working in the garage and on the grounds.

As I walked alongside the couple I sensed that I would not be frequenting the kitchen as I did in the past. I also came to the conclusion that even if I did I wouldn't be as comfortable there as I was when Pat ruled the roost.

* * *

Sitting in a booth in a coffee shop on the Upper West Side of

Manhattan in New York City one day before taking the train back to Tarrytown, I overheard a young man singing in the booth next to me. What got my attention was not the resonance of his voice – which was pronounced and notable – but its distinct Irish accent. The man (who I guessed to be a few years older than me) was singing a song and seemingly talking at the same time.

The mellifluous voice singing the recognisable Irish song obliged me to introduce myself. When I turned my head in his direction I said with as much humour as I could muster, "You're not from Dublin, sure you're not?"

Without hesitation and with a sense of pride the voice bellowed at me, "I'm from Armagh!"

Defensively and at the same time wanting to be friendly, I responded, "I'm from Dublin!"

The man then laughed and reached to shake my hand. "A jackeen, is it?"

For a moment I felt I had intruded on the fellow's privacy and with the little knowledge I had of the rivalry between Irish counties I felt more than a bit insecure – even a tinge fearful. The term *jackeen* was a sobriquet used to refer to people from Dublin by the natives of other Irish counties; the "jack" in the word had an etymology that historically associated it with the "Union Jack", England's flag. Given that my father had once served in the British army, I felt even more vulnerable.

Just as I withdrew my hand the man from Armagh got up and joined me in the booth I was sitting in.

"Do you do any singin'?" he asked me.

For fun I mockingly belted out, *"In Dublin's Fair City where the girls are so pretty!"*

He then reached back over to the booth he had been sitting in and retrieved his coffee cup.

"Have ya done any actin'?" he queried me.

"Done a bit," I said and told him about my vast experience of playing two bit parts on television.

When I introduced myself and asked him his name, he replied, "Just call me the Man from Armagh! Listen t'me – Ted Hanley – a fellow across the street – is puttin' together a group of Irish actors and singers to go on tour of Connecticut. He asked me to find a few more Paddies. Ya want a job?"

Thinking I had all of a sudden got lucky I quickly answered, "Yes."

Then unhesitatingly and with a happy smile on his face he introduced himself: "My name is Tommy Makem from the County Armagh."

The Man from Armagh informed me that the production he was helping put together was low in budget but high in quality. A few minutes later and without any kind of introduction I was sitting in Ted Hanley's apartment across the street with about five or six other young Irishmen and a few older women. I learned from the Man from Armagh that Ted Hanley was an Irish-American who wanted to break into show business and came up with the idea of forming a group of Irish-born thespians and singers and sending them on a tour of Irish-American bastions in the nearby state of Connecticut. The idea was to put on two one-act plays – in this case Millington Synge's *Riders to the Sea* and Yeats' *The Pot of Broth*. In between the plays the group would sing at least half a dozen Irish ditties. Both of the plays and all of the songs were public domain and didn't require any payment for usage. Mr. Hanley, the producer, informed the six or seven of us who were sitting in front of him that we were all cast in the show. None of us aspiring actors and singers even had to read a line from a play or sing a note from a song for him. He assigned each and every one of us the part we were to play and the songs we were to sing. I was given the part of the young son in the *Riders to the Sea* play and I was to learn the lyrics to about five or six songs. The songs were old traditional numbers and all of us already knew the lyrics. The parts in the two plays were tiny and they wouldn't require much memorising. Mr. Hanley gave us a piece of paper with instructions on how to get to an empty warehouse the following Monday that was adjacent to a Catholic school somewhere in Yonkers. It turned out that Ted's father was a janitor at the Catholic school and had the keys to the warehouse. This was another indication of how low the budget for the proposed tour was to be.

* * *

Back in Tarrytown later that evening I informed Mr. and Mrs. Axe of my new adventure and got their blessings to go forth. The following week I rehearsed the plays and sang the songs in the warehouse in Yonkers. A man with a very Greek-sounding name was in charge of directing the production and the scuttlebutt was that he was a former employee of the Greek diner where I first met the man from Armagh. One fact that stood out very clearly about the Greek director was that his command of the English language was very much in its elementary stage. A consequence of being exposed to this kind of mixed linguistics was that the cast under his command thought they were in plays by Sophocles and Euripides. The Greek director however left the singing of *Galway Bay*, *Molly Malone* and *The Girl from Donegal* to the Man from Armagh. The set for the play I was in had rolled-down red-painted bedsheets for the four walls of an Irish cottage.

The first show of the tour opened in Bridgeport, Connecticut, to a half-empty house. This impacted on our yet-to-be-paid salary but we were promised that when we opened the next night in New London, Connecticut, we would be fully compensated. The 'company' of the 'Irish Players' arrived in a theatre in New London and prepared for the second show. This night the cast was told that the show would open with one of the two plays instead of the musical number that opened the show the previous night. It also meant that I was on stage and ready to roll when the call for "places" was given.

The curtain went up. I stood on the stage with the actress Mary Boylan who played my mother and noticed that the vast auditorium of several hundred seats had only two people sitting in the back row. Mary looked out at the two people who were now making out in the back and said out loud, "Fuck 'em! I'm not going on with this!"

I agreed wholeheartedly and both of us walked off the stage. Backstage the rest of the cast and the two crew members, one being Mr. Hanley and the other unidentified individual who spoke Greek, protested our stage desertion. The chorus, including the Man from Armagh sided with us. Within fifteen minutes the tour of the 'Irish Players' came to a sudden and sad end.

With my bag in hand and while standing in the lobby of the theatre later that night the Man from Armagh came up to me and offered a gentle apology to me and the rest of the cast. Before he turned to go his own way I reached out to him and asked him what his plans were for the future and he said he'd "continue to look for acting work in Manhattan. Absent that, I'll keep on singing."

Several years later I met the Bard of Armagh, Tommy Makem, outside Carnegie Hall where he was appearing on stage with the Clancy Brothers.

* * *

Early Monday evening the Axes and I went to the Metropolitan Club for dinner and then to the opera. While I drove home Mr. and Mrs. Axe got into a debate about the performances in the opera *Rigoletto* which we had just seen. Mrs. Axe favoured the singer who played the Duke of Mantua whereas Mr. Axe seemed to gravitate to the one who performed Rigoletto. I sided with Mr. Axe and supported him because I identified with Rigoletto, the hunchbacked jester. Identifying with people with deformities might have had something to do with my Catholic past.

The Dublin of my childhood was diminishing like a distant star in the galaxies but, like a lingering hangover or the pain of rejection, it was not yet gone from my mind. Very welcome was the fact that living in New York was different: very different. Yet it wasn't difficult for me to fall back into memories of my past. In fact there were many hours and days that I couldn't escape it.

* * *

Morning, noon and night for the next month I spent as little time in the kitchen as I could. I made sure I got up earlier every morning than I usually did and consumed my breakfast before the *gendarmes* arrived. I would greet the couple entering the kitchen as I was exiting it. Part of what made my relationship awkward with the French couple was that they were not sure or aware of what my position and relationship with the Axes was. Neither I – nor presumably Mr. or Mrs. Axe – made an effort to explain what was perplexing even for us. They were likely confused by my presence when I accompanied Mrs. Axe as she gave them a tour of the castle. My propensity to prepare my own meals and sit alone at the kitchen table was likely seen in their eyes as an insult to their professionalism. I would not have been insulted if the culinary duo had looked upon me as the house cat. There were times when I actually felt that I was. The new reality of who controlled and commanded the kitchen was beginning to look more and more like the Battle of Borodino. Had the French not made so many tactical mistakes when invading Russia in 1812 Napoleon's legacy might be more venerable. The times when we mutually occupied the kitchen I couldn't help but notice that the couple approached the preparation of Mr. Axe's meals as if they were field commanders in a military campaign designed by Robespierre. They watched over Mr. Axe's eggs, bacon and toast with such strict culinary methodology it often looked as if they were painting a portrait of the man's appetite. After breakfast they readied and organised what Mr. Axe was having for lunch. When they completed that chore, they re-decorated the dining-room table by placing flowers all over it only to be told to remove them by Mr. Axe who preferred to have books in front of him rather than flowers. Because of the language barrier I was limited in my efforts to make a suggestion of any kind regarding anything that concerned Mr. and Mrs. Axe. Adele and Jacque soon learned however that only occasionally did Mr. and Mrs. Axe sit together for dinner. Often the labour of love they invested in their efforts to showcase their gastronomic talents went unnoticed and even unappreciated. For me, the couple made the friendly terrain of the kitchen a less friendly place. Eventually I minimised my time and partly lost my desire to be in it. In a very short period of time the once big open friendly kitchen went from being a home to being more like The Bastille at the height of its storming.

A few times I was called on by Mrs. Axe to take Adele and

Jacque to town and show them the shops and markets wherein they bought food and supplies for the castle. This activity did have its benefits. I learned how to smell and inspect food and even how to prepare it for anyone with a discerning taste. And as if by osmosis my French improved. For that I was thankful.

* * *

One evening I was just about to get into my car and drive to town when Mr. and Mrs. Axe pulled up alongside me. They had been out for the day visiting their house on Long Island. Mr. Axe asked me where I was heading off to but because my intentions were to go down the pub I told him I was going to have a mechanic look at my car. I made up a story about how the brakes weren't working properly.

As I stood next to the passenger side conversing, the subject of the French couple came up and Mr. Axe asked me if I liked them or not. I responded by telling him I should have paid more attention in high school to my French teacher. He responded by telling me that I should have paid more attention to him when he made the effort to tutor me in the subject. Mrs. Axe then said something to him in French which I didn't understand. After a few seconds of silence Mr. Axe wanted to know – before I chalked up another year of not attending – if I still had plans to attend college. Mrs. Axe answered for me and said I did but that there was no hurry, given the fact that I already had a secure job with a bright future place, provided I paid attention to some of the senior executives in the office. She informed Mr. Axe, however, that some of the reports she received on my work performance weren't altogether sterling. She was referring to my attitude and work commitment at the office.

Since I had returned from my theatrical odyssey I'd been spending a lot of my time in the office but it was reported to her that I sometimes didn't come back to work after lunch break. Almost every day I found myself immersed in reading financial newspapers and quoting stock-market trends and changing prices in commercial goods and services over the phone to several associates who sat at their nearby desks calculating and digesting the information for further use. In reality it was not the kind of activity I looked forward to when I got up every morning and sometimes when I was in town I couldn't bring myself back to the office. I was so tired of office work I not only couldn't concentrate or enjoy my present state of affairs, I hardly had the energy or the desire to think about a future.

The unexpected and spontaneous conversation with Mr. Axe led me to talking about the profession of acting. My limited experience in it had gone to my head and I began to promulgate and expound on the infinite idiosyncrasies of it. I told Mr. Axe that I had extended his invitation to Hurd Hatfield to visit the castle when it was convenient for him. Mr. Axe replied that he looked forward to meeting the actor and admitted he was a fan of any actor who had a booming stage voice and a Shakespearean presence. These credentials Mr. Hatfield certainly had. Mr. Axe then bellowed out: *"Now go we in content to liberty and not to banishment!"*

Mrs. Axe reminded me of the vicissitudes of the acting profession and encouraged me to think of it more as a hobby than a way to make a living. I wanted to argue back but because I was so attached to her I simply wasn't able to. I felt it would not only be difficult but close to inconceivable for me not to pay attention to her. A day or even an hour didn't go by without her being on my mind. On a daily basis I seemed to live in a drifting limbo that sometimes made me feel secure in her presence. Other days I might just as easily have been floating about in a mist of purgatory that clouded my vision and sense of a future. Since I had experienced a different life with my job in the theatre recently, I had come to believe that I was more and more in control of who I was and what I wanted to do with myself.

Still, and paradoxically, the more independent I felt I was becoming of Mrs. Axe, the more a part of me wanted to hang on and cling to her. It was as if some unseen beast was biting the back of my neck. What I was beginning to see more and more clearly was that I wanted to leave her and my life in the castle more out of the pain of ambivalence than out of the pursuit of fantasy. From the mornings when I served her breakfast, the drives and tours about Westchester County on weekends and the moments of physical embracing, I boiled in a stew of emotional and physical confusion. Also living in such close proximity to Mr. Axe, while my obsession with his wife continued was like living in a prison that had no doors, keys or guards. Nevertheless something kept pulling at me that reminded and encouraged me to step out of Mrs. Axe's shadow and experience life without her. At times I felt I had fallen into a dangerous whirlpool and I wasn't sure if I wanted to drown in the water or swim my way out of it. In the tumult, indecisiveness and confusion that rolled about in my mind I accused and blamed myself for being of two minds.

Living in the castle in many ways was adventuresome and at times exciting. I had met and talked with many people I'd not likely meet or know if I was living elsewhere. The intellectual and cultural life at the castle was in many ways comparable to attending college twenty-four hours a day.

Mr. Axe reminded me that if I wanted a compass that would guide me towards a future I should revisit my past. He specifically referred to my parents and Dublin.

This moment standing outside the car gifted him with the opportunity to expound on his awareness of Sigmund Freud: "Think back, Gabriel. Think back."

Mrs. Axe joined in and unhesitatingly added, "Yes, Gabriel. Emerson is right. He knows what he's talking about."

In my present frame of mind my relationship with the lady holding the steering wheel of the car was becoming more and more awkward. And although my past was slowly fading from me I couldn't see myself living a life in the castle and a future with Mrs. Axe at the same time. However, I wasn't able to imagine my present without her and this condition of consciousness was tormenting. Every day I was so enmeshed and entwined in a half state of awareness that I began to question my ability to think straight.

As I stood and listened and thought and answered questions, I was becoming exhausted and wearied. My attitude while I stood outside of the car was changing from that of a happy surprise to a not so pleasant one. My answers sounded angry and I involuntarily displayed an unwelcome and unappreciated demeanour. Certainly not something that the Axes wanted to hear or even be a part of and, before I could step away, Mrs. Axe drove away from me.

I waited a few moments and digested the awkward confrontation. A few seconds later I was driving out of the driveway and on my way to the pub in Tarrytown.

* * *

I revisited the local watering hole in Tarrytown, after having avoided it for about two months, because I felt obliged to tell

Frank Dillon in detail what had transpired in my life since I got my first acting job. Supporting my motivation to revisit the pub now was the French Disconnection and the loss of my base at the castle, the kitchen being no longer a place for me to loiter in.

I had missed the old tavern, which had been an oasis for me almost since the first day I arrived in Tarrytown, the place where I found a welcome noisy ruckus crowd when the loneliness, isolation and silent world of the castle was leaning heavily on me. In some instances my attendance at the pub substituted for the neglected practice of religion for me. The path from being observant to the observed suited my frame of mind as I got older. I keenly missed the pub recently as most of my high school classmates had gone off to college and only returned on holidays. Some simply came back at Christmas. When they did and when I met up with them they had changed so much I felt I had less and less in common with them. As a consequence of not having applied and gone off to college with my graduating class, my social life in Tarrytown was limited and in many ways restricted to the carnival atmosphere in the pub.

However, I had stayed away from the pub and that was partly because I was a bit shy about meeting up with Frank again. I had hoped over the past few months that he had recovered from the trauma of his visit to New York City but I wasn't sure. I imagined Frank had taken it upon himself to blame me for his bad day in New York. But when I entered the pub he almost fell off his stool and was insistent on hearing all about my experiences since the night he leapt from my car and went into hibernation. He grabbed hold of me and became effusive and complimentary to me about what he considered to be my success. I played down any and all compliments that were thrown at me by the gang at the bar. I did however insist on buying Frank a drink. He accepted and ordered whiskey. As soon as he swallowed the stuff he once again began to brag about his future as an actor. This time however his focus and concentration was on going to Los Angeles. He had become more and more convinced that California was the place for him. I told him I had made friends with some of the actors I appeared with on the stage in Pennsylvania and a few had given me their phone numbers out there. Frank demanded I tell him everything I knew about them. I told him I acted on the stage with Hurd Hatfield, Robert Redford and Louise Fletcher. And that Mr. Hatfield had given me the name of his agent in Hollywood. I related also that I had met Peggy McCay, an exceptional actress who was leaving New Hope at the time of my arrival, after appearing with James Whitmore in the previous play, *The Summer of the Seventeenth Doll*. I gossiped about how I joined her and James Whitmore and some of her fellow actors for a drink at The Inn and that Peggy took note of the fact that I was Irish, and with a perfect Irish accent invited me to call her should I ever be in Los Angeles.

Frank ordered another drink and I paid for it. Sitting next to Frank was Wayne Franklin who also ordered a whiskey and signalled to me that I might cover it – which I did. Encouraging me to blabber on, Frank wanted to know what my response was to James Whitmore. I told him it wasn't James Whitmore who offered me his phone number but Peggy McCay. When Peggy had suggested I give her a call if I ever made it to Los Angeles, I responded with a voice as American as I could conjure and proclaimed that I would nail her phone number to the back of my head. At the time my effort to affect an American accent was met with laughter. But I took it to be a warm and welcoming kind of response. Proof of this was that everybody sitting around the table ordered me a beer. Of the six beers that arrived I could only consume one of them. The five other beers were quickly disposed of by the three others actors and two actresses of which Peggy was one. This kind of fellowship and 'sharing' was common among vagabonds in the past and as far as I was concerned it was still practised among actors and actresses. It was this kind of thinking that brought me back to visit Frank at the bar. I ordered a whiskey for myself and almost consumed it before the bartender had time to withdraw the bottle from the shot glass. Then with more confidence than I'd had in a long time I decided I was going to celebrate something I had been thinking seriously about for over a month. I had now finally come to the conclusion that I was simply not cut out for office work and I planned on telling Mrs. Axe that I was seriously thinking of leaving Tarrytown and quitting work at the castle. Frank and the others raised their glasses and drank to my intentions. A surge of liquor-coated courage came on me and I began asking myself questions: such as, why did Mrs. Axe change my daily routine and schedule of serving her breakfast every morning? My sense of it was that she wanted those observing our behaviour and friendship to look at me from a different perspective – and especially Mr. Axe. And why in the mornings when I showed up for work in the office did she take on the mantle of the 'boss' and chief executive and act when I was in her presence with other members of her staff as if I was a twin to one of the wastepaper baskets? Thoughts in my head began to unravel and I felt that I was walking on marbles and was about to fall flat on the floor. I kept on babbling to myself until Frank Dillon told me to calm down and sit back on the bar stool I didn't know I had stepped off.

At about the same time my friend, neighbour and self-anointed protector entered the pub. Sergeant Gilroy took one look at me and shook his head and, with as definite a negative gesture as I had ever witnessed drunk or sober, said to me with a deep tone of paternal care in his voice, "I saw your car outside and you can't drive tonight."

I wondered for a moment if he had truly spotted my car or if he had been told to keep track of my travels. In the past Mrs. Axe had alerted him to what she characterised as my "impulsive behaviour". It was because of this that I sometimes avoided going to the pub in case my uniformed neighbour dropped in on me.

Tonight as I looked directly at him I accepted that he had my interests at heart. Sergeant Gilroy didn't have a mean bone in his body. The first thing that came to my mind was what we had in common and without hesitation I spoke in a clear voice, "John, you should be in Ireland."

John laughed, "You should stop drinking and you should be home and I'm going to see to it that you get there safely."

Those were the last words I remember hearing that night.

* * *

The next morning when I woke up I was lying on my bed fully dressed and almost in the identical position and state of mind as when I first came to the castle close to four years earlier. I turned to face the morning sunshine coming through the drawn curtains, which cast light on the bed I was lying in. Although the window was closed I thought I heard the flapping of my shirt when I first put it out to dry back then. When I turned back from the window I remembered that the old suitcase I brought with me from Ireland was still under the bed.

With the thought of leaving the castle and Tarrytown still in my head I jumped off the bed and pulled the suitcase out from its dark entombed shelter. The clasps were still un-lockable and the leather was even more faded than when I first separated myself from it. I touched it again for the first time in years and though I was still suffering from a hangover from the previous night, I thought I heard it snoring, and yet again I was reminded of my father. He was known in my family more for his snoring nose than from anything he said or accomplished during his waking hours. The suitcase had a life of its own and in its own inanimate way it could have easily contained the history of the Walsh family. Certainly I believed that my childhood was inside of it and was trying to get out. My past and my present seemed to be joined this morning in a ritual of giving birth to the unknown. Almost four years my life at the castle had gone by and I still couldn't comprehensively define my everyday life or my dreams to anyone or even to myself for that matter. In my confusion it seemed to me that in dreams the logic and reality of life is transformed into a private universe and where one has to not only live alone but to dream alone.

When I descended from my half-comatose state the first thing I was thankful for was that Sergeant Gilroy was on duty the night before. How he got me home and deposited me in my room I couldn't remember. I worried for a moment if Mr. or Mrs. Axe might have played a part in transporting me to my room. I was to find out later that it was the French couple who assisted Sergeant Gilroy in depositing me on my slumber sack.

After dismissing the approach of curiosity regarding what happened to me the previous night, I immediately jumped off the bed and looked down at the parking lot and happily saw my car parked there. John Gilroy had managed again to save me from myself and I was once again thankful to him.

This being a Saturday morning I knew I'd be seeing Mrs. Axe wearing earrings and dressed in attire that didn't reflect the business executive she was during the week.

* * *

Ossining, a town north of Tarrytown, was situated high on the embankment of the Hudson River and its view and vantage point afforded its residents a unique vista of the great waterway. Ossining was famous for being the location for Sing Sing Prison. Sing Sing was where Jules and Ethel Rosenberg were executed for espionage in 1953. Years ago in Dublin I saw a film that took place in Sing Sing. I think George Raft was the star in it.

Sitting on a bench near the summer school I attended in Ossining Mrs. Axe and I tested and ate a few apples she had bought at a nearby fruit-and-vegetable stand. The day had started off like a day where introspection was non-existent and illusions were many. Mrs. Axe was in great form when she asked me to take the drive and I was as usual more than happy that she did. Mr. Axe had gone into the city to meet up with college friends at the Metropolitan Club and that fact brought a settling and contented feeling to Mrs. Axe.

As I continued to look out at the great river in the distance I remembered the struggle I had in trying to make up the two credits I needed to get my high school diploma. Also my youthful and deep infatuation with Muriel came back into my mind. I wondered as I sat on the bench in Ossining this fall day where I'd likely be if Muriel had not fallen for someone else when she went away to college. Since my relationship with her had come to an end and the transformation of my ambiguous friendship with Mrs. Axe had begun, I felt I was exiled to an existence of introspection and isolation.

Although Muriel had gone from my life she still remained a warm and tender memory. I was lucky that my foray into the boxing world that her father supervised didn't leave me with a broken nose. As I looked at the river I had visions that Muriel had married the young man she met at Bennington. Since that day in her dorm when she introduced me to her new paramour I convinced myself that she had forgotten about me. Had I her ear today as I looked at my life since we went our separate ways, I would have quoted Blake again: "*A robin redbreast in a cage puts all Heaven in a rage.*"

The time and consequence of being frightened by those who attempted to educate me with a bamboo cane and a leather strap back in Dublin was always loitering in the shadows of my mind. I had struggled to keep up with my classmates but lack of an earlier focus on learning and knowledge was becoming more and more evident as I slow-danced through high school. I had signed up for an academic programme that led to having college ambitions but I wasn't and hadn't been prepared for the task and my neglected and almost non-existent academic past in Dublin was quickly catching up with me. My mind and energy with regard to school back home was almost totally invested in not wanting to enter the front gate of the Christian Brothers School in Dublin. The consistent corporal punishment schooldays in Dublin were more like being a prisoner in a penitentiary that advocated closing a mind rather than opening it. In Dublin I was obliged to go to school for pain and punishment rather than for academic or social enlightenment.

While we sat on a bench taking in the vista Mrs. Axe mentioned that Father Leo had temporarily returned to Ireland to instruct novices of his religious order in their calling and she would likely not be seeing him for at least the next six months. She joked that Father Leo had apparently converted everybody in Paterson New Jersey. The news that he was far away filled me with a tinge of satisfaction and I was glad that he would not, at least for now or in the near future, be asking me to confess. Without giving it much thought I mentioned that Father Leo had on more than one occasion requested to hear my confession and a few times he seemed to insist on it. When I told Mrs. Axe this she almost swallowed the entire apple she was biting into. The implications of me confessing my 'sins' to one of her best friends went from her being shocked to having a big smile on her face. It wasn't difficult for me to imagine what thoughts went through her mind. After a moment or two of pensive contemplation she turned and looked at me directly. The look in her eyes was definitely a command for me to continue with my story. Confessing to the 'sins' of the flesh and naming the person in the confidential and holy ritual of the Catholic Church was something that Mrs. Axe probably never thought about. I reassured her that my obedience to the sacraments had long evaporated and there was no chance on earth that Father Leo would ever hear me confessing to anything. I reiterated that I had stopped going to Confession many months ago and under the pain of death Father Leo would be the last person I'd confess to. Mrs. Axe laughed and then went back to munching on the apple and staring out at the Hudson River in the distance. While her eyes appeared to be focused on the far side of the Hudson River she began to talk once more about her youthful ambition to be a violinist and what classical music meant to her when she was much younger.

"I really never lingered on that part of myself. I wasn't really that possessed or obsessed or whatever it is that glues one to any or one way of thinking." She stopped, turned in my direction, looked at me for a split second then went back to what she appeared to be focusing on in her mind. "Margaret Sheridan had it but I don't."

Whether it was the fall air or the taste of the apple she was eating that caused her to fall into a sentimental mood I didn't know or question. She had in the past talked about her youthful artistic impulse even when she wasn't eating an apple. She admitted to me, although I accepted the fact that she was really talking to herself, that one of the great attractions she had for Maggie Sheridan was the fact that Maggie was totally committed to her art and that she devoted her life to opera and sacrificed just about everything else that might have made her a happier person. Her admiration for Maggie was as palpable as the apple she held in her hand. Sharing reminiscences about Maggie was always a subject we both enjoyed. When we were unable to share a different subject we resorted to talking about our friend the opera diva. But Maggie had been gone from our lives for a considerable time and there was less and less a need or an opportunity to invoke her memory.

When we stopped talking about Maggie we fell into a silence. It was as if both of us were afraid or even unable to talk to each other about each other. The night before when I was intoxicated I was determined to tell her I wanted to go to Los Angeles and throw my fantasy impulses to the wind. I was secure in the fact that I had made a few contacts out there and I would likely not be adrift when I went in search of whatever it was that was pulling at me. I retreated into my mind in search of a statement that would prove I knew what I was talking about and what I was doing. I had trouble finding any.

Amazingly then, and as if I had told her to say it, Mrs. Axe turned to me and recited: "*Too long a sacrifice can make a stone of the Heart.*"

240

I practically fell backwards when she quoted the line from a William Butler Yeats poem. Never before had she resorted to poetry or metaphor in our conversations. She loved the theatre and the opera but her affinity for them was essentially passive. When she did debate and argue about the arts it was a sign that she was either intoxicated or happy with something she kept secret and didn't talk about. Taking time out to discuss the merits of the creative impulse was not a subject she spent much time or energy on. This had always been the domain of Mr. Axe and I took it today that the puzzling person sitting next to me had wanted to talk to me about all kinds of things but couldn't put it in her own words.

After she quoted the line of the poem to me I knew then and there she knew what I was thinking and what I wanted to do. It was also the first moment that I felt we were the same person with the same wants and wishes at the same time. I sat dumbstruck and became more and more in awe of Mrs. Axe than I had ever been. Feeling more confident in her company than I had since I met her I managed to tell her I planned on leaving Tarrytown and the castle in about a week and that I was going to give living in Los Angeles a try – the implications being that I was going to pursue a career as an actor. Surprising me more than when she recited the poem, Mrs. Axe asked me with a tone of encouragement in her voice to make sure she knew where I could be reached when I settled in a new abode. She also advised me to make sure I had my car serviced as well as fitting it with four new tyres. And with a smile that was almost at the point of evolving into a laugh she advised me to make sure before I took to the road that I had enough money in my pocket as well.

For the next five minutes or so I found myself stretched out across her lap and holding on to her as tightly as I could. Then she gently pushed me aside, got up from the bench and reminded me that we had a date for the opera on Monday night.

* * *

When I pulled the old suitcase from under my bed it was like pulling the skin and skull from the front of my brain and seeing half if not all of my life fall from my head to the floor. The suitcase was old, frayed, tattered and consistent with just about the way my father who originally owned it lived and thought. For a moment I hesitated and wondered if I should even be bothered with it at all. Even though it made no practical sense I decided that for personal and maybe emotional reasons I would take possession of the thing again. When I first opened it the sight of a colourful pair of socks – which had been given to me by my sister Rita when I left Ireland – impacted on me as if I was kneeling in a confession box all over again. I had forgotten all about the socks but as I held them in my hand it occurred to me that I chose to keep them in the suitcase and not wear them in fear of wearing them out. I wanted to keep them as 'new' because everything in my past was 'second-hand'.

The suitcase was lying open like a whale's mouth and it looked like it wanted to swallow me. I wasn't confident that what was in my head and my body were going in the same direction. One minute I felt like falling into the suitcase and closing it on top of me. The next moment I felt like pushing it as far away from me as I could. Regardless of whether I could get away from it or fall into it, it brought back images of Dublin and my family.

For the most part Dublin was a combination of a seminary, a convent and a prison. The prison aspect of it might be attributed to the fact that, because of a close physical resemblance to my father, I innocently but painfully reminded my mother of the man she married and as a consequence my face was slapped more times than it was washed. Being unable to express her anger at her husband my mother vicariously slapped the son who was, as she often blurted out, "The spittin' image of *him*!" Yet paradoxically I was in some bizarre and unhealthy way responsible for keeping my parents together. My presence in the house afforded my mother a form of physical therapy. She took her anger out on me because of my resemblance to my father. I was an easy and convenient target for her whenever she felt disappointed in her husband and life in general. In a not-so-obscure way my mother and father were a bit like Medea and Jason in Euripides' play *Medea*. My father displayed his contempt for my mother's lower position on the social scale by constantly ignoring her presence. My mother in turn reacted by obsessing on the teachings of the Church and bestowing on all of her children a complex of fear and guilt that was grotto in size. For years I walked about Dublin and wandered about my house, not sure if I was being welcomed in or being thrown out, because of my physical resemblance to my father. To say I suffered from an identity complex might well be an understatement. With little clarity that could illuminate my present at the time or any grasp of a future, I lived in my home like a weed struggling for survival in a bed of concrete. Having been born into a family of ten children I sensed that my brothers and sisters and I were different vegetables growing up in a small and crowded garden. Who was a carrot, a head of cabbage, a turnip, a potato or a weed was anybody's guess. Each of my siblings appeared to be caught in a traffic jam, all rushing to get out of each other's way without really knowing where they were going. My home was a bit like a dog pound for stray dogs: five brothers and five sisters each barking and yelping as if they were a threat to each other's existence, all panicked and anxious to escape the bewildered reality of having been born into a family that never got to know each other.

As I continued to slowly pack the suitcase I began to weaken and had second thoughts about what I was doing. Yet something kept impressing on my brain that I was doing the right thing. I felt secure in the fact that I believed I knew more about what I wanted than what I didn't want.

To further motivate myself to leave the castle I thought back to the morning when I was working on the breakfast shift in the Shelbourne Hotel in Dublin. That part of my life was my compass and I leaned on it whenever I felt apprehensive. What caused the change in direction was when I made the decision to take Maggie Sheridan's breakfast tray to her room after others shunned and rejected the chore. A reason as to why I took no notice of the warnings about Maggie's wrath might have had to do with the struggles I had often encountered in my own home with my own family. The lack of fear or even intimidation might easily have been born out of my own family struggles. The task of facing and confronting a disgruntled customer was, as far as I was concerned, bereft of fear. Maggie was a lonely person who had reached the heights in her chosen career but had almost just as quickly descended from the pinnacle of her success and for many years after she exuded loneliness that was embedded in her eyes. She appeared to be looking for something that had been lost since the beginning of time: certainly since the beginning of her time. Having portrayed so many tragic characters in her life she might have felt she had been totally disconnected from any and every human emotion. Seeing her that morning half stretched out on the bedroom floor in the hotel and

244

wrongfully assuming she wanted her breakfast served there presumably triggered a moment of innocence she might not have encountered since she left the operatic world. I had come to know and learn more about her after she died than when she was alive. Had she picked me out to spite other members of the hotel staff or did she want to do something for herself at this stage of her life? Her life on the operatic stage had ceased and her voice was confined to recordings she had made when she was younger and in her prime. Cio-Cio San, the character she sang in Puccini's *Madame Butterfly*, was now a faded poster that lined the inside of her large travelling suitcase when she travelled from place to place. Her opera posters and her old travelling trunk that was really the centre of her life didn't accompany her to the grave. A sad part of Maggie's life was that her career never afforded her financial independence. Had it not been for the benevolence of the Axes she might well have had to retreat to a convent in Ireland and spend the rest of her days under the care of a charitable clergy.

I was never really sure what my relationship with Maggie truly was. Maybe the beauty and the definition of a relationship is not knowing what it truly is. Unlike many workers at the hotel, I felt comfortable in Maggie's presence and always believed she was deep down an affectionate person. Her life, as she may have envisioned it, might have in some way, shape or form been reaching back for a connection to her beginnings when she was consigned to a convent in Dublin after both her parents passed away when she was very young. Was I that connection, I wondered to myself as I considered packing the old suitcase. The shadow of the orphan in Maggie might also have reflected in me even though both of us had parents and siblings. Maggie's parents had died when she was young.

Maggie had spent her early years in a convent in Dublin after both her parents passed away. It was there she got picked out by a nun who heard her singing in the convent choir. The nun coached and encouraged Maggie's singing voice and in many ways gave her the confidence to be a singer when she was left without parents. The nun at the convent was a reassuring presence for Maggie and in no small way did that translate into her being successful later in life. Maggie Sheridan went from singing in Dublin as a young girl, to London when she got a bit older and her voice matured, to Italy and fame at La Scala. In spite of her fame in Italy Maggie always carried around with her the aura that she was essentially alone. No matter what large-brimmed hat she wore or dresses that looked as if they had come out of a recent opera performance, Maggie had that sad and questioning look in her eyes that reflected dissatisfaction with life. It was as if she was still waiting for some part of it to come and claim her. The friendship I had with Maggie, as far as I was concerned, had more to do with lonely souls spontaneously colliding and reaching out to each other.

I then made a hasty decision to return the suitcase to its dark grave under my bed but I changed my mind because the suitcase in its shaggy neglected presence reminded me of my father and his youthful ambitions that were never realised. Memories of my father didn't and couldn't exist independent of shades and shadows of my mother in the illusions I suddenly found myself wrapped up in. Paddy couldn't compliment Molly and she wouldn't trust him if he did. Molly and Paddy would not be able to handle such a change. Anything that reflected on either of them in a positive way would bring on nightmares to both of them while sleeping in the same old bed at night. Thinking back and half wishing they were in the room with me, I was reminded again of the amount of time and energy my parents devoted to self-deprivation in their lives. It was remarkable in the extreme.

As I forced myself to dwell on past remembrances I wished I could tell my mother that I was leaving home again even though we'd had almost no contact since the day she saw me off at the train station in Dublin four years earlier. By now everything that happened to me in America seemed to pale in comparison to the rush of blood and nerves that was assaulting my brain. I was tempted again to kick the old suitcase back under the bed but I resisted the urge. The cold hungry days in Dublin, the sadistic Christian Brothers and priests who liked to slap my face, seemed unimportant but still close.

This day, feeling somewhat insecure about my decision to leave the castle, I found myself adrift between the conflicting thoughts there were flooding into my brain. Almost like a monstrous ghost rising up from the depths of my imagination, I decided I wanted to test the power of pain and suffering that so hypnotised my mother, my father and brothers and sisters in Ireland. I attempted to visualise the event at Calvary hiding at the bottom of the suitcase and considered if I should keep it open or not. The crucifix, the ever-present image of pain and suffering, assaulted my mind, and I felt as if a heavy cross had fallen from the ceiling and cracked open my skull, allowing the hundreds of youthful memories to escape from the captivity of my mind. The echoes of my cries, confessions and prayers resonated in my head like a flock of frightened birds ascending from a still lake. In my temporary diffused state of mind I involuntarily begged for forgiveness for sins I hadn't committed. Like a drunk who had made his first pledge never to drink again I threw the last of my personal belongings into the suitcase and attempted to close it, but was quickly reminded that one of the clasps was missing from the thing and, if I didn't put a strap or a strong string of twine around it, it could never be completely closed. I managed in the end to tie it securely. The sight of the closed suitcase was another reminder of the morning I first packed and tied it shut.

Feeling drained, fatigued and even fearful as to what I was about to do with my life I then lay down on the bed and tried to re-imagine the journey all over again, just to make sure I wasn't dreaming. The expressions of wishing and wanting and the voices of the other passengers on board the ship I sailed on four years earlier flooded into my mind. They had bags, rags and suitcases and many of their faces were as prominent and as real as the tattered leather suitcase that was now ready for yet another journey. I tried to remember some passengers I had met on the ship coming over. Faces and expressions of all kinds and the stories behind them came flooding into my head. I wondered how they were greeted and what they might be doing now four years later. Like myself, many had spent their lives wishing, waiting and saving up for the day they could leave Ireland and come to America. Down to a person, all had relatives in America and were greeted and welcomed at the boat when it came into the dock in New York City.

Where were they now? And what happened to them? After the hurry and fuss of disembarking and the dockside greetings, those I had travelled across the ocean with had vanished into the American landscape. Where were the men from Cork and Donegal gone to? What happened to the man who was carried off the ship on a stretcher? I hoped he had survived. He was a great companion to me.

In a very short period of time my mind came back to the present and I was reminded again by the presence of the suitcase that I had more miles to go in life. Half frozen in time I continued to fall deeply into my life in Dublin years earlier. My family and neighbourhood had forged my fears, pain and ambitions a long time ago. The consistency of my family's estrangement was something no member of my family ignored or disregarded and I realised now as I planned another journey that I was no exception to that sad reality. Since my arrival in America I had spent very little time looking back or recollecting any aspect of my childhood. The days were rare indeed when I looked back in warm sentiment. I spent much of my early childhood sneaking into the cinemas of Dublin to escape from a reality that darkened every moon I looked up to. I don't know if it's a record or not but as a child I spent more time talking to myself than I did to anybody else. Why did I talk to myself so much? I think it was because in my childhood no one talked to me in a manner that made much sense. My past in Ireland had made sure that adulthood came to me prematurely and as I looked back I didn't find the image positive or welcoming. I'd been officially working and earning a living since the age of thirteen.

Unofficially I was earning pennies since the age of seven. In some ways I was still wrapped in a perspective of self-inflicted social status. What that meant to me was that I was always in a constant state of 'hoping' but what I was hoping for I was never really sure. In some ways I might only have been qualified to embrace my past. And when that was done I could only imagine myself wishing it would go away.

I stopped thinking and patiently listened to the silence that followed. After a few moments of absorbing the silence I got up from my bed and looked out the window at the estate below me and the Hudson River in the distance. I could also see my old car below in the parking lot. It was tuned up and waiting to take me to another place that might only exist in my mind. I turned away from the window, picked up the suitcase and walked out of the room I had spent the last four and a half years in.

* * *

Thirty minutes or so later, standing in the foyer, I hugged both Mr. and Mrs. Axe and said goodbye to them. It was not a time for words and few were spoken. Minutes later in my old car I exited the estate gates and left the castle behind me and began the long drive to California.

If you enjoyed
I Dream Alone by Gabriel Walsh
why not try
Maggie's Breakfast also published by Poolbeg?
Here's a sneak preview.

GABRIEL WALSH

Maggie's Breakfast

POOLBEG

Dublin

My mother looked through the curtains, saw who was at the door and without looking back at me said "Hide!"

I was sitting in front of the fireplace counting the sparks that were floating up the chimney. As the front door was opened, I ran and hid under the small table.

The priest entered the house and my mother greeted him with a reverential bow.

With a voice that was known to knock cups off their saucers Father Joe Devine bellowed out, "Mornin', Missus!" With hat in hand he stepped into the middle of the room and viewed all the holy pictures and statues my mother had accumulated over the years. He probably thought it was as good a place as any for a miracle to occur.

Father Joe Devine was referred to by my father as 'Holy Divine' and by us thereafter as 'Father Divine'. He was also known as 'Sheep Dog' because of his habit of roaming about on his bicycle rounding up errant parishioners and herding them with due violence into the church for 'retreats' and other 'devotions'.

Rumour in the neighbourhood had it that in his earlier years he had been thrown out of a cloistered order in County Waterford because of his unnatural fixation on the Virgin Mary. Instead of money, he carried around in his pockets small mini-statues of the religious figure. It was believed that when he went to bed at night he placed a life-size statue of the Virgin next to the foot of his bed. The religious order required Joe 'Divine' to take a vow of silence but he couldn't stop talking about the Blessed Virgin and he was asked to leave the monastery. The irrational relationship Joe had with the Virgin Mary tarnished the image of the holy order. A hundred or so reclusive men who were pledged to a vow of silence in a hidden-away monastery didn't appreciate Joe Devine's very vocal obsession. Also, when Joe left the cloistered monastery, his fellow monks made sure he took his collection of plaster statues with him.

Now the Oblates Parish of Mary Immaculate in Inchicore was blessed with Father Joe, a man with deep roots in County Waterford who preferred to speak Gaelic rather than English and had little sympathy for Dublin people. He was a replacement for a priest who was exiled to Donegal by the Bishop of Dublin after he was accused by several of his parishioners of unpriestly activities. The nature of his unpriestly conduct was never made public and no one who attended Mass or received Communion in the parish ever asked why. Some parishioners were heard to say that he had plans to "Christianise Ireland properly". The parish in North Donegal was at the edge of the Atlantic Ocean and, because of the fierce cold weather there, it was said that it was only accessible during the summer months. So whatever his crimes or misdemeanours, the errant priest was well out of the way of the Bishop of Dublin.

"Mornin', Father," my mother finally and humbly said to the man who stood in front of her, dressed from head to toe in black.

Father Joe stood in the centre of the room, spoke about the Virgin Mary and looked like he was about to burst and drown the whole country in holy water.

"The blessed Mother of God stands alone and crownless watching over all of us who pray to go to Heaven. The Mother of God has withstood storms and bitter cold winters, facing and comforting all who come by Her feet to pray."

The big old statue he was referring to was there since the local church was built and nobody paid much attention to it before Father Divine arrived.

From under the old wooden table I could hear the priest's notorious voice and I trembled with fear. When he stepped close to the table I noticed his black shiny shoes. They had thick soles on them as if they had been repaired twice.

"The Virgin Mary is the closest to God that any imaginable person or thing could be. Anything she says, you can be sure God pays attention to." Father Joe then knocked on the table with his knuckles. "Mrs. Walsh, I'm here on a duty to honour Our Lady. How many times, and I needn't ask you this, but how many times have you knelt down before the Mother of God and asked her for guidance and blessings?"

My mother's voice rang out, "Many times, Father!"

"I know you have, Mrs. Walsh, and I also know that the Mother of God hasn't forgotten. She keeps a long and remembered record of your prayers."

My mother, feeling blessed, stepped closer to the man in black. "Wasn't I only there meself this mornin' after Mass offerin' up me prayers, Father. That's as true as Christ is in Heaven!"

Our Lady's statue outside the church was standing on a high pedestal surmounting the gate that led into the church-yard. She had a big rosary beads over her arm but she didn't have a crown or a halo over her head. What she did have was a man who was resolved to do something about it.

"Have you anything to offer, honour and beautify the statue of Our Holy Mother?" he asked my mother.

My mother's response was typical of her. "The few ha'pence I've left over wouldn't be enough to buy a bottle of holy water, Father."

Father Divine wasn't satisfied with my mother's answer so he walked about the room inspecting everything in the place. From where I was sitting under the table, I could smell the polish on his shiny shoes. He continued to walk about looking at everything – the pictures on the wall and every bit of furniture my mother had collected since she was married. He even lifted up the kettles and pots in the fireplace.

Finally convinced that my mother had nothing of value in the house to offer the Virgin, he walked to the door and, turning, reached out as if to shake her hand. But he took her left hand, not her right hand.

On the fourth finger of her left hand was her wedding ring. The ring that bonded my parents in marriage and perhaps more than anything else the object that kept them in the holy miserable state of matrimony. Maybe the only happy memory my parents ever experienced together. Perhaps the one thing of value in my mother's life, the thing that empowered her to endure pain and discomfort. The wedding ring on her finger was more than a bond to her: it was a sacrament. Whatever the pain, anger, and confusion, the ring held my parents together like no other force. It might even have been the only worthy thing she admired about my father. My mother's life was reflected in its shine. The band of gold had endured countless floor-scrubbings and thousands of laundry-washes. It had been there when arses were wiped and piss-pots emptied. It had been there when potatoes were peeled and when pigs' cheeks were cooked. It had touched shop stalls and meat counters when she reached out for bargains or charity. It felt my mother's breath when she prayed a thousand prayers with her hands joined. Every saint and statue in Dublin had had their image reflected in my mother's wedding ring when she prayed to them at one time or another.

Father Joe held onto my mother's hand as if he was proposing marriage to her. When he spoke his voice had changed dramatically.

"The Holy Mother of God would be eternally grateful if you could donate this ring to her crown, Mrs. Walsh. I know she'd look down on you and anoint you. If you do, it would be placed in her crown with other gold rings from other women and wives in the parish."

"Ah, Paddy put that on me finger," my mother said sadly.

"Our Blessed Lady will be crowned in May – the month of Our Blessed Virgin, Mrs. Walsh."

My mother then knelt down on the scrubbed wooden floor and offered a prayer. "Jesus, Mary and Joseph, I offer you me heart and me soul!" Her thick brown stockings had holes in them and her knees were showing.

She then arose and in an obedient manner presented her hand to the priest.

As he stood by the door in his crusade to undo contentment, Father Devine separated the wedding ring from my mother's finger. He told her it would be forever a star in the new crown of the Virgin Mary. God would look with special affection on her for giving such a gift to his Mother and she could have a front-row seat when the time came for the consecration of the Virgin's crown.

After a quick blessing and the Sign of the Cross Father Divine made a hasty exit.

My mother, who couldn't afford a pint of milk, felt she had achieved something close to sainthood.

Within a few minutes of Father Divine's departure my father came hurrying in the door. He looked pale and exhausted. He had encountered the man from Waterford who had told him about the wedding ring sacrificed so the Virgin Mary could have her crown. When my father entered the house he walked to the table I was still sitting under. He then called to my mother who was cleaning out the fireplace.

"I want to talk to ya! I want to talk to ya now!"

"About what?" my mother responded with a tone of guilt that you could cut with a knife.

My father raised his voice louder than I had ever heard in my entire life. "Isn't there somethin' missing from your finger?"

"What?" my mother answered.

It was the first direct confrontation I had witnessed in a long time.

"You had a ring on there, didn't ya?"

"I had."

"Where's it?"

"Me weddin' ring?"

"Yes. You only had one bloody ring!" my father yelled. "Where's the bloody ring I bought ya?"

Molly began to peel a potato as if to avoid his wrath. After a second or two Paddy took the potato from her hand and threw it across the room. It landed in the fireplace.

My father was then hit with what he hated to hear most.

"What good are you? You're just a labourer! You've no trade! Nobody has any need for ex-soldiers. And if they served in the English army they have even less use for them. All of Ireland knows that!"

Paddy retreated like a soldier who had run out of ammunition or one who'd got fed up with firing at the same target.

"Where's the ring I bought ya? Where's the wedding ring I spent me savin's on? Where is it?"

He then began to cry.

I wanted to crawl out from under the table but I was afraid to.

My mother, with a sense of sacrament in her voice, continued: "The Holy Mother of God will be wearing the ring in her crown."

My father fired off one last shot. "Why the hell didn't you give her the wedding dress as well?" Holding on to his suspenders he retreated like a wounded soldier to the bedroom. It was the only place he could hide.

* * *

Murphy's barbershop was located not too far from the foundry. At the time it was Inchicore's only beauty salon. I was sitting on the curb outside the shop with Danny Murphy, a boy about the age of seven, the same age as myself and the son of the owner.

"Come in here, Danny, and mind the shop." Mr. Murphy's hands were shaking and his tongue was sticking out of his mouth. "I need to go get a pint before I drop dead on the floor. I'm goin' across the street for a drop of porter. Keep the lock on the door and let nobody in. I'll be back in a bit. Y'hear me, son?"

"Yis," Danny said.

Mr. Murphy took off his apron, shook the hairs off it, put his overcoat on, reached for his hat, covered his bald head and walked out the door.

Danny looked at me. "Give me a hand with the hair," he said, imitating his father's demanding voice.

"What d'ya want me t'do?" I asked.

"Put the dirty hair in the barrel in the back room."

I grabbed as much hair off the floor as my hands could hold, walked to the back room and pushed the stack of greasy hair into a big cardboard barrel. Half of the hair stuck to me. My face, ears and nose were covered with it. I walked back to the front room and saw Danny wearing his father's apron and holding the hair-snippers in his hand.

"When I grow up I'm goin' to be the barber here. And if you're me pal you'll help me get a start."

For a second or two I wasn't sure what Danny was talking about.

"Let me do it," he said.

"Do what?" I asked.

"Let me give you a haircut."

I crawled into the chair in front of the big mirror. Danny tied a striped apron around my neck and within seconds he was snipping away at my head. Twice he snipped my ears and made me bleed. I had hair and blood-spots all over me. I looked like Magua, in *The Last of the Mohicans*. I started to cry.

As Danny tried to reassure me about my bleeding ears, a knock came to the door. "Me dad is back," he mumbled.

Mr. Murphy's voice yelled out, "Open the damn door, Danny!"

Danny sat down on the floor and began to cry. "I'll be kill't! I'll be kill't!" he moaned painfully. He was so frightened he couldn't shake the scissors out of his hand and stabbed me with it again and again as he tried. He looked like he was lock-jawed and dead at the same time.

Mr. Murphy's voice bellowed even louder than before. "Open the fuckin' door!"

Danny started to cry and pray at the same time. "Holy Mary, full of something, and Jesus, say something to me father!"

I became so frightened I began to pray also. "*Oh my God, I'm heartily sorry for having offended Thee!*"

Danny stuck his hand to my mouth. "Don't pray so loud! He'll hear you!"

I was now very worried and choking at the same time. For what seemed to be forever, I couldn't talk. Danny shifted his hand a bit and now I couldn't breathe either but I could hear Mr. Murphy yelling.

"Open the damn door or I'll whip the shite out of ya! I swear to Christ you won't sit on your arse for a month!"

Danny then pissed in his trousers. Mr. Murphy kicked on the door again. In panic I leaped from the chair, ran to the back room and jumped into the big barrel of hair. I had hair in my ears, my nose, my eyes, my mouth, my pockets, my shoes and down the back of my neck. I closed my eyes and hoped I could just fall asleep and forget everything.

"Open the door! Open the blasted door! Y'hear me? Open the bloody door, Danny!" Mr. Murphy yelled again.

Danny rushed into the back room and looked down at me hiding under a mountain of hair.

"Me father's drunk and I'll be kill't if he finds out what I did to ya."

I wasn't able to help him. I was imprisoned in a barrel of dirty hair that up until a few hours earlier belonged to half the men of Inchicore.

Mr. Murphy was going crazy. "*Open the bloody door before I kick the thing in! Y'hear me? D'y'hear me? Open the door!*"

Danny ran back to the front room. I heard the sound of the front door opening and said a few prayers to myself – "*Glory be to the Father and to the Son and the Holy Ghost!*" and "*Hail Mary, full of grace, the Lord is with Thee, blessed art Thou amongst women and blessed is the fruit of Thy womb, Jesus!*"

From the front room I heard a loud noise. It sounded as if Mr. Murphy had thrown the wooden bench at Danny.

Danny let out a scream. "*Don't hit me! Don't hit me!*"

There was a loud grunt from Mr. Murphy as if he had missed hitting Danny with the wooden bench. "What in the name of Christ are ya up to? Why didn't ya open up for me? Why? You're a right git, ya scruffy little bollocks! Get home with yourself!"

The door slammed. All was quiet again. They were both gone.

I was terrified of what my mother would say about my hair when I got home. I planned on telling her that I'd been praying all evening and had said more prayers in one hour than I had in a week. I wanted to tell her I said the Act of Contrition and the Our Father so many times I could sing them backwards.

After about fifteen minutes I climbed out of the container and walked into the front room. I tried to open the front door but it was locked. I then went into the back room, climbed to the small ventilator window, crawled out sideways and fell into the back alley.

* * *

"Sacred Heart of Jesus, what happened to you?"

My ears had two red streaks of blood dripping down the sides of my neck and face. My head looked even worse. My mother's face appeared to turn purple when she saw me. She quickly grabbed my hand, led me to the big mirror that was hanging over the picture of the Sacred Heart of Jesus. I stared at the plaster statue and for a moment wondered if it had real blood dripping from its heart. For a very short time I was dreaming that Danny Murphy hadn't really operated on my head and the greasy snippets of hair that were pasted to every part of my body weren't really there at all.

My dream was cut short when I felt my mother's hand on the back of my neck.

"Jesus, Mary and Joseph, you're unrecognisable!" She was having convulsions and hit me again and again on the back of my head.

A big bang went off in my left ear. Her hand felt like a shovel.

"You bloody git! You'll make a holy show of me if you show up for school looking like that! You'll be thrown out!"

She walloped my left ear with her other hand and I heard a bell ring. Its gong seemed to last forever but then all went silent.

A week or so later my ear was still paining me. My mother then took me to Saint Vincent's hospital and had a doctor look at it. After putting a small light beam into my ear he told my mother I should cut down on salt and stop eating eggs altogether. It was easy to give up the eggs because I only had one every second Sunday.

* * *

On Friday mornings the Sisters of Mercy from nearby Goldenbridge Convent went around the neighbourhood in a horse and cart with a big barrel of hot mashed potatoes and parts from a slaughtered pig. Where they got the pig carcasses from I never knew and I didn't want to know either. The smell of hot potatoes from the barrel on the horse-drawn wagon signalled to families like mine that it was time to eat. I approached the nuns' wagon with my can which had a smiling cow's face on the outside label. Fresh milk was expensive and rationed at the time. Condensed milk was donated by the Saint Vincent de Paul Society. With my family, the condensed milk lasted for about two days. After that the can was discarded, but the remnants of the condensed milk inside the can remained and tasted like sweet glue. I stood in line with other children but by the time the wagon got close to my house the barrel of mashed potatoes was almost depleted. Exercising her last charitable impulse of the day the nun scraped the bottom of the barrel and filled my can with crusty burnt mashed potatoes. It was just the way I liked them.

The Saint Vincent de Paul Society periodically dropped off a voucher for a pair of new shoes or sandals to every family on Nash Street. Children who went to school barefoot were singled out for the benefit. My mother decided that it was my turn to take advantage of the shoe voucher because the toes on my feet were withering away with chilblains from walking to school every day barefoot. Molly went with the voucher to Cleary's on O'Connell Street for a pair of sandals for me and brought them home in a box but even with the coldest toes in Ireland she wouldn't let me wear them right away. She insisted I wait till Sunday and wear the sandals to Mass. After that she said I could do what I liked with them. For the rest of the week I went to school in my bare feet, thinking about my new sandals that were in a box under my mother's bed. Saturday night came and I washed my feet and went to bed with such great anticipation of wearing a new pair of sandals I couldn't fall asleep. The next morning my mother handed me my new sandals. I was so sleepy I could hardly see them. Instead of shoes or boots with laces, my sandals had buckles, silver buckles that took only a second to fasten. The sandals were the first new thing I had ever owned and were a perfect fit. When I put them on my feet I thought I had died, gone to heaven and sprouted wings. In a hurry to feel the sandals on my feet I ran out the door and headed for Mass. On my way to the church I kept looking down at my feet. It felt so good I thought I was in a bus or riding a bicycle. Inside the church I kept gazing downwards at my feet. While I was doing that a person behind me slapped me on the head and told me to look up at the altar and pay attention. As soon as Mass ended I was determined to form a relationship with the leather items that covered my feet. I ran up towards the canal to test the sandals. I wanted to show them off to anybody I'd meet. I felt so free I could have jumped over the moon. When I got to the canal I decided to cross over to the other side. As I stepped on the footbridge that allowed one to cross over the canal, my right foot got caught in the chain that secured the wooden crossing. To free myself I yanked my foot and was quickly separated from the sandal that covered it. It fell into the water where it went under and drowned. I never saw it again.

When I came home with one sandal my mother threw me out of the house and I sat on the sidewalk and cried till sunset. Monday morning I was back in school in my bare feet.

* * *

I woke up in the middle of the night and my jaw was so swollen I looked like I had a doorknob in my mouth. The next morning, after a night of me screaming in agony, my mother dragged me by the scruff of the neck to the community dentist.

After we'd sat in a crowded waiting room for about two hours, a man in a white coat with the spots of blood on it came out and looked around. Behind him was a nun praying silently. The man in the white coat pointed his finger at me, then called to my mother: "He's next!" He then turned to the nun and whispered something into her ear. The nun began to pray out loud.

The nun came over to me and asked me if I had made my First Holy Communion. My mother answered for me and said I hadn't but I would soon. The nun asked my mother if I was baptised. My mother said I was. The nun then led me and my mother into a room where the man in the white coat told me to step into the dentist's chair. He looked in my mouth.

"Half of them have to come out," he said.

"Only take the bad ones out, sir," my mother pleaded.

"Sure most of them are bad," the dentist said.

The nun blessed herself as if on cue.

The dentist then took another look at my decaying teeth. "I assume he's been baptised?" He smiled and squinted towards the nun who nodded while kissing the rosary beads she was holding. "I'm afraid I'll have to put him to sleep," he added.

"Ah Jesus, can't you help him without puttin' the gas-bag on him, sir?" my mother begged.

"I'll give it a try, missus," the dentist replied.

He then put a pair of pliers into my mouth, got a grip on one of the teeth in the back that had a big black hole in it and began to pull. The dentist continued to pull and pull. I was spitting blood like a loose water tap and crying even louder. I screamed so loud I almost swallowed the pliers and the hand of the dentist as well. The tooth would not come out.

The dentist then looked again at my mother and the nun. "I was afraid of this," he said. He then reached for a rubber bag that was on the shelf behind him. The bag looked like a recently extracted cow's liver and smelled as bad. "Take a deep breath," the man with the bloodstains on his white coat said to me. Before I could inhale anything he slammed the slippery-looking cow's liver flat on my face as if he was slamming an insect with the heel of his shoe. I could hear the nun praying louder as I screamed, pushed and attempted to resist being knocked out by the rubbery bag that was smothering me. In seconds I was gone, way gone. Where I sailed to I don't know. When I came to the nun was still praying and I had fewer teeth in my mouth than ever before.

* * *

Receiving your First Communion showed everybody in the church that you were in a State of Grace and if you died a second after you received Communion you'd go directly up to Heaven because your soul was clean and white. At the age of seven, receiving Holy Communion gave you the right to walk to the altar and receive the sacrament with grown-ups. Many families walked up to the altar and received Communion together. First, of course, you had to make your First Confession and confess all your sins to the priest.

The Communion wafer that the priest stuck in your mouth was made at the biscuit factory. It was a small round light papery wafer that you had to swallow the second the priest placed it on your tongue. It was a sin to let it touch your teeth because if you did it meant you took a bite out of God. The Sacrament of Communion was like a passport to

Heaven. Receiving it meant you had no sins or black marks on your soul. You had a white soul and that was the only kind of soul that got you by the guards at Heaven's gate.

After you received your First Communion you were allowed to walk around the neighbourhood, knock on doors and show people that you were saved from punishment for your sins. When friends, relatives and neighbours saw you dressed up in your new suit with the white ribbon on your lapel, they gave whatever they could afford and congratulated you on avoiding the fires of Hell or Purgatory.

My First Holy Communion got off to an odd start. At Goldenbridge Convent which I was attending, Sister Charlotte approached me in the middle of class one day with a big happy smile on her face.

"Did you get your Communion suit?" she asked me.

I didn't know what to answer. I knew my mother had gone to the Iveagh Market looking for a suit for me but she hadn't told me if she'd found one or not.

"After class I want you to stay in your seat. Will you do that?" the nun asked me.

I could never say no to Sister Charlotte. Had she told me to walk backwards on my head, I would have. I would do anything for her but I was afraid to tell her that.

She was so beautiful I couldn't stop thinking about her even when school was over. I didn't know why my body was reacting the way it was. All of Sister Charlotte's prayers and promises were like Christmas presents. She made me believe that all things and all people were good. Even if I had no shoes on my feet Sister Charlotte convinced me that I didn't really need them. "Ah, you've such a good pair of feet, Gabriel! It would be a shame to cover them up with shoes or sandals," she'd say to me. I felt so happy and comfortable in Sister Charlotte's presence I forgot about everything else in my life. Sister Charlotte was my Guardian Angel. Guardian Angels were to remind you not to commit a sin when you were tempted. I asked myself every day in school: What would Sister Charlotte say if she knew I wanted to kiss her?

When the bell rang for the end of school that day, I remained in my seat. After the class had emptied out, a woman who used to cook in the convent kitchen came into the classroom with a big brown-paper bag.

"It's all here, Sister. Clean and pressed. Like new," she said and handed the bag to Sister Charlotte.

"Come up, Gabriel."

I timidly got up from my seat and walked to the head of the class.

"Congratulations, Gabriel, on making your First Holy Communion this week," she said.

The woman who'd brought the brown-paper bag in blessed herself and moved her lips as if she was saying a prayer.

Sister Charlotte then took a grey jacket and trousers out of the bag. "I think this will fit you, Gabriel."

The woman stepped forward. "Stretch out your arms," she said to me.

I stretched my arms out like the man on the cross. The woman placed my arms into the sleeves. "The jacket fits him," she said, turning back to Sister Charlotte.

Sister Charlotte smiled. "This suit used to belong to one of my young brothers, Gabriel. He's a lot older than you and he's living in England. It's been hanging in my room for years. I've kept it in mothballs."

"That's where I keep me husband," the woman said.

Sister Charlotte laughed out loud.

The woman measured the trousers to my knees. They too seemed to fit.

Sister Charlotte stepped back and took a look at me.

"I have a confession to make, Gabriel."

I thought she was going to say she loved me. My blood boiled and my face turned red.

"I've tried to fit this suit on boys for the last three years and it didn't fit any of them. When you first came into my class, you reminded me of my young brother. I prayed that the day would come when you could wear his suit, and now you're going to. Your poor mother will be happy about that, won't she?"

"She will and thanks very much," I said.

Sister Charlotte then put a white ribbon on the lapel of the jacket. "Wear this on your lapel when you receive your Communion on Friday, Gabriel."

The ribbon was snow white and brand new. It was to be my badge of honour when I received my First Communion from the priest.

The sister also gave me a new prayer book with a picture of Jesus on the front of it.

"You can say your prayers with this book, Gabriel. Whenever you're having trouble with everything that goes on around you, open this and read it. Making your First Communion gives you rights and responsibilities. Your Holy Communion Day is one of the most important days of your life."

As I stood in front of my Guardian Angel she reached back to her desk and handed me a small box. "Open it," she said with a glowing light in her eyes.

I fumbled with the box but managed to open it without much trouble. Inside the box was a pair of new brown shoes. I almost passed out from the smell of the new leather.

"Wear them with your suit when you make your Communion," the nun said. "Tie the laces tight so they won't fall off your feet."

I was so fixated on Sister Charlotte I wasn't able to concentrate on what she was saying to me. I felt trapped in a cage of pure love. My skin was boiling and I felt as if my hair was on fire. I could hardly breathe. I was convinced I was committing sin.

A week after I made my Communion I went to Confession and told the priest that I wanted Sister Charlotte to be my mother. The priest told me I had a mother and I shouldn't be thinking of having another one. I told the priest that I was always wishing I could see Sister Charlotte in a dress instead of the black habit she wore. And I wondered if she painted her legs brown like my oldest sister Mary did before she left home and got married. I told the priest that I had a dream when I imagined Sister Charlotte wearing almost no clothes at all. For the act of committing sin by "thought" the priest told me to say the rosary every day for two weeks as well as six Acts of Contrition.

Sister Charlotte was the nicest person I ever met. The more I got to know her the more I believed she was a real saint who should have been living up in heaven. She told me she prayed for me and hoped that I would find everything I ever wanted out of life. She said she prayed that I would even find my lost sandal. "Gabriel, you will find your sandal. You will have new sandals with silver buckles on them as well."

I had fantasies of kissing her but I knew that was a serious sin. Nuns didn't kiss or be kissed. But I think I was the only boy in her class that she held hands with. Every day she'd look into my eyes and smile and say nice things to me. In the back of my mind I kept telling her I loved her and that I wanted to see her every day for the rest of my life.

Sister Charlotte was talking about how a star in the sky guided the Three Wise Men to Bethlehem when another nun came rushing into the class and whispered in her ear. The two nuns then walked to the classroom door and opened it wide.

"Everybody go home and quickly!" they said.

The room emptied in a hurry. I didn't know what was going on and most of us in the class started to cry. One boy who wasn't crying said the Devil had escaped from hell and he was being chased all around Dublin by Catholic angels. That bit of information made us feel better. We knew no devil could beat up God's angels and when the Devil was caught he would be sent back down to hell and Dublin would again be safe for us to sit in school or do anything we wanted. Then in a fit of panic Sister Charlotte started to herd us out of the convent. When we got to the school gate another nun yelled out, "Infestation!" The boy who said the Devil had escaped from hell said "infestation" meant mortal sin. There was no escape from that unless you went to Confession and confessed all your sins and really meant it. I was trying to think of how many mortal sins I had committed when another nun called out to the Mother Superior of the convent: "Lice! Lice!" The Mother Superior blessed herself in a hurry. Lice weren't mortal sins. They were bugs with legs growing everywhere that crawled on your head and in your hair. The dogs and cats and the birds in the trees had lice. Mice had lice. Somebody said the cause of the lice was eating the dead rabbits the dogs dropped on the street.

When I got home my sisters and brothers were sitting outside on the kerb. They had been told the same thing in their schools. My sisters and brothers and all the boys and girls on the street had lice in their hair. A man came by and left a big bottle of Lysol outside our hall door. He was from some government agency and he said there was a state of emergency in Dublin because of the lice. The government handed out fine-toothed combs and paper with drawings of the lice on them. I think they drew the picture of the lice so the mothers wouldn't confuse them with mice or rats or stray kittens or anything else that was on the loose in Dublin. All the mothers in Dublin had a big combing job every night after dinner. My mother searched our hair for lice then crushed them with her thumbnail. Crack and splatter! Poor head! Poor mothers! Poor lice! Poor Dublin!

After the lice infestation and when everybody was back in school, still smelling of Lysol, Sister Charlotte called me to the head of the class and handed me six shiny new pennies. The six pennies Sister Charlotte gave me was the most money I had ever had in my life. She also presented me with a birthday cake. It was my very first present ever and the closest I had ever been to anything that had cream on top of it. *Happy Birthday* was written on top of the cake. Sister Charlotte held me by the hand and told me to smile and be happy about everything. With great difficulty and shyness I managed to lift my chin and look in her eyes. I thought I was going to die when I made eye contact with her. Angels and Heaven and happiness were floating all about me. I didn't want to stop looking. Her face was the sun shining through on a cold rainy day. I didn't know who I was any more so I started to cry.

Sister Charlotte wiped away the tears that were falling from my eyes with her fingers. She smiled at me and told me it was not a bad thing if I cried my eyes out in front of her. When she said that I stopped crying. She then walked me back to my seat and sat me down. The other boys in the class were watching with looks of serious confusion on their faces. I sat in silence and felt numb.

Sister Charlotte came back to me with the cake in a box tied with a red ribbon. "Open this when you go home, Gabriel, and share it with your family. Your mother will be happy, I'm sure of it! And a big happy birthday to you, Gabriel!"

Sister Charlotte turned to the class and asked the other boys to sing "Happy Birthday" to me. The classroom thundered with the sound. When the school bell rang she asked me to stay in my seat. She then walked up to me and wished me a happy birthday again. As I picked up my cake and was about to walk out of the classroom, she took my hand in hers.

"Gabriel," she said and went silent for a moment or two. She looked down at my two feet as if to make sure I was wearing the shoes she gave me. She then looked in my eyes again.

I was consumed by shyness, fear and confusion. Since I first met her I believed she was my Guardian Angel with white wings growing out of her shoulders. Her magical presence made everything in my life bright and clear.

Almost at the exact moment when I felt I didn't exist at all, she whispered, "Gabriel, in a few months you'll be transferring to Saint Michael's Christian Brothers School. The brothers are fine teachers. They'll help prepare you for the day when you'll be going out in the world looking for a job."

The thought of me ever having a job was as far away as my entering Heaven. I'd have to be dead first to get there. My father and loads of other men were always looking for jobs.

"You'll soon be gone from the convent here. You know that, don't you?"

I was so shy I could only nod my head. Sister Charlotte continued to talk. What she had to say came close to erasing me from the page of life that my name was written on.

"I'm to leave the convent soon."

I stood, feeling half paralysed.

Sister Charlotte continued. "I'm going away to Africa to join my fellow sisters there. My order has encouraged me to go and I've accepted. I won't be in class when you come here next week. I wasn't going to tell you or the class and I didn't, until now." Then she leaned towards me and kissed me on the forehead.

* * *

If you enjoyed this preview of
Maggie's Breakfast by Gabriel Walsh,
why not order the full book online
@ www.poolbeg.com